Democracy, Politics & Governance

Democracy, Politics & Governance

A. Surya Prakash

PRABHAT PAPERBACKS

Published by
PRABHAT PAPERBACKS
4/19 Asaf Ali Road,
New Delhi-110 002 (INDIA)
e-mail: prabhatbooks@gmail.com

ISBN 978-93-5521-168-2
DEMOCRACY, POLITICS & GOVERNANCE
by A. Surya Prakash

Edition
First, 2022

Price
₹ 500.00 (Rupees Five Hundred only)

Printed at
R-Tech Offset Printers, Delhi

Preface

My tryst with the media began when I joined the Indian Express, Bangalore as an apprentice 50 years ago. As I look back at the last half a century, one event which is permanently etched in my memory is the dreaded Emergency imposed by Indira Gandhi in June, 1975. With this decision, the then prime minister turned a vibrant democracy into a dictatorship and trampled upon the rights of all institutions including the parliament, the judiciary and the media.

There are many reasons why the Emergency has defined my journalism and my politics. One among them is the decision of the Indira Gandhi government to subject several newspapers including *The Indian Express* to pre-censorship and to appoint the Inspector-General of Police (IGP), Karnataka as the Chief Censor in the state. As a result, all editorial matter including editorials, columns and news reports had to be sent to his office for clearance. The IGP had a battery of information department officials and policemen to assist him in this task. They would edit out sentences critical of the government and only the version approved by the Chief Censor could go to print. In other words, a man in uniform had virtually become our Editor! It is simply not possible to forget the humiliation that the government of the day heaped on media professionals.

This experience of mine has substantially influenced my 'politics'. By 'politics', I mean the political line that I have pursued in my writings. If a reader were to pull out a common strand, it would be my belief in the core values in the Indian Constitution and the democratic way of life and my aversion to anything which is said or done which weakens the unity and integrity of India.

I believe that India is the most vibrant democracy in the world and also the most diverse society in the world. Be it religion, ethnicity or language (the last language census said Indians spoke over 120 languages and 170 dialects), there is no other nation in the world which is as heterogeneous as ours. In fact, the concept of unity in the midst of such plurality is unheard of elsewhere–history has shown that just a Shia-Sunni or a Protestant-Catholic divide is enough to break up nations. But 1.4 billion citizens of India have proved that unity in diversity is not just a slogan but a living creed.

This has been possible because of the constitution, which guarantees a liberal, democratic and secular environment. This is indeed an extraordinary document that provides enough vents for all of us to periodically let off stream. The shrillness of the debate may confound a visitor, but Indians are generally used to high decibel arguments.

When India became independent, Western politicians and scholars were rather sceptical about the survival of India as a democratic nation. They felt that the social, economic and political diversity would drag this nation down. Even now, they may mock at the 104 times we have amended our constitution, but this should not trouble us. We know how to manage our affairs and what is best for us. The era of prescriptions is over. Long years ago, Mahatma Gandhi had spoken about the virtues of man-made texts and had said that one important quality was that they were open to emendations.

The American statesman, Thomas Jefferson has also made a very significant observation that justifies constitutional amendments, when needed. He said, "We must consider every generation as a distinct nation, with the right of the will of the majority to bind themselves, but none to bind the succeeding generation… ."

Another strand that could emerge is my strong aversion to the persistent attempts by the English-educated elite to negate India's civilisational greatness and run down the majority that so willingly opted for a democratic way of life at a time when the country was partitioned by those who believed in a theocratic state. Also, the one-sided prescriptions which smacked of pseudo-secularism, which was much in evidence when the Nehruvians controlled the levers of power.

I do believe that a common code should guide all citizens. I would also argue that citizens of every democratic nation, which guarantees equality and fundamental freedoms to all, must acknowledge the fact that they enjoy those freedoms because that is the will of the majority. Those who have the misfortune of being born in theocratic and autocratic nations are aware of this truth.

When I reflect over the five decades which have gone by, I must acknowledge the faith and confidence that my parents–Parvatamma and A.N. Anantaramaiah–reposed in me as I stepped into the world of journalism–a profession they knew nothing about. In fact, the only thing my father knew about journalists in those days was that these were (mostly) men with many vices and huge egos and generally in high spirits! He had heard that a journalist was one who was paid 'per column, per inch or perhaps!' Yet, he never for once doubted my ability to find my way through this labyrinth and reach a stage of stability and dignity.

There are many others in this long journey who have meant a lot to me. Some of them are: S.K. Seshadri, a Bangalore journalist and family friend who helped me find my first job; V.N. Subba Rao, the Chief Reporter of *The Indian Express*, Bangalore who gave me my first break; Arun Shourie, then Executive Editor of *The Indian Express*, who got me over to the national capital and gave me the space needed to pursue my professional goals; S. Gurumurthy, a friend, philosopher and guide whose advice has been invaluable in the later part of my professional journey; Chandan Mitra, who gave me editorial latitude in *The Pioneer* when few others were willing to do so; Ramoji Rao, the Chairman of the Ramoji Group, for his constant encouragement and support; and Pushpa Girimaji, my wife, who, while pursuing her exceptionally people-centric journalism, has constantly been an invaluable companion and voltage stabiliser.

My thanks are due to G.S. Vasu, Editor, *The New Indian Express*; and Navin Upadhyay, Executive Editor, *The Pioneer* for readily giving their consent for using articles published in their newspapers in this book.

—A. Surya Prakash

Contents

Chapter-3: OUR DEMOCRACY

Chapter-4: OUR COURTS

Chapter-5: OUR MEDIA

Chapter-6: THE SECULAR & THE PSEUDO-SECULAR

Chapter-9: **THE EMERGENCY**

Chapter-10: **GOVERNANCE**

Chapter-1

OUR CONSTITUTION

Wisdom of the Makers of our Constitution

As the nation grapples with its biggest public health crisis, and disparate political parties and groups squabble over arrangements to fight the pandemic, one must thank the country's Constitution makers for giving us a basic law that enables us to have one central command in times of national emergencies.

Apart from specific emergency provisions, the makers have provided for a fairly large concurrent list in the Constitution's seventh schedule that gives the Centre greater manoeuvrability in times of crisis.

The Disaster Management Act (DMA), which is being fully deployed to impose lockdowns and regulate the conduct of citizens to contain the spread of the coronavirus, is a case in point. This Act, passed by Parliament in 2005, has enabled the Centre to lay down rules and ensure strict compliance across the country. Its significance can be gauged from the fact that at last count, there were over 40 political parties governing the 28 states and a couple of union territories that have Assemblies. One wonders what could have happened if this law had not been enacted.

When the country's Constitution was drafted, the Constituent Assembly witnessed an intense debate on the kind of federal structure that India should have. Dr. B.R. Ambedkar, Chairman of the Drafting Committee, explained to the House that the Indian brand of federalism was distinct from that of the US or Australia and although it was federal, it had strong unitary features to cope with emergencies. In his concluding remarks on the Constitution on 25 November, 1949, he addressed the complaint that there was too much centralisation and the states had been reduced to municipalities. Describing this as an exaggeration, he explained that the basic principle of federalism was the demarcation of the legislative and executive authority of the Centre and states in the Constitution itself. Therefore, he said, "The charge that centralisation is defeating federalism must fail".

As regards the second charge that the Centre had been given the power to override the states, Ambedkar admitted that this was true, but clarified that the overriding powers do not form the normal features of the Constitution. They are to be deployed only in certain exigencies. "Their use and operations are expressly confined to emergencies only."

He obviously had in mind not only the articles in the Constitution regarding proclamation of an emergency but also the powers vested in the Centre in the Union List and Concurrent List. For example, Item 23 under the Concurrent List gives the Centre the power to make law with respect to "prevention of the extension from one state to another of infectious and contagious diseases or pests affecting men, animals and plants".

The DMA Act defines disaster as "a catastrophe, mishap, calamity or grave occurrence..." and several of its provisions empower the Centre to take charge when disaster strikes, issue directions and ensure compliance. The series of orders issued by the Union home secretary regarding the lockdown flow from these provisions.

Some of these orders also expressly put the onus on the district administrations in the country and make it clear that the district magistrates and the superintendents of police "will be personally liable for implementation of these directions and lockdown measures issued under the above mentioned orders".

This is to ensure that the orders are not flouted because generally the district magistrates and superintendents of police are drawn from the central services and they are well acquainted with the consequences of non-compliance in these matters. Apart from the provisions in the Concurrent List and the DMA, the Epidemic Diseases Act, 1897 also arms the Centre with powers to handle epidemics.

In addition, the Constitution vests residuary power in the Centre. That is why noted constitutional experts like K.C. Wheare say that India is "a unitary state with subsidiary federal features rather than a federal state with subsidiary unitary features". Ivor Jennings feels that India is a federation "with a strong centralising tendency".

Why did our Constitution makers vest the residuary powers in the Centre? Dr. Ambedkar held the view that the residual loyalty of the citizen in an emergency must be to the Centre and not to the constituent states. For, it is only the Centre that can work for a common end and for the general interests of the country as a whole.

He also explained the role and responsibility of the states when some contingencies arise. "No more than this—that in an emergency, they (the states) should take into consideration alongside their own local interests, the opinions and interests of the nation as a whole."

When Dr. Ambedkar and his colleagues drafted the Constitution, India was virtually a one-party nation with the Congress in complete command both at the federal level and in the provinces. They may not have anticipated over 40 political parties in diverse, at times bizarre combinations, ruling the states, as is the case now. But given the country's social, economic and cultural diversity, they did anticipate the mushrooming of different ideologies and political parties. We owe it to their foresight for creating the constitutional mechanism to cope with national emergencies like this pandemic.

While one must work in a spirit of cooperative federalism, those who govern the states must respect the wisdom of the nation's founding fathers. While some peripheral disagreements between the Centre and the states are natural, a calamity of this magnitude calls for national unity and unequivocal commitment to the constitutional mandate.

The New India Express, 10 June, 2020

□

Stormy Amendments

The Indian Constitution has been amended 104 times and many of the modifications, including the ones passed by Parliament during the dreaded Emergency, have been extensively discussed. But there has not been sufficient debate on the amendment that started it all— the controversial "First Amendment." It was mooted by the first Prime Minister of India, Jawaharlal Nehru, in May 1951 within 15 months of the adoption of the Constitution the previous year. The intent was to impose restrictions on freedom of speech and other fundamental rights and to save anti-zamindari laws. These amendments, which were carried out by the Provisional Parliament, were meant to overcome judicial verdicts that struck down laws that affected the Press and individual freedom.

The statement of Objects and Reasons appended to the First Amendment Act said that certain difficulties had cropped up in the working of the Constitution because of judicial decisions, especially with regard to the fundamental rights. The citizen's right to freedom of speech and expression, guaranteed under Article-19(1)(a), "had been held by some courts to be so comprehensive as not to render a person culpable even if he advocates murder and other crimes of violence." Therefore, restrictions were sought to be fortified in the name of "public order", "friendly relations with foreign states" and "incitement to an offence."

There is much debate on the use and misuse of the sedition law these days but what is not well known is that one of the purposes of Nehru's First Amendment was to fortify Section-124A of the Indian Penal Code (IPC) under which the charge of sedition is pinned on individuals for speaking or writing against the State.

Credit goes to Tripurdaman Singh, a post-doctoral fellow at the Institute of Commonwealth Studies, University of London, for throwing light on the politics surrounding this event in his exceptionally readable book, Sixteen Stormy Days—The Story of the First Amendment to the Constitution of India, published by Penguin.

The First Amendment needs to be remembered for many things, including the first major clash between the President and the Prime Minister; the introduction of "reasonable restrictions" in Article-19(2) in the Constitution; and the idea of placing legislation in the Ninth Schedule so as to insulate them from judicial review.

It is indeed a fascinating story with many sub-plots such as the debate over "reasonable restrictions." Nehru wanted to impose "restrictions" on freedom of speech and expression in the light of some cases pertaining to the media. In Romesh Thappar *vs* the State of Madras, the Supreme Court had held in May 1950 that a Madras State law barring entry and circulation of the petitioner's magazine, Crossroads, on the ground that it disturbed "public order" was unconstitutional as the Constitution did not provide for it. Further, it said, "liberty of circulation is as essential to that freedom (of propagation of ideas) as that of the publication." In Brij Bhushan *vs* the State of Delhi (the Organiser case), the magazine was subjected to pre-censorship because the then Nehru Government did not like what it was saying about Pakistan. The magazine challenged the order and the Supreme Court held that pre-censorship violated Article-19(1)(a). In Master Tara Singh's case, the East Punjab High Court had held that Section-124(A) (sedition) and Section-153(A) of the IPC were violative of the fundamental rights guaranteed under Article 19.

Nehru felt frustrated by these judicial pronouncements and wanted to remedy the situation via the First Amendment. He wanted restrictions imposed on the freedom of speech and expression in the name of "public order", "friendly relations with foreign states" and "incitement to an offence." Senior parliamentarians, including members of the Congress, wanted the restrictions to be circumscribed by the word "reasonable." Nehru did not like it one bit. In the midst of the raging controversy, he wrote to T.T. Krishnamachari, Congress leader and MP, and confessed that he did not like the word "reasonable" before "restrictions" because it would be an invitation for every such case to go to the courts.

However, eventually, he yielded when he found that there were many in the Congress Parliamentary Party (CPP) who disagreed with him. In fact, as the author notes, 77 MPs wrote to him asking for a free vote on the First Amendment. That was when Nehru realised that the game was up and he gave in to the popular demand to make the restrictions "reasonable." Thanks to Syama Prasad Mukherjee, Acharya Kripalani and other stalwarts in the Congress, the Supreme Court has had the constitutional mandate over the last seven decades to examine whether the laws made by Parliament and the State legislatures, imposing restrictions on free speech, are "reasonable" or not.

Former President Rajendra Prasad, Syama Prasad Mukherjee, Acharya Kripalani, H.N. Kunzru and many other leading parliamentarians questioned Nehru's intentions and warned him about the dangerous precedent he was creating. But Nehru was adamant— the judiciary and the Press had to be reined in. The leaders felt that the Constitution should, if necessary, be amended after the first general election and the constitution of the two Houses—the Lok Sabha and the Rajya Sabha. They argued that a single chamber, the Provisional Parliament, was not competent to amend the Constitution when Article-368 prescribed the procedure to be followed by the two Houses.

During the debate, Kameshwar Singh accused Nehru of "sowing the seed of executive despotism." Syama Prasad Mukherjee had said that Nehru was "disfiguring" the Constitution by bringing in "public order" as a restriction. He said, "It is the beginning of the encroachment of liberty of the people of free India." His words have proved to be prophetic.

The President repeatedly clashed with Nehru on the latter's proposals and even asked senior Congress leader, Alladi Krishnaswamy Aiyyar, whether he could give his assent to an unconstitutional legislation when he is under oath to "preserve, protect and defend" the Constitution.

The First Amendment also introduced Article-31(B), to add the Ninth Schedule, which the author describes as a "Constitutional vault," to bar judicial review of laws placed in the schedule. Syama Prasad Mukherjee warned Nehru against creating such a precedent and said, "any nonsensical law can be put there" and placed beyond judicial review. Sure enough, Nehru's daughter, former Prime Minister Indira Gandhi, misused this provision on many occasions.

Tripurdaman Singh calls the Ninth Schedule "constitutional skulduggery" and says it granted constitutional protection to the Constitution's abusers. All the evidence he gathers compels the author to deliver a harsh indictment. He says, "In the reckless, impetuous bid to establish the Government's supremacy and open the constitutional doors to the Congress' social revolution... all caution had been thrown to the wind. The creation of the Nehruvian State demanded constitutional blood—and the Prime Minister and his acolytes were willing to spill it..."

The Pioneer, 16 June, 2020

□

The Nation's Constitution is under Threat

The continued opposition to the Citizenship (Amendment) Act (CAA) passed by Parliament and the preparation of the National Population Register (NPR) by several state governments that are antagonistic to the present dispensation at the Centre and their threatening postures towards the Union government do not augur well for our Republic and constitutional well-being.

The CAA, which is now the law of the land, has amended the Citizenship Act to provide succour to Hindus, Sikhs, Buddhists, Jains, Parsis and Christians, who, because of religious persecution in Pakistan, Afghanistan and Bangladesh, crossed over to India before 31 December, 2014 and are living in our country without any legal status. These nations are Islamic states, meaning Islam is the state religion there. Thus, automatically, unlike in India, adherents of all religions other than Islam, are second- or third-class citizens. Therefore, all non-Muslims are constitutionally inferior and this has conditioned the majority to ill-treat the religious minorities in these nations.

Since Partition, Hindus and other minorities have been subjected to all forms of harassment and cruelty in these nations, forcing them to either convert to Islam or flee. As a result, the population of Hindus in undivided Pakistan, which was around 24% in the mid-1940s, has crashed to just 1.7%. Similarly, in Bangladesh, which was earlier East Pakistan, the percentage of Hindus has crashed from 30% to about 7%. This should also answer the question as to why the Muslims are left out of the list of persecuted minorities under the CAA.

First of all, they are not "minorities" and secondly, it is laughable to say that Muslims are "persecuted" by an Islamic state. The CAA seeks to offer some help to these subjugated minorities and to only those who entered India before the cut-off date. In other words, this is not an open-ended scheme to allow for future migrants from these nations. Nor does it have anything to do with citizens of India, whether Hindu or Muslim.

Given this reality, the attempt by the Communists, Congress and others opposed to the BJP to spread the word that the CAA is against the Muslim citizens of India is blatantly false. This Act seeks to provide succour to persecuted religious minorities in Islamic states and this is in line with Bharatiya dharma and our constitutional dharma as well. Those opposing this are abetting the non-secular, non-democratic behaviour of the citizens of Islamic nations across India's border, and will thereby lose the moral right to talk about these values in India.

The Communists and Congress are also spreading canards about the NPR, the compilation of which is critical for policy formulation in the country. Both these parties have been roundly rejected in the last parliamentary election in May 2019. In fact, although the Communists hog 30-40% of the airtime on television debates, public support for these parties has fallen dramatically. In the 2004 Lok Sabha election, the two main Communist parties had a combined vote share of 7.07%. In 2014, this was down to 4.07%, and in 2019, it crashed to 2.36%. So, it appears JNU is their last bastion, and in combination with the Congress, these two parties are seeking to avenge their electoral humiliation by whipping up passions against the government that has received overwhelming public support.

Meanwhile, the Kerala, Punjab and Rajasthan Assemblies have all passed resolutions asking Parliament to repeal the CAA. Three other developments in recent weeks are extremely worrying. One, several chief ministers have declared that they will not implement the CAA in their states; two, the disgraceful decision to bring children to protest sites and to get them to raise foul, abusive slogans against a duly elected prime minister; and three, telling the Muslims not to respond to queries from enumerators who are tasked to prepare the NPR.

Every chief minister and politician in the country who has declared that CAA will not be implemented in his or her state must immediately withdraw that statement, because it will amount to challenging the supremacy of the Constitution. Parliament is empowered to make laws regarding citizenship, naturalisation and aliens under item 17 in the Union List and no state or individual has the right to say that the law made by Parliament will not be implemented. If the CMs persist with this line, it will amount to a constitutional breakdown and the consequences will be terrible because the overwhelming majority in this country swears by the Constitution and will not allow a few malcontents in our politics to disturb its rhythm and balance.

Secondly, the decision by protestors to bring kids to protest sites and to get them to hurl abuses at PM Narendra Modi is another act of brinkmanship which no reasonable person will support. Lastly, asking Muslims to boycott the NPR is equally risky, because any attempt to stymie the working of a duly elected government at the federal level will have its own implications. Those who are encouraging such tendencies are treading a dangerous path. It is indeed unfortunate that one has to make such a gloomy prognosis about what lies ahead, around the time the nation is celebrating Republic Day. The majority has to be alert to ensure that the Constitution and the democratic way of life remain undisturbed.

The New Indian Express 20 Jan, 2020

□

Uniform Civil Code: How did we get here?

The decision of the All India Muslim Personal Law Board (AIMPLB) to establish Sharia courts in all districts across the country has stirred up a controversy and brought us back to the debate on the fundamentals of a secular state, which began in the Constituent Assembly over seven decades ago. It now appears the concerns expressed by some eminent lawmakers in that Assembly, including Dr B.R. Ambedkar, over objections to a common civil code, have come to haunt us all over again. Political developments in recent years and the appeasement policies of several parties including the Congress are the consequences of the congenital maladies that the Nehruvian establishment injected into India's polity at the time of the nation's independence.

The Constituent Assembly began its sessions on 9 December, 1946. Eight months hence India gained independence and the Muslims of India succeeded in dividing the country and creating a separate Islamic State: Pakistan. Even two years after Partition, Muslim members of this Assembly, who represented the Muslims who preferred to stay back in secular India, raised demands such as for a separate electorate and successfully stalled the proposal for a common civil code. The vehemence with which they protested the constitutional provision to enable the drafting of a common civil code shocked many members of the Assembly including Dr. Ambedkar.

Here are some excerpts of the debate in the Constituent Assembly on 23 November, 1948. Now that the AIMPLB is planning to have a separate legal and judicial network across the country to deal with matters pertaining to civil law, readers will realise the price the country is paying today for Jawaharlal Nehru's pusillanimity at the time of independence and the shadow that this has cast on the secular aspirations of a majority of Indians.

When the issue came up for discussion in the Constituent Assembly, Mohammed Ismail Sahib, Nazirudin Ahmad, Mahboob Ali Baig Sahib Bahdur, Pocker Sahib Bahdur and Hussain Imam vehemently opposed the Article which said "The state shall endeavour to secure for citizens a uniform civil code throughout the territory of India." Baig Sahib Bahdur claimed that as far as Muslims were concerned, their laws of succession, inheritance, marriage and divorce are completely dependent upon their religion. Other Muslim members echoed this sentiment.

Mohammed Ismail Sahib claimed a uniform civil code will generate disharmony whereas "if people are allowed to follow their own personal law, there will be no discontent". Pocker Sahib Bahdur claimed that the Article was "a tyrannous provision which ought not to be tolerated". Baig Sahib Bahdur put forth a convoluted interpretation of secularism. He said that in a secular state, citizens belonging to different communities must have the freedom to observe their own life and their own personal laws. Pocker Sahib Bahdur claimed that it was the duty of the majority to secure the sacred rights of every minority.

K.M. Munshi challenged both of them: "Nowhere in advanced Muslim countries the personal law of each minority has been recognised as so sacrosanct as to prevent the enactment of a civil code. Take for instance Turkey or Egypt. No minority in these countries is permitted to have such rights." He said that most Muslims showed no such consideration to the Khojas and Cutchi Memons, who wanted to have their own personal laws. Therefore, he pooh-poohed their claim that the personal laws of minorities were always respected in other parts of the world.

Alladi Krishnaswami Ayyar also challenged the contentions of the Muslim members. He asked whether these arguments would promote "the welding together [of] a single nation, or is this country to be kept up always as a series of competing communities?" Further, when the British introduced one criminal law for the entire country, the Muslims had no objection. Nor did they object to a common law on contracts and such other laws. He felt that "the only community that is willing to adapt itself to changing times seems to be the majority community in the country"—the point often reiterated by Hindus today.

Dr. Ambedkar said he was surprised to hear Muslims had always followed their own personal laws because there was a uniform criminal code, a common transfer of property act, a Negotiable Instruments Act, etc. in existence. In other words, there is already a uniform civil code and the idea is to extend it to marriage and succession. Dr. Ambedkar challenged the claim of Muslim members that many of the practices came from the Koran and so, for 1,350 years, it has been practiced by Muslims. He said, for example, the North-West Frontier Province followed Hindu Law in regard to succession and other matters until 1935. In the Malabar region, Marumakkathayam—a matriarchal law—applied not only to the Hindus but to the Muslims as well.

So it is incorrect to say that "the Muslim Law has been an immutable law ... from ancient times". Therefore, "I am certain that it would not be open to any Muslim to say that the framers of the civil code had done great violence to the sentiments of the Muslim community."In order to put off the discussion on the common civil code, Nazirudin Ahmad claimed that the Constituent Assembly was ahead of its time. He said he had no doubt that one day, the civil code would be uniform. This was wishful thinking indeed, as the recent decision of the AIMPLB shows. This is one of Nehru's monstrous follies. His pursuit of a fake brand of secularism encouraged the Muslim minority to retain its separateness and thus impede national integration. Future generations of Indians will pay the price.

The New Indian Express, 17 July, 2018

□

Your Indian Citizenship is not so Fragile

The agitation against the Citizenship (Amendment) Act, the National Population Register and related matters, triggered largely by fears that the Centre will deprive millions of Muslim citizens of their citizenship, is one of the most bogus agitations that this writer has witnessed over the last 50 years. The CAA has nothing to do with Indian citizens. It only seeks to provide citizenship to a limited number of people who have been persecuted in India's three Islamic neighbours. The premise on which the agitation is being carried on is completely baseless and indicative of the extent of mischief a bunch of malcontents can do when the electorate rejects their agenda.

More importantly, anyone who reads The Citizenship Act, 1955 (the whole Act and not just the 2019 amendment to it) will realise how water-tight the citizenship of a natural-born citizen (a citizen born on Indian soil) is under this Act and that in reality, no one has the power to take it away. Section 3 of the Citizenship Act, 1955, describes citizens of India "by birth". It says: "Every person born in India (a) on or after the 26th of January, 1950 but before the first day of July, 1987; (b) on or after the first day of July, 1987 but before the commencement of the Citizenship (Amendment) Act, 2003 and either of whose parents is a citizen of India at the time of his birth; (c) on or after the commencement of the Citizenship (Amendment) Act, 2003 where (i) both his parents are citizens of India; or one of whose parents is a citizen of India and the other is not an illegal migrant at the time of his birth."

As can be seen, probably 99% or more of the citizens of India fall in this category called "citizens by birth" and they belong to all religions—Hindus, Muslims, Christians, etc. Such citizens are also known as "natural-born" citizens. These citizens are distinct from naturalised citizens and indeed constitute the highest class of citizens (for example in the US, only a natural-born citizen can be the President). These citizens (this writer included) do not "apply" for citizenship. They become citizens with the first breath of life. They do not make an oath swearing allegiance to the Constitution of India as their every breath is deemed allegiance. They can give up their Indian citizenship but no power can deprive them of their citizenship. Among such citizens, those who commit rape and murder can be hanged for the offence, if the law so provides, but their citizenship cannot be snatched away. The Act does not provide for it. They will take their citizenship to the gallows. Such is the quality of this citizenship.

The Citizenship Act offers other categories of citizenship like Citizenship by Registration (Section-5) and Citizenship by Naturalisation (Section-6). These are basically for foreigners who wish to settle in India and seek Indian citizenship or persons of Indian origin living abroad who want to return to India and live as citizens in this country. There is another category—foreigners who marry Indian citizens and settle down in India. For example, Ms Sonia Gandhi, the interim president of the Congress, is an Italian expatriate who moved to India after her marriage to Rajiv Gandhi in 1968. Under Section-5, Indian citizenship can be granted to a person coming via the registration route. There is a similar provision under Section-6 for expatriates who apply for Indian citizenship through "naturalisation". In both cases, citizenship is granted, subject to conditions and restrictions, and only after they make the oath of allegiance.

In Ms Gandhi's case, as per the law at that time, she could have applied for Indian citizenship five years after marriage, but she did so after 15 years on 7 April, 1983 and was granted citizenship on 30 April 1983. Despite being an Italian citizen in 1980, she illegally entered the electoral rolls that year and following a complaint, her name was deleted from the rolls. However, that is another story for another day. But how is all this relevant, one may ask. These facts are relevant because unlike natural-born citizens, the citizenship of a 'naturalised' citizen like her is extremely vulnerable and is subject to several conditions and restrictions. Further, if such a citizen violates any of those conditions, their citizenship can be cancelled. Section 10 of the Citizenship Act lists out the situations in which a citizen by naturalisation can be deprived of his or her citizenship.

It says that if the registration or certificate of naturalisation was obtained by "means of fraud, false representation or the concealment of a material fact; or that citizen has shown himself by act or speech to be disloyal or disaffected towards the Constitution of India as by law established; or that citizen has, during any war in which India may be engaged, unlawfully traded or communicated with an enemy...; or that citizen has been ordinarily resident out of India for a continuous period of seven years", that person's citizenship can be cancelled. Further, unlike citizens by birth, a naturalised citizen has to swear allegiance to the Constitution of India. It cannot be taken for granted.

Every Muslim citizen who is swayed by the anti-CAA argument must ask themselves the following questions, in order to know the quality of citizenship they enjoy: Did he/she ever "apply" for citizenship like Ms Gandhi? Was he/she ever asked to swear allegiance to our Constitution, like Ms Gandhi was?

So this is the power and quality of the citizenship of 99% of citizens under the Citizenship Act, 1955, but the Congress, after its decimation in the 2019 Lok Sabha polls, wants Muslims of India to believe that their citizenship is fragile. This is nothing but an attempt to spread falsehood and disaffection and could even be seen as an attempt to overthrow a duly elected government through guile and subterfuge. Proud natural-born citizens of India—Hindu, Muslim, Christian, Sikh, Jain, Buddhist, Parsi, Jew—must see through this game and disengage themselves from this campaign, which is dangerous for our democracy and for our constitutional well-being.

The New Indian Express, 3 March, 2020

□

Abrogation of Articles-370 and 35A

August 5 marked the first anniversary of the abrogation of the special status of Jammu & Kashmir and conversion of the erstwhile state into two Union Territories—Jammu & Kashmir and Ladakh. But more than all this, it has meant the constitutional mainstreaming of this erstwhile state and an end to the shameful, discriminatory and undemocratic policies pursued by an entrenched elite for seven decades.

In one sudden political strike, executed with surgical precision a year ago, Prime Minister Narendra Modi and Home Minister Amit Shah abrogated the provisions—Article-370 and Article-35A—that went against the core values of our Constitution and ensured that finally everyone in Jammu & Kashmir secured the rights and privileges available to citizens all over the country.

Looking at the changes brought about in the past 12 months, it is obvious that the Union government has pulled out all the stops to ensure that everyone living in the two Union Territories would get a sense of the egalitarian principles that are firmly embedded in India's Constitution. These developments extend to a wide range of issues like social and political equality, education, jobs, reservations and other rights enjoyed by the underprivileged in the rest of the country.

It is indeed creditable that the government has ensured that all this has been achieved within a span of 12 months. For the first time after seven decades, the Indian Constitution and all the 890 Central laws are fully applicable to J&K. This has meant the application of 170 more Central laws to J&K, including progressive laws such as the Scheduled Caste and the Scheduled Tribes (Prevention of Atrocities) Act, 1954, the Whistle Blowers Protection Act, 2014, the National Commission for Safai Karamcharis Act, 1993, the Scheduled Tribes and Other Traditional Forest Dwellers (Recognition of Forests Rights) Act, 2007, the National Commission for Minorities Act, and the Right of Children to Free and Compulsory Education Act, 2009.

The question we need to ask is why the leadership of the Congress, Left parties and the state parties did not allow such crucial laws which protect the Dalits and other disadvantaged groups to be implemented in the erstwhile state for all these years. Another discriminatory legal provision, which prevented women in J&K from retaining their rights if they married outside the state, has been put to an end.

The treatment meted out to around 10,000 municipal workers (*safai karamcharis*) in the erstwhile state was equally shameful. They were denied citizenship, access to education and jobs. Now, the municipal workers have become legitimate domiciles in the Union Territory with access to all rights and privileges and the Dalits and the tribal communities have got their due, as in other states. How could such discrimination happen within the geography of independent, democratic India all these years? What explanation do the Nehru-Gandhis, the Abdullahs, the Muftis, the Congress Party, the communists and their fellow travellers have for this? Why did the communists, the so-called standard-bearers of the working class, not take up the cause of the Dalits and safai karamcharis in J&K?

Apart from these initiatives, the last 12 months have seen several other momentous developments. The first of these is the rehabilitation of the Kashmiri Pandits, who were hounded out of the Valley 30 years ago by militants. The ethnic cleansing of nearly four lakh Kashmiris belonging to the Hindu minority remained a blot on India's secular credentials. In the year gone by, 4,000 of them have got jobs in the UT and many others are listed for employment. Also, over 20,000 refugees from West Pakistan, who were treated as aliens in their own country and denied all rights, have been given domicile rights and financial assistance of Rs. 5.50 lakh per family.

The follow-up after the constitution of the two Union Territories has been swift. Simple rules have been formulated for issuing domicile certificates—this will create a much-needed level-playing field for all residents. The J&K government has also initiated a massive recruitment drive to fill up 10,000 vacancies in the local government; another drive to fill up 25,000 posts is in the pipeline. Also on the anvil are revised rules to enable the hitherto disadvantaged groups like Scheduled Tribes, OBCs and economically weaker sections to get employment.

Other measures which have ensured mainstreaming of the region are the enforcement of the Right to Information Act, 2005, direct supervision of the Central Vigilance Commission with regard to anti-corruption cases and the setting up of the 18th Bench of the Central Administrative Tribunal (CAT) for the UTs of J&K and Ladakh.

The decision to make Ladakh a separate Union Territory has been hailed by the people of the region. It seemed inevitable because of the discrimination suffered by the region at the hands of the political leadership of the erstwhile state. The Union government has initiated innumerable measures to put Ladakh on the road to development. This includes work on massive infrastructure projects in both the UTs.

One year ago, the CPM described the abrogation as "an attack on democracy, secularism and the Constitution". Equally amusing was the statement of the Congress leader, Rahul Gandhi that "the nation is made by its people, not plots of land". Really? If so, are not the Kashmiri Pandits, Dalits, tribal folk, municipal workers, people?

As one sees the fundamental changes brought about in the two UTs, they remind us of the monstrous failure of the Congress leadership which lacked the courage and confidence to correct these wrongs and hence chose to tout pusillanimity as an act of great statesmanship. As a result, J&K slipped away from the liberal, secular and democratic traditions that India stood for. But that is now a thing of the past. It is now time to celebrate the new beginning.

The New Indian Express, 6 August, 2020

□

Working of Constitution: Some Home Truths

On November 26, Parliament observed Constitution Day and leaders of various political parties hailed the Republic's founding fathers for their diligence and foresight while drafting the country's Constitution. Since we happen to be the world's largest democracy and also the most diverse society, the success of the democratic process over the last six decades is certainly a matter of pride for every Indian citizen. This is the most extraordinary human experiment in the world because nowhere else can one find democracy co-existing with such poverty and diversity. Therefore, despite all their faults and inadequacies, all stake-holders in the democratic process deserve congratulations and they include the people, their representatives and all the political parties.

Among political parties, the Congress Party takes pride in the fact that it led the freedom movement and played a key role in Constitution-making. While speaking in the Lok Sabha, the Congress President, Ms Sonia Gandhi drew attention to this fact and said the history of our Constitution is "inextricably linked with that of the freedom movement and therefore of the Congress Party." This is indeed true and this very fact imposes a special responsibility on India's oldest party to uphold the highest values embedded in our Constitution.

The Congress President also said the Constitution had seen over a hundred amendments, "a number of them in response to changing circumstances and emerging challenges." This is also true, though not all amendments would stand the scrutiny of even those who have only a nodding acquaintance with the core principles enshrined in democratic constitutions. An unfortunate example of this would be the 39th Amendment, which nullified the June, 1975 verdict of the Allahabad High Court which had found then Prime Minister Indira Gandhi guilty of corrupt electoral practice.

This amendment was hustled through the two Houses of Parliament and state assemblies in order to prohibit the Courts from entertaining election petitions against the Prime Minister. In gross violation of parliamentary rules, it was introduced and passed in the Lok Sabha on 7 August, 1975 and again introduced and passed in Rajya Sabha on the very next day. Then a miracle happened! As many as 17 state assemblies, summoned on Saturday, August 9, ratified this amendment and an amenable President gave his assent on Sunday, August 10 and the ever-obliging civil servants of those days opened offices that very Sunday to notify the amendment. Why this break-neck speed, you may ask? Because the Supreme Court was to hear Indira Gandhi's petition on August 11 and the government's lawyers had to tell the court that the Constitution stood amended and Parliament had decreed that election petitions against the Prime Minister were henceforth out-of-bounds for it!

In the course of her speech, Ms. Gandhi quoted Dr. Ambedkar as having said: "However good a Constitution may be, it is sure to turn out bad because those who are called to work it happen to be a bad lot." Ms Gandhi also said, "the ideals and principles that are embedded in our Constitution and that have inspired us for decades are now under assault. What we have witnessed these past few months particularly are a complete negation of what our Constitution stands for and guarantees."

If we reflect over the events during the dreaded Emergency in 1975-77, when the Congress Party imposed a dictatorship in the country and flung the core values of our Constitution out of the window, we realise how true Dr. Ambedkar was. It will also help us get a correct gauge of current political disturbances if we juxtapose the present debate on so-called intolerance with the horrendous assault on our democratic system 40 years ago.

The 39th Amendment was just for starters. It put the then Prime Minister above the law and nullified Article 14 which guaranteed equality before the law to all citizens. But the final nail in the coffin was the 42th Amendment which clipped the wings of the judiciary, removed, brick by brick, the foundations on which the document stood and did such violence to the basic principles enshrined in it that the Constitution eventually became a poor caricature of what Dr Ambedkar and his colleagues had given us.

The 42th Amendment introduced two provisions which can only be described as reprehensible. First, it abolished the need for quorum in Parliament and the state legislatures. The Constitution stipulates that at least ten per cent of the members must be present in the Houses to transact business. This was done away with, thus making it possible for just a handful of Congress MPs to sit late in Parliament and make laws for the country. Fortunately, the Janata Party, which defeated the Congress Party in the 1977 Lok Sabha election, corrected the mischief and restored the Constitution to its original, pristine glory.

The other provision, which should make any democrat hang his head in shame, was that which empowered the President to amend the Constitution through an executive order! As anyone with a nodding acquaintance with the Constitution is aware, it is very difficult to amend the Constitution because the government of the day cannot even change a full stop or a comma in it without securing the support of two-thirds of the members in each House of Parliament. Further, if the amendment involves the rights of the states, the assemblies of at least one half of the states will have to ratify the amendment. Only then can the amendment be made. The Congress Party found this to be too much of a rigmarole and authorized the President to "adapt or modify the provision in the Constitution) to remove the difficulty" through an executive order.

Apart from the Indian President during the Emergency, the only other heads of state to have had the power to amend their constitutions through executive order were Hitler and Mussolini! The Congress President concluded her speech on the Constitution by saying "it is to the protection and advancement of constitutional processes that we must re-dedicate ourselves."

It is indeed an irony that the Congress Party, which was at the vanguard of the freedom movement and constitution-making, later became the party which mutilated the Constitution and robbed it of its founding principles like equality before law, right to life and liberty and fundamental rights including the right to freedom of expression. Therefore, every citizen must feel gratified that this party is now committed to advancement of constitutional processes. This augurs well for our democratic well-being.

The New Indian Express, 8 December, 2015

□

Recalling Ambedkar's Advice

The nation observed Ambedkar Jayanti on April 14 around the time when there were disturbances in some parts of the country consequent to a judgement of the Supreme Court regarding the enforcement of The Scheduled Castes and the Scheduled Tribes (Prevention of Atrocities) Act, 1989. Much of the protests have been triggered by opponents of the Bharatiya Janata Party (BJP) who have tried to lay the blame at this party's door in a bid to generate hostility against it among the Dalits, even as the Narendra Modi government filed a review petition in the apex court.

The political twist given to the court's judgment and the violence on the streets is truly unfortunate because it goes against the firm advice given by Dr. Ambedkar when the Constituent Assembly adopted the Constitution. Once the Constitution is adopted, he said, citizens must abandon the unconstitutional path to put forth their grievances. In the judgment that has triggered the agitation, the court said that there was misuse of the Act by vested interests to settle political scores, etc. It said that the underprivileged need to be protected against any atrocities to give effect to the Constitutional ideals and the Atrocities Act has been enacted with this objective.

It added: "At the same time, the said Act cannot be converted into a charter for exploitation or oppression by any unscrupulous person or by police for extraneous reasons against other citizens as has been found on several occasions in decisions referred to above. Any harassment of an innocent citizen, irrespective of caste or religion, is against the guarantee of the Constitution. This Court must enforce such a guarantee. Law should not result in caste hatred. The preamble to the Constitution, which is the guiding star for interpretation, incorporates the values of liberty, equality and fraternity". Also, the Act was "not intended to deter public servants from performing their bona fide duties".

Following the court's judgment on March 20, agitators took to the streets and a Bharat Bandh was organised against what they called the "dilution" of the Act. They said the judgment would completely nullify the main purpose of the Act and actually protect the perpetrators of atrocities against the Dalits. While some questioned the theory that the Act was being misused, others said the premise on which the court had drawn its conclusions was incorrect.

There were also the argument that this would completely jeopardise the efforts of the Indian state to protect the Scheduled Castes and Scheduled Tribes, who have faced and continue to face oppression across the country. These arguments found resonance in many quarters. The Narendra Modi government promptly filed for a review of the judgment. It took the stand that offences under this Act were heinous crimes committed to humiliate and subjugate SCs and STs. It said the government was committed to ensuring the well-being of the Dalits and tribals and that it did not agree with the reasoning of the Supreme Court.

Law Minister Ravi Shankar Prasad said it was important to note that the Union Government was not a party to the proceedings at all and therefore, a very comprehensive review petition had been filed. The government also noted that less than 25 per cent of the cases filed under the Act resulted in conviction of accused persons. Therefore, the court's judgement would only further impede justice for the victims of atrocities.

The government felt that the accusations hurled at it by its opponents were baseless because it enjoyed the confidence of the Dalits. Electoral studies have shown that the BJP's share of the Dalit vote jumped from 12 per cent in 2009 to 24 per cent in 2014. Also, the party bagged 66 of the 131 Lok Sabha seats reserved for Dalits and tribals in the country. While doing so, it had completely wrecked the electoral base of the pro-Dalit Bahujan Samaj Party, which did not win a single reserved seat. The Congress also saw its Dalit base erode.

Speaking in the Constituent Assembly on 25 November, 1949, Dr. Ambedkar cautioned the citizens and told them what they should do if they wished to maintain democracy "not merely in form, but also in fact". He said, "The first thing in my judgement we must do is to hold fast to constitutional methods of achieving our social and economic objectives. It means we must abandon the bloody methods of revolution. It means we must abandon the method of civil disobedience, non-cooperation and satyagraha. When there was no way left for constitutional methods of achieving economic and social objectives, there was a great deal of justification for unconstitutional methods. But where constitutional methods are open, there can be no justification for these unconstitutional methods. These methods are nothing but the grammar of anarchy, and the sooner they are abandoned, the better for us".

Now that the Union Government has filed a strong review petition on their behalf, the Dalits and the tribal communities which are anguished over the court order, must allow the judicial process to take its course. Any group or community that feels aggrieved about something, must remember

Dr. Ambedkar's sage counsel, because, as he has warned, violent methods of protest could imperil democracy.

The New Indian Express, 24 April, 2018

□

Chapter-2

OUR PARLIAMENT

Parliament @ 60—A Balance Sheet

As the two Houses of Parliament celebrate their Sixtieth Birthday on May 13 (they came into being on 13 May, 1952), parliamentarians are in a celebratory mood and are preparing for a special sitting on that day, despite it being a Sunday.

However, as all Indians know, the Sixtieth birthday (Shashtaabdi Poorthi) is also a day for some sober reflection on life gone by and on what lies ahead. So, away from the din in the two chambers, there is need for some quite stock-taking on the efficacy, relevance and standing of these two democratic bodies that are at the apex of our democratic structure.

How have these two Houses functioned over the last 60 years? How representative are they? Have they fulfilled their mandate of overseeing the work of the executive, keeping the government on its toes and protecting the interests of the people? Are our MPs still committed to public welfare? Do they take their parliamentary duties seriously? Given the constraints of space, let us attempt to answer at least some of these questions.

Since this is a birthday celebration, it would be in the fitness of things to begin on a positive note. The biggest achievement of the two Houses of Parliament is that they are far more representative of the Indian people now than they were 60 years ago. We can now see the occupational democratisation of the Lok Sabha. Almost half the members of the First Lok Sabha comprised of Lawyers (36 per cent), Journalists and Writers (10 per cent) and most of them came from dominant Hindu castes. The political empowerment of hitherto disadvantaged groups has brought about a change over the last two decades and the composition of the Lok Sabha is far more balanced now in terms of occupation, caste and class of members. The First Lok Sabha had 112 non-matriculates. This came down to 19 in the 14 Lok Sabha. Again, the first Lok Sabha had 277 graduates, post graduates and doctorates. In the 14 Lok Sabha as many as 428 members could boast of such qualifications. The political empowerment of the less privileged has also changed the composition of the state assemblies for the better and this in turn has changed the composition of the Rajya Sabha because the assemblies elected Rajya Sabha Members. The Upper House too has begun to mirror the social, political and economic diversity of Indian society.

A couple of other developments that are of a positive nature are the introduction of the committee system and the televising of parliamentary proceedings by Speaker Shivraj Patil in 1993. The constitution of department-related committees has improved parliament's oversight functions and has nudged MPs towards specialisation. The televising of parliament has lifted the purdah on parliament and enabled people to see it in its true colours. It has also improved the sartorial sense of MPs if nothing else!

However, there are many items of the negative list: The Question Hour has lost its zing. The inquisitorial nature of this hour which one saw in parliament up to the late 1980s when ministers trembled at the thought of being subjected to harsh interrogation by the likes of Bhupesh Gupta, Indrajit Gupta, Atal Behari Vajpayee, Madhu Limaye, Piloo Mody and Madhu Dandavate are over. Today, MPs who are ill-prepared or lack the moral courage to pin down ministers appear uncertain and nervous and ministers like P. Chidambaram, who are wanting in democratic etiquette, talk down to them! Many other parliamentary instruments like Adjournment Motions, Call Attention Motions and Short Duration Questions have become rusted. The government is no longer afraid of the opposition, because the latter is not clothed in moral authority any more. Compare this to the situation in 1957 when a question put by Feroze Gandhi, an MP belonging to the ruling party led to the unearthing of the LIC-Mundhra Scandal and the eventual resignation of the then Finance Minister Mr. T.T. Krishnamachari.

Yet another troubling statistic is the decline in the number of sittings of parliament per year. In the 1950s, parliament had an average of 123 sittings, in the 1960s it rose to 138 sittings. This had declined drastically to just 78 sittings in the year 2003. In recent years, the total sittings per year is down by about 30 per cent compared to the situation in the 1960s. The irony is that while the work of government is expanding, the work of parliament which has oversight responsibilities is declining. How do MPs keep a watch on the working of government?

While sittings per year and time allocated for budgetary matters is down, there is a sharp rise in the time lost in disruptions and in the cost of parliament. The 11 Lok Sabha lost 5 per cent of its time to disruptions. This rose to over 10 per cent in the 12 Lok Sabha and 22.40 per cent in the 13 Lok Sabha. In the 14 and 15 Lok Sabha, at least 30 per cent of the time has been lost to disruptions in session after session.

As regards individual MPs, the report card is disappointing. The distance between MPs and the electors is growing; the motto in the 1950s was simple living, high thinking. Now it is high living, no thinking. MPs want to flaunt their power and wealth and stay away from the Aam Aadmi. They want red beacons (lal bathis) atop their cars; they are obsessed with their privileges and have a disdain for ethics; they neglect parliamentary duties; attendance is abysmal during passage of bills and there is high absenteeism in committees (50 per cent). The list is endless and all this has taken its toll on the working parliament.

On the issue of maintaining standards in public life, India's parliament started on the right note when it decided to expel H.G. Mudgal, a member, for advancing the cause of the Bombay Bullion Association in the House for a price. After much negotiation and haggling, he accepted an advance of Rs. 2700 and raised questions of behalf bullion merchants. But that was in 1951 in what is known as the Provisional Parliament that existed prior to the constitution of the two Houses in May, 1952. However, after the Lok Sabha and Rajya Sabha came into being, a certain laxity crept in when it came to moral and ethical issues. Parliament watched in silence when a member forged the signatures of 20 MPs on a memorandum submitted to the Union Commerce Minister on behalf of liquor importers from Yanam and Mahe, former French territories. The MP was prosecuted, sentenced and jailed by the court, but there was no admonition or punishment by parliament. Sensing public resentment, Speaker Shivraj Patil proposed a Code of Conduct for legislators in the early 1990s and the Privileges Committee of the Lok Sabha followed this up with a recommendation that parliament adopt the Code of Conduct and establish a committee to look into both privileges and ethics. These developments led to the establishment of ethics committees in the two houses, but the committees have by and large remained dormant.

Parliament therefore needed a major jolt to get it out of its stupor and to understand the growing public concern over the fall in ethical standards among MPs. This happened with two sting operations conducted by television professionals in 2005. The first of these exposed a "Cash for Questions" Scam in our parliament. MPs were willing to raise questions in parliament for a price (Rs. 30,000 to Rs. 1.10 lakh). The tapes aired on a TV channel came as a shock to the people. Swift action followed. The two Houses referred the matter to committees and on the basis of their reports 11 MPs were expelled from parliament. Around the same time, there was another expose vis-à-vis the MPLAD Scheme. A TV channel showed four MPs or their personal staff demanding money to recommend projects under this scheme. Here again, based a committee's findings, the MPs were reprimanded and suspended from parliament for a while. But the most shocking case was that of a Lok Sabha Member who was into human trafficking. He was caught smuggling a woman to Canada on his wife's passport. Action was swift. He was and criminally prosecuted and later expelled from the House.

So, what does the balance sheet look like? As stated earlier, the most positive development over the last 60 years is the political empowerment of disadvantaged groups, introduction of the committee system and better policing of members. However, we still need to address the issue of dysfunctionality of parliament (loss of over 30 per cent of parliamentary time to disruptions), MPs' disdain for law making and the absence of periodic audit of the working of parliament by independent citizens.

A beginning can be made with a review of the practice and procedure of parliament. This has never been more pressing. Though the two Houses have been in existence for 54 years, we have not had an independent audit of the working of parliament and this has contributed in no small measure to the growing hiatus between this elected body and the people. A look at the quality of debates and the efficacy of parliamentary instruments will give us an idea of how far removed we are from that ideal parliament that we all thought we would have after independence.

Finally, since it's the 60th birthday of our parliament, let us end our diagnosis on a positive note by borrowing a phrase from Atal Bihari Vajpayee. Our parliament is 60, but it will neither tire, nor retire! Instead, it will go on to perpetuity and hopefully become more efficient and more responsive to the aspirations of the people.

VIF, 13 May, 2012

□

Rajya Sabha: What was it Meant to be?

The National Democratic Alliance (NDA) government is expected to improve its numbers in the Rajya Sabha after the present round of biennial elections, but it is still some distance away from gaining a majority in this House. Which means that the ruling coalition, which is around 50 short of the mid-way mark in the 245-member House, will still be hostage to the obstructionist tactics of a hostile opposition.

The Modi government is not the first government to cope with the disjunction in numbers in the two Houses. Except Jawaharlal Nehru and Lal Bahadur Shastri, who enjoyed majorities in the Upper House throughout their tenures, all other governments have had to deal with difficult situations brought about by a shortage of numbers in this House.

However, among political parties, the Congress party is the only one which has enjoyed a comfortable majority in the Rajya Sabha, either on its own or with its allies for much of its tenure. After the two Houses were constituted in 1952, the Congress enjoyed a comfortable majority in the Rajya Sabha. To begin with, it had 146 members in a House of 216. Later its strength went up to 186. Prime Minister Indira Gandhi too could bank on a majority when she entered office. Prime Minister Rajiv Gandhi too enjoyed a comfortable majority in the Upper House for most part of his tenure from 1984-89.

The Bharatiya Janata Party (BJP) has not been so lucky. When the coalition headed by the party ruled India between 1998-2004, it had just 45 MPs in this House and just around 80 for the entire coalition. Narendra Modi too has begun his innings with 47 BJP MPs in this House and the support of about 30 others from the coalition.

So, what does one do when a party or coalition secures a decisive mandate in a Lok Sabha election, but finds that all its plans are stymied by the Rajya Sabha where it is in a hopeless minority? Going by the debates in the Constituent Assembly, it is clear that the Constitution-makers did not anticipate that the Upper House could become an impediment to law-making and governance.

They also did not envision a situation where in some decades after the Constitution came into being, the country's polity would become so fractured as to squeeze and marginalise national parties and nurture dozens of regional, denominational and caste-based parties in the states, leading to representation of a plethora of these parties in the Upper House. In 1952, there were just six recognised political parties in the Rajya Sabha. Today, there are 27. The debates show that despite opposition in some quarters, most members of the Constituent Assembly favoured a second chamber because they felt erudite members of this House, who are not trapped in the political thicket like Lok Sabha members, would view legislation more dispassionately and thus provide critical value addition to law-making.

That is why they ensured that both Houses stood on an equal footing when it came to law-making except in regard to money bills. Here, the Constitution-makers made it clear that it was entirely up to the Lok Sabha to accept or reject the advice of the Rajya Sabha. In other words, if there was disagreement between the two Houses on a money bill, the Lok Sabha's view would prevail.

In respect of all other bills, if the Upper House disagreed, the only way out was to call a joint sitting of the two Houses to consider a disputed legislative measure. But, this provision is not available with respect to constitution amendment bills. Such bill require the approval of two-thirds of the members present and voting, in both Houses. With these safeguards, Constitution-makers felt they had done a good balancing act. In the Constituent Assembly, there was stiff opposition to the constitution of an Upper House. One member, Mohd Tahir said the Upper House would be an imperialist tool used to negate the democratic atmosphere in the other House.

Prof Shibban Lal Saxena was even more vocal. He said in no country had the Upper House helped progress. "It has always acted as a sort of hindrance to quick progress". It was not a good idea because India needed to catch up with the world and had to implement its programmes with rapidity in the next five to 10 years. In this scenario, the Upper House would be "a clog in the wheel of progress". The most vociferous supporter of the idea of a second chamber was N Gopalaswami Ayyangar, who had moved the resolution in this regard. He said, the second chamber would ensure "dignified debates" and it would "delay legislation" until "the passions of the moment have subsided".

He said the second chamber is "an instrument by which we delay action" and also give "seasoned people" who would bring their learning (which we do not ordinarily associate with the House of the People), to the House. He, however, assured the sceptics that he and his colleagues in the committee which drafted this provision had taken care to ensure that the Upper House "does not prove a clog either to legislation or administration".

In other words, by stripping the second chamber of the power to veto a money bill, the Constitution-makers felt that they had struck a balance and that the Upper House would not be a hindrance to governance. Would they say that if they saw how the Rajya Sabha functions today?

The New Indian Express, 7 June, 2016

□

When Upper House has the upper Hand

Prime Minister Narendra Modi may have secured the people's mandate in May 2014, but as the political conflict over the land acquisition Bill shows, his plans could get stymied because of his minority status in the Rajya Sabha. Since one-third of the seats of this House are filled afresh in biennial elections from State Assemblies, he will need a lucky run at the hustings in many States over the next four years, if he is to gain control of the Upper House. Meanwhile, what happens to his electoral promises which need to be translated into law.

It is said that the politics of confrontation between the two principal players—the Bharatiya Janata Party and the Congress—could lead to a possible joint sitting of the two Houses of Parliament to secure passage of the controversial Bill. But, even this option could be dicey because of the strong reservations that many of the BJP's allies have, vis-à-vis the land acquisition law. An analysis of the strength of political parties in the Rajya Sabha since its inception shows that only two Prime Ministers—Jawaharlal Nehru and lal Bahadur Shastri—enjoyed a clear majority in this House throughout their tenures, and nine Prime Ministers were crippled by the lack of numbers.

The two Houses of Parliament were constituted for the first time in 1952. Though the Rajya Sabha today has 245 members, this was not always the case. It had 216 members to begin with and the Congress opened its innings in this House with 146 members—

more than a two-thirds majority. This ballooned into a three-fourths majority in 1956. In fact, throughout the tenure of the first Prime Minister, Jawaharlal Nehru, the strength of the Congress in this House ranged from 146 to 186. The party had 166 MPs in the Upper House when he died in 1964. His daughter Indira Gandhi too began her innings in 1966 with a comfortable majority in this House, but lost this perch after the famous Congress split in 1969. Her wing of the Congress became a minority with 99 MPs when 42 members broke away to form the Congress (O). This situation prevailed for three years until 1972, but she regained her majority in this House until she was trounced in the 1977 lok Sabha poll. Prime Minister Morarji Desai too had to make do without a majority in this House during his tenure between 1977-79.

Thanks to defections from the other half of the Congress, Indira Gandhi secured a majority in the Rajya Sabha when she returned to power in 1980. Prime Minister Rajiv Gandhi too enjoyed a comfortable majority in this House for four years, but his strength dipped to 108 in a House of 245 following the Bofors scandal and the split engineered by VP Singh. The next Congress Prime Minister, P.V. Narasimha Rao, was not so lucky. Not only did he run a minority Government with just 232 MPs in the Lok Sabha and some ad hoc support from an assortment of parties, he also had to contend with a minority status in the Rajya Sabha where his strength ranged from 85-99.

The National Democratic Alliance Government helmed by Mr Atal Bihari Vajpayee between 1988 and 2004 too survived on depleted oxygen in the Upper House. The strength of the BJP, which constituted the core of this alliance, ranged from just 45-49, and his biggest ally in the House was the Telugu Desam Party with 13 members.

The United Progressive Alliance that dislodged the NDA, also had problems in garnering support in the Rajya Sabha. The strength of the Congress, which formed the core of this alliance, ranged from 71-73 throughout its 10 years in power. It got some additional support from allies and a string of small parties and independents. But, it banked heavily on ad hoc, tactical support offered by parties outside the alliance, such as the Rashtriya Janata

Dal, the Bahujan Samaj Party and the two communist parties.

The Jan Sangh, the precursor to the BJP, had one seat in the Rajya Sabha in 1952. As a party, the BJP acquired some strength only in the 1990s when it crossed the 40 mark. In the last two decades, its strength in this House has hovered between 41 and 51. All this has serious consequences for law-making and governance because the Constitution stipulates that all Bills, except money Bills, have to be passed by both Houses of Parliament. If a Bill that is passed by one House is rejected by the other or the two Houses disagree on amendments to be made in the Bill, Article-108 authorises the President to summon the two Houses to meet in a joint-sitting to deliberate and vote on the Bill.

A joint-sitting of the two Houses of Parliament was called for the first time when the Rajya Sabha disagreed with the lok Sabha on the Dowry Prohibition Bill in 1961. But this was not because the ruling party was short of numbers. Prime Minister Jawaharlal Nehru commanded a strength of 164 in the Rajya Sabha at that time. This was an instance of genuine disagreement over a proposed law among members of the two Houses.

The ruling Janata Party Government sought a joint-sitting in May 1978, to secure passage of the Banking Service Commission (Repeal) Bill, 1977, which was rejected by the Congress-dominated Rajya Sabha. The third time a joint-sitting became necessary was in 2002, when the Vajpayee Government wanted to see through the Prevention of Terrorism Bill, which was vehemently opposed by the Congress in the Upper House.

As stated earlier, only Jawaharlal Nehru and lal Bahadur Shastri had a clear majority in the Rajya Sabha throughout their tenures. Apart from them, only two other Prime Ministers managed a majority in that House for a substantial part of their innings (for 12 out of 17 years, in the case of Indira Gandhi; and four out of five years, in Rajiv Gandhi's case). Also, no Prime Minister has had majority support in that House for the last 26 years. The proliferation of regional parties clubbed with the impatience of the electorate leading to frequent turnover of parties has resulted in a major legislative gridlock in the Rajya Sabha since 1989.

This may call for a fresh look at the constitutional provisions relating to law-making because of the grave implications that this legislative logjam has on the working of duly elected Governments. Are we ready for this.

The Daily Pioneer, 14 April, 2015

□

Tyranny of The Minority in Parliament

The Winter Session of Parliament ended with the customary lament over the dysfunctionality of Parliament. Both the Houses faced many disruptions over intractable political issues as a result of which the Narendra Modi government could not push through much of the legislative work it had placed on the agenda. The helplessness of the government once again raised the question as to whether an obstinate opposition, which is determined to obstruct Parliament, can virtually undo the mandate of 2014 by disrupting the legislative plans of a duly-elected government. Though generally statements by the government and the opposition parties on who was responsible for the singular failure of the country's apex legislative body to function with some modicum of efficiency and seriousness, become part of the blame game that goes on after a session, there appears to be more than a grain of truth in Parliamentary Affairs Minister Mr. Venkaiah Naidu's argument about what went wrong this time.

He accused the Congress Party of coming up with "manufactured" excuses to disrupt proceedings in the two Houses on a day-to-day basis. The Congress Party's disruptive techniques resulted in nearly fifty per cent of the Rajya Sabha's time being lost to disruptions and adjournments. The Bharatiya Janata Party (BJP) is in a hopeless minority in the Upper House and the Congress Party, which has close to 70 members in the House, has been using its numbers to stall the legislative agenda of the government.

The Chairman of the Rajya Sabha, Mr Hamid Ansari, has been voicing his concern over the poor output of the Upper House in recent times. After the Winter Session, he said the Rajya Sabha seemed to be "singularly unproductive" in regard to legislative work during the Session. But, even more worrying is the virtual washout of Question Hour in the Upper House. PRS Legislative Research, which does a fine job of tracking Parliament, has reported that the Question Hour worked for just 2.4 hours in the entire session in this House which meant it functioned for just 14 per cent of its allotted time.

Nothing symbolises the failure of the parliamentary process more than the collapse of Question Hour. This hour holds the key to accountability and is central to Parliament carrying out its oversight responsibilities. Over the last sixty years, it has been the most effective hour for MPs who wish to keep the government on its toes. It enables them to question and virtually cross-examine ministers, so much so that ministers spend hours in understanding issues and preparing their answers. It is for this reason that the Question Hour is the most dreaded hour for ministers. Therefore, when the opposition raises issues and disrupts the Question Hour, the happiest members of the House are the Union Ministers.

The disrupters also do violence to the concept of accountability because MPs, specially those in the opposition benches, lose the right to question government and demand answers. The biggest loser from the disruption of Question Hour is therefore the opposition. It is therefore tragic to see the opposition throw away such an important parliamentary weapon which enables it to keep the government on track.

Another factor that needs to be taken note of is the rising cost of Parliament. Over the last six decades, there has been a phenomenal rise in the cost of Parliament. It rose from `36,000 a day in the 1950s to over `1.23 crore per day in 2004. In recent years, it was close to `2 crore per day or `29,000 per minute. These figures show a huge escalation in costs and therefore, it is only natural for the people to expect Parliament to work. If the people do not get value for money, the efficacy of the parliamentary system is certain to be called into question.

If a duly elected government is not allowed to legislate and bring in laws to fulfil its electoral promises, the entire democratic process becomes dysfunctional. Democracy is all about plurality and space for different points of view. Over the years, India's social diversity has metamorphosed into political diversity and resulted in the emergence of a plethora of political parties representing a wide range of interests from religion to region to caste. Over the last quarter of a century, even political parties that came under the broad Mandal umbrella have splintered into parties representing specific castes and sub-castes. Similarly parties representing regional aspirations have splintered or given way to newer formations. The best example is the emergence of the Telugu Desam in 1982 as a party representing Telugu pride and making inroads into Congress bastions all over undivided Andhra Pradesh. Thereafter, the Telangana Rashtra Samithi (TRS) came on the scene to slice away this vote bank and carve out a separate constituency to represent the aspirations of Telangana. The shavings and sub-shavings of the erstwhile Janata Party of yore pop up in different states representing different aspirations.

The people will begin to see the plurality in our politics as a hindrance to governance. This could once again strengthen the argument for one-party rule or pave the way for anarchy. During the Jawaharlal Nehru, Indira Gandhi eras, when India was largely under one-party rule and the Congress Party not only held the reins of the federal government but also of a majority of the states, one often worried about the tyranny of the majority. This tyranny unfortunately led to some of the most draconian constitutional amendments, including one which abolished the need for quorum for the two Houses of Parliament and the state legislatures to transact legislative business and to make laws.

After the defeat of the Rajiv Gandhi Government in 1989, no government has been able to muster a clear majority in the Rajya Sabha. While many coalitions have come to power since then either through a clear mandate for a pre-Lok Sabha poll arrangement or through post-poll negotiations, every government has had to cope with an adverse situation in the Rajya Sabha.

This is so because most of the seats in the Upper House are

filled via biennial elections in which MLAs are the electors and the party elected to govern at the federal level does not enjoy majorities in that many state assemblies in order to gain a majority in this House. This vicious dysjunction between the complexion of the two Houses is a political reality for a quarter of a century, but never before has this problem resulted in derailing the people's mandate.

We must now worry about the tyranny of the minority!

The New Indian Express, 6 January, 2016

□

Privileges that have Made them Masters

The 69th Independence Day made our hearts swell with pride when we thought of the significant achievements India has made on several fronts including all round economic growth, industrialisation, food production, poverty alleviation, literacy and education, and the media and the information technology boom. However, while there is much to cheer about, Indians are deeply troubled by the fractured nature of the polity, the confrontational nature of our politics and the virtual dysfunctionality of our various democratic bodies.

This is indeed sad and ironic because we take pride in being the biggest and most vibrant democracy in the world with 814 million electors and the capacity to hold relatively free and fair elections. But, contrast this with what happens once an election is over. The latest example is the complete washout of the Monsoon Session of Parliament, that 'concluded' last week without transacting any worthwhile business.

Starting with the apex legislature, most of our democratic bodies are seriously impaired and the downslide has been on over the last 25 years. The deterioration can be seen on various counts. The number of sittings per year of the two Houses of Parliament and the State Assemblies have crashed; in the 1950s and 1960s, our MPs and MlAs saw themselves as servants of the people.

Now, they perceive themselves as the masters; in the early years after independence, our MPs and MlAs did not want any salaries or perks. They saw their work as public service. Present day MPs and MlAs are constantly asking for more and in some States, their demands are insatiable; again, in the days gone by, rich politicians felt embarrassed to display their wealth. Today, dozens of politicians are worth hundreds of crores and they openly flaunt it; finally, in the past, there would be occasional scandals and the guilty would be punished. Now, there is a scandal a day and no one gets punished!

Let us start with sittings of our democratic bodies. For example, in the initial decades after independence, Parliament and the State Assemblies used to meet for 120 to 140 days in a year. In recent years, the two Houses of Parliament meet for about 70 days, whereas the situation is indeed deplorable in the States. Most State Assemblies meet for just 25 to 30 days! Even here, since political fights break out every day and our representatives have no forum to represent us. Then, who is to represent us and where?

Talking of salaries, when the first MPs' salaries Bill was debated in the Lok Sabha in the 1950s, several MPs opposed it and some even said that they would not draw the salary (Rs. 300 per month) even if the House were to pass the Bill. Today, an MP gets close to one lakh rupees as salary and constituency allowance plus an addition sum for secretarial assistance. But more than the salary, MPs and legislators in the States get a basket of unusual perks that their counterparts elsewhere are not entitled to and yet keep asking for more. Sometimes they make rather strange demands.

For example, two years ago, 100 MPs wrote to the Speaker of the Lok Sabha and demanded that they be permitted to have red beacons atop their cars in Delhi. When the media asked some of the MPs why they wanted lal battis, some of them said it would deter Delhi police from issuing them challans when they violate traffic rules!

This is where we differ from Western democracies. Although MPs in wealthy nations like Britain, America and Germany are themselves fairly well-to-do, they do not flaunt their wealth or status. Many British and German MPs go on bicycles to Parliament. They also get a small allowance per mile if they bicycle to work. They have no fear of personal security. Nor do they worry about what people will say if they travel on a bicycle. Many MPs and Ministers in Britain, Germany, Sweden and Norway use the local metro or bus to go to office. In some of these countries, even the Prime Ministers use the metro to get to work. In India, MPs come to Parliament in big and expensive cars because they believe that they cannot command the respect of their electors if they do not flaunt their wealth.

The moral decline is also too perceptible for anyone to gloss over. In the 1950s, the Mudgal case was the only prominent one of corruption involving an MP (there were some involving Ministers though). HG Mudgal was accused of taking a fee from the Bombay Bullion Merchants Association to espouse their cause in Parliament. He had taken an advance of Rs. 2,700 and Prime Minister Jawaharlal Nehru moved a resolution to expel him from Parliament.

Ten years ago, a major scandal rocked Parliament. A sting operation in December 2005, caught 11 MPs who were ready to table questions for a price. One MP demanded a 'fee' of Rs. 30,000 while another put his price up and collected Rs. 1,10,000 to do the job. The people were aghast to see the tapes aired by a news channel. All of them were expelled after the parliamentary investigations.

Soon thereafter, another set of four MPs was trapped in another sting operation and reprimanded by Parliament for improper conduct while assigning projects under the Member of Parliament local Area Development Scheme.

But, what really takes the cake is the arrest of an MP by the Delhi police in a human trafficking racket some years ago. This MP, who hailed from Gujarat, showed a woman from Punjab as his wife, secured a passport for her on this false pretext and for a fee, flew to Canada with her and returned alone. The woman of course became an illegal immigrant in that country!

This case tells us a lot about our political system, the degeneration of our institutions and the gross misuse of privileges by a section of our representatives. The reluctance or incapacity of political parties and parliamentary institutions to enforce norms has hurt the image of democratic institutions.

Parliament will find it difficult to redeem itself in the eyes of the people if it fails to wield the stick. The list of complaints against MPs is a long one. They are accused of sub-letting their official quarters, 'selling' domestic gas connection coupons and even encouraging relatives and friends to travel ticket-less in first class AC coaches on our trains. All this must end. Only then will August 15 celebrations be really meaningful.

The Pioneer, 18 August, 2015

□

Wayward MPs bring Infamy to Parliament

The rowdy behaviour of Ravindra Gaikwad, Member of the Lok Sabha, with a senior official of Air India and his shameful boast before TV cameras that he beat the official 25 times with his slippers, has shocked the conscience of the nation. But, what is even more worrying is the deafening silence of most parliamentarians and their unwillingness to speak up for the people and against such blatant hooliganism by a colleague who has sullied the image of India's apex legislature.

This shocking incident also brings us back to the core issue—the reluctance of Parliament to enforce a code of conduct and to discipline unruly MPs. Members of a committee that probed the Mudgal Affair in the provisional Parliament in 1951 drew up a code of conduct for MPs. A fresh attempt was made by Speaker Shivraj Patil in 1993, leading to the establishment of the ethics committee in both Houses, but precious little has been done to regulate the conduct of MPs. While our MPs are extremely conscious of their privileges, Parliament has failed to enforce ethics and punish gross misbehaviour.

The Gaikwad incident would never have taken place, if past incidents of gross misbehaviour had been punished. Our MPs are entitled to travel free in air conditioned first class coaches on Indian Railways. They also get 32 air tickets to travel within the country, apart from air tickets from their constituency to attend sessions of Parliament. Yet, there have been cases of MPs' families traveling ticket less on trains. There have also been instances of MPs and their companions threatening and assaulting genuine passengers who object to these ticket less VIPs usurping their seats. Such instances are not uncommon. But, we never hear of Parliament punishing MPs who misuse their privileges in this manner.

The Gaikwad case is just the latest in a series of such instances concerning unruly MPs. Here is an example from the past, which tells us a lot about how MPs behave and how our Parliament responds to complaints regarding their misconduct. An IAS officer was traveling with his family in the first class compartment of the New Delhi-Calcutta Rajdhani Express on October 28, 1992. Two MPs from Bihar boarded the train at Gomoh and Dhanbad stations. The first MP walked into the compartment at Gomoh with three men, two of whom were his bodyguards, and the other a security personnel in uniform. The MP asked the bonafide passenger to vacate his reserved seat. When the passenger refused, the MP's bodyguards beat him up, brandished their revolvers and threatened to shoot him. This passenger and his family were traumatised a second time when the second MP entered the compartment at Dhanbad. It was now the turn of the second MP and his 10 armed supporters to thrash the passenger. They even tried to throw him out onto the station platform. This incident was widely reported in the media but Parliament did nothing to punish the rowdy MPs. There are many more such cases both on the railways and airlines since then, but such MPs have never been punished.

The list of complaints against our representatives is only growing by the day. One of the reasons for such misbehaviour is the prevailing misunderstanding about their "privileges" and the false sense of importance that our representatives carry on their shoulders as a result. The presiding officers of the two Houses of Parliament and the legislatures in the States should educate members about the meaning of parliamentary privilege and the reason why some special privileges are bestowed on MPs and MlAs.

M.N. Kaul and S.L. Shakdher, the authors of the basic text on parliamentary procedure and rules have explained these issues most succinctly. They point out that the object of privilege is to safeguard freedom, authority and dignity of Parliament and that "privilege" means the rights and immunities enjoyed by each House of Parliament, its committees and its members. Privileges are granted to MPs and MlAs so that they may perform their duties in Parliament and the State Assemblies without let or hindrance. However, it is not a licence for criminal misconduct or for them to ride rough shod over bonafide passengers.

Parliament has been extremely lenient towards such MPs in the past, leading to the present situation. For example, an MP—Jaswant Singh Bishnoi—was downgraded from first class AC to second AC—to accommodate a High Court judge (who was above him in order of precedence) on a Delhi-Jodhpur train in August, 2000. The MP raised such a shindy that the Committee of Privileges of the lok Sabha hauled up the entire railway board and submitted a 75-page report in defence of the MP's conduct.

In December, 2011, 18 MPs from Uttar Pradesh and Bihar complained to the Railway Minister about ill-treatment at the hands of the railways because they were downgraded from first class to second class AC on the Patna-Delhi Rajdhani Express.

MPs just board trains at will and expect bonafide passengers to be dislodged. The railway officials said out of 22 first class berths, only six were vacant and were given to MPs. The rest were accommodated in second class AC coaches, but this was infra dig for our MPs. The hapless Minister apologised to these MPs in Parliament and transferred out a senior railway official.

The obnoxious behaviour of the MPs on the Rajdhani Express in 1992 prompted a media veteran—Nikhil Chakravarthy—to ask in his column in The Pioneer: "One would be enlightened as to what measures of discipline are enforced upon people's representatives by the leaders of their party, and also by the Speaker of the lok Sabha, who has been informed of their misdemeanor—amounting to a Member of Parliament terrorising citizens of the country—which should invite disqualification from the membership of the august House. Unless appropriate punishment is meted out, infamy will infest the institution itself—and thereby it will lose its very occupation".

Twenty five years after this incident, Nikhil Chakravarthy's words sound prophetic when we see and hear an MP publicly boast that he landed 25 blows on an Air India official with his slippers. If Parliament had a quarter century ago put the right of the people, who elect MPs, above that the "privilege" of MPs to indulge in such gross misdemeanor, we would never have the Gaikwad incident now. The Bihar MPs lowered the dignity of Parliament. Gaikwad has done it now. How long will Parliament prefer infamy to enforcing discipline among its members.

The Pioneer, 28 March, 2017

□

Who will Stem the Rot in Legislatures?

The recent judgment of the Supreme Court on the criminalisation of politics has taken voters a few steps towards making an informed choice in exercising their franchise, but the hopes of debarring those facing criminal cases from contesting elections seem a bit too distant. This is because of the apex court's view that while entry of criminals into legislative bodies is like a "termite to the citadel of democracy," it cannot make the law to keep them out. That, the court said, is the domain of Parliament, an institution that is yet to show a firmness of resolve to stem the rot.

Over the years the apex court has spearheaded measures to ensure that voters have adequate information on election candidates. The court's directives have ensured that candidates have to file affidavits containing their educational qualification, assets and liabilities and criminal record.

In the latest judgment, the court has gone further and said political parties that give tickets to persons with criminal cases pending against them must publicise the information on the party websites. In addition, the candidate and the political party must issue a declaration in "widely circulated" newspapers about the candidates' criminal records and must give "wide publicity" to this at least thrice on the electronic media after the nomination is filed. The court expressed "immense anguish" at the rising number of individuals with criminal records entering legislative bodies in the country, but refrained from debarring such individuals from contesting elections.

It said the time has come for Parliament to "make law to ensure that persons facing serious criminal cases do not enter into the political stream." The court recalled the opinion of the Law Commission that persons against whom serious criminal charges have been framed in a court be barred from contesting elections. The Commission's recommendation "vividly exhibits the concern of the society", the court said.

The court also wanted Parliament to make it mandatory for political parties to revoke the membership of persons charged with "heinous and grievous offences" and not give them tickets to contest elections. It said this will go a long way in decriminalising politics. This judgment reminds us of the Supreme Court's verdict in the infamous JMM case, which was about the bribing of MPs to ensure the defeat of a no-confidence motion brought against the P.V. Narasimha Rao government in 1993.

Rao headed a minority government and the numbers in the Lok Sabha were precariously stacked against him. He was accused of buying the support of ten MPs to survive the vote in the Lok Sabha. Four of these MPs belonged to the Jharkhand Mukti Morcha (JMM) and they were paid ` 2.8 crore in total in lieu of their support. This cash-for-vote deal helped Rao defeat the no-confidence motion on 28 July, 1993 by 265 votes to 251.

What happened before and after the vote in the House was nothing short of a scandal. A prominent party leader from Karnataka flew to New Delhi with the bribe money in a huge suitcase. The suitcase burst open on the conveyor belt in the Delhi airport and fellow passengers were aghast to see bundles of currency notes strewn all over the place.

Even more hilarious was what happened after the vote in the House—the JMM MPs took the bribe money in gunny sacks to a branch of a nationalized bank in Delhi and asked the manager to deposit it in their accounts! But none of these MPs was punished for accepting a bribe to vote in a certain way in the Lok Sabha and deposit the bribe money openly in a bank.

These corrupt MPs went scot free because the Supreme Court held that Article 105 of the Constitution shielded them from prosecution. Article-105(1) says MPs shall enjoy freedom of speech in Parliament. Article-105(2) says no MP "shall be liable to any proceedings in any court in respect of anything said or any vote given by him in Parliament".

In this case, the MPs who took bribes were prosecuted under the Prevention of Corruption Act. But the MPs argued that they cannot be prosecuted for what they said or did in Parliament. The court found merit in this argument. It said the alleged bribe-takers who had voted in the House were "entitled to the immunity conferred by Article-105(2)". However, the court said the bribe-givers should be prosecuted, as also the bribe takers who did not vote. It said only those who voted were protected by Article-105(2).

While the Supreme Court's constitutional correctness is understandable, the consequence of all this—especially the precipitous fall in the quality of men and women entering our legislatures—is plainly evident. We need not be surprised if many legislators see this as licence for gross misconduct, and assume they are outside the moral and ethical framework within which the law and the courts expect public servants to live.

It would be futile to expect Parliament, which has been, at best, just a spectator to the criminalisation of politics, to now suddenly pay heed to the apex court's recent judgment. The decision to give party tickets is based on the ability of the candidate to win, and the number of legislators with criminal records has been on the rise over the years. Will Parliament share the apex court's concern and anxiety and bring in a law to keep criminals out? India's apex legislature must prove the sceptics wrong!

The New Indian Express, 9 October, 2018

□

Impeachment: The Chairman was Right

Since leaders of the Congress Party are unhappy with the Chairman of the Rajya Sabha for rejecting the notice of impeachment against Chief Justice Dipak Misra, it is worth reflecting over the conduct of this party vis-a-vis impeachment of judges in the past.

As discussed in the previous column, Mr. G.S. Dhillon, the Speaker of the Lok Sabha during Indira Gandhi's prime ministership in 1970, rejected an impeachment notice against a judge of the Supreme Court at the preliminary stage on the ground that it was frivolous. Then why deny Mr. Naidu the right to do so in respect of Chief Justice Dipak Misra?

Secondly, if the party is so worried about the image of the judiciary, why did it not vote in favour of the motion to remove Justice V. Ramaswami, who faced grave charges of misbehavior, in the Lok Sabha in 1993?

Since a quarter century has gone by since the Ramaswami impeachment saga, it is necessary to jog public memory about what this case was all about. The notice of motion for removal of Justice V. Ramaswami of the Supreme Court was sent by Madhu Dandavate and 107 other MPs on 21 February, 1991 to the Speaker of the Lok Sabha. It related to acts of misbehavior during Justice Ramaswami's tenure as Chief Justice of Punjab and Haryana between 1987-89. The allegations made against the judge indicated gross misuse of office and included: Purchasing furniture, carpets etc. for the High Court and for his residence worth about Rs. 50 lakh from hand-picked dealers at highly inflated rates and without inviting tenders; purchasing more than Rs. 13 lakh worth of furniture, carpets etc.

For his official residence when he was entitled to spend only Rs. 38,500; purchasing silver maces worth Rs. 3.60 lakh at highly inflated prices from a firm in his home town without inviting bids even after other judges opposed the move as being wholly unnecessary and a relic of the colonial past; and that he misused public funds and built up a residential telephone bill of Rs. 9.10 lakh in Chandigarh and even made the high court pay for his residential telephone bills in Madras. But the most shameful charges were that he got himself reimbursed for fake petrol and car repair bills; that he misappropriated furniture and other items purchased from court funds for his official residence; and that he replaced several items of furniture, carpets and suitcases purchased with public funds for his residence with old and inferior quality items!

There is a lot more, but for the sake of brevity, many more instances of petty behavior of the judge are not listed here. I do not think there has ever been a more scandalous charge-sheet against a senior member of the judiciary. Yet, Mr. Kapil Sibal was his chief defender and the Congress Party chose not to impeach him!

Mr. Rabi Ray, the Speaker, admitted the motion and constituted an inquiry committee comprising Justice P.B. Sawant of the Supreme Court, Justice P.D. Desai, Chief Justice of the High Court of Bombay, and Justice O. Chinnappa Reddy, former judge of the Supreme Court. This committee, which submitted its report to the Speaker in July, 1992, came up with a damning indictment of Justice Ramaswami.

It said: "Justice Ramaswami's conduct... discloses willful and gross misuse of office, purposeful and persistent negligence in the discharge of duties, intentional and habitual extravagance at the cost of the public exchequer, moral turpitude by using public funds for private purposes in diverse ways and reckless disregard of statutory rules and brings disrepute to the high judicial office and dishonor to the institution of judiciary and undermines the faith and confidence which the public reposes in the administration of justice.

The acts are of such a nature that his continuance in office will be prejudicial to the administration of justice and to the public interest". Also, there was something very petty about the conduct of this judge, because the committee found many articles missing when he handed over his official residence in Chandigarh. Among them were five new suitcases, which he got the High Court to purchase just before his elevation to the Supreme Court!

This must certainly be the severest indictment of a judge of the apex court .Yet, despite such a damning indictment, the Congress Party chose to let him off the hook when the motion for his impeachment was put to vote in the Lok Sabha in May, 1993 and Mr Sibal played the role of this judge's chief defender.

Yet another judge who faced grave charges of misbehavior was Justice Soumitra Sen, judge of the Calcutta High Court. He was charged with misappropriating Rs. 33.22 lakh which he had received in his capacity as Receiver appointed by the High Court of Calcutta.

Unlike the Ramaswami and the Sen cases where grave charges were made against the judges and the accusations were backed by compelling evidence, the signatories to the motion against CJI Misra appeared to be "unsure of their own case". The RS Chairman said, for example, the signatories said in one allegation that the Chief Justice "may have been involved in a conspiracy of paying illegal gratification". At another place they said "he (CJI) too was likely to fall within the scope of investigation". Therefore, Mr. Naidu said "in the absence of credible and verifiable information placed before me... it would be an inappropriate and irresponsible act to accept statements which have little empirical basis".

Anyone who compares the petition filed against CJI Misra with the weighty petitions filed against Justice Ramaswami and Justice Sen will clearly see the difference.

Finally, a word about the Congress Party's commitment to an independent judiciary. The party campaigned vigorously for a "committed" judiciary in the 1970s—meaning committed to the party and its leader Indira Gandhi, after the Supreme Court ruled that the basic structure of the Constitution cannot be amended.

The party also brought in the 42nd Amendment to strip

the higher judiciary of its powers. The respect the party had for the Supreme Court is best explained by what its leaders said in Parliament during the debate on the 42nd Amendment. Here is a glimpse:

C.M. Stephen: Now the power of this Parliament (through the 42nd Amendment) is declared to be out of bounds for any court. It is left to the courts whether they should defy it. I do not know whether they will have the temerity to do that but if they do... that will be a bad day for the judiciary. The committee of the House is sitting with regard to the enquiry into the conduct of judges and all that. We have got our methods, our machinery.

Swaran Singh: Unfortunately, the courts transgressed the limits prescribed for them. It is a crude sort of invasion. NKP Salve: In the life of every nation ...there comes a time when the Constitution has to be saved from the court and the court from itself. The new crop of Congresspersons must acquaint themselves with the history of their party vis-a-vis our Constitution and judiciary.

The New Indian Express, 9 May, 2018

□

Congress cannot have Leader of the Opposition Status

Throughout Jawaharlal Nehru's prime ministership, India never had a Leader of the Opposition because no political party commanded one-tenth of the strength of the Lok Sabha. Similarly, there was no LOP for 15 of the 16 years when Indira Gandhi was Prime Minister and during 1984-89 when Rajiv Gandhi was at the helm. Not once during those 32 years when the Nehru-Gandhis were at the helm did the Congress Party ever consider altering the rule drafted by Mavalankar.

The leader of the Congress Party will once again not have the status of Leader of the Opposition (LOP) in the Lok Sabha because the party has failed to win ten per cent of the seats in the House in the 2019.

The rule for granting the Leader of the Opposition status in the House was drafted by G.V. Mavalankar, the first Speaker of the Lok Sabha and has been followed since then. As per this rule, a party must have at least 10 per cent of the strength in order to qualify to be designated as a parliamentary party and the leader of the largest such parliamentary party in the opposition ranks is designated as the Leader of the Opposition (LOP).

When the Congress Party won just 44 seats in 2014, its leader in the House failed to qualify as LOP. Again, in 2019, the party has bagged just 52 seats and has fallen short of the magic number (55) to get the status. Five years ago, the Congress Party and many of its fellow travelers argued that democracy would be in danger if its leader was not accorded the status of LOP in the House.

Those who took this line were hiding a dreadful truth, namely that throughout Jawaharlal Nehru's prime ministership, India never had a Leader of the Opposition because no political party commanded one-tenth of the strength of the Lok Sabha. Similarly, there was no LOP for 15 of the 16 years Indira Gandhi was Prime Minister and during 1984-89 when Rajiv Gandhi was at the helm. Not once during those 32 years when the NehruGandhis were at the helm did the Congress Party ever consider altering the rule drafted by Mavalankar.

According to Kaul and Shakdher, the conditions laid down by Mavalankar for an association of members to be recognised as a parliamentary party were as follows: They must have a distinct ideology and programme which they have announced prior to the election and on which they have been elected and "they should form a homogenous unit capable of developing into a well-knit entity"; they should have an organisation both inside and outside the House, their number should not be less than the quorum fixed to constitute a sitting of the House, which is one-tenth of the total membership.

These principles were later embodied in Direction 121 (1) of the Directions by the Speaker, Lok Sabha. Many decades later, they were incorporated in The Leaders and Chief Whips of Recognised Parties and Groups in Parliament (facilities) Act, 1998.

In the present case, this means that a political party must have at least 55 MPs to be recognised as a parliamentary party and to get the LOP position. India got its first leader of Opposition in 1969—a good 17 years after the first general election held in 1952. Ram Subhag Singh became the LOP when the Congress split and 60 of its MPs moved to the opposition benches. He remained in office until the dissolution of the Lok Sabha in December, 1970.

In the 1971 poll, no party in the opposition secured ten per cent of the seats and so, did not have the LOP status. Indira Gandhi had won a massive majority in that election and the Communist Party of India (Marxist) with 25 seats was the largest party in the opposition In the Seventh and Eighth Lok Sabhas constituted in 1980 and 1984 the Congress registered huge victories and won

353 and 404 seats respectively. There was no LOP in either of these Houses.

The largest party in opposition in 1984 was the Telugu Desam Party with 30 MPs. In the 10th Lok Sabha, the Congress returned to power heading a minority Government with 232 seats. The BJP secured 120 seats and its leader was given the LOP status. In the 11th Lok Sabha election, again the BJP with 161 held the LOP position. In the 12th Lok Sabha formed in 1998 and the 13th Lok Sabha constituted a year later, the Congress with 141 seats and 114 seats respectively, got this status.

In the 14th and the 15th Lok Sabhas, the Congress came to power under the United Progressive Alliance umbrella, and the BJP secured 145 and 116 seats respectively to retain the LOP status.

In the 16th Lok Sabha, the Congress Party's strength crashed to 44 and the BJP has secured a handsome victory with 282 seats.

In the new Lok Sabha, the BJP has 303 seats and the Congress just 52. Five years ago, the Congress argued that the statutory limitations should be overlooked because the LOP is now a member of many key committees to appoint Information Commissioners, Chairperson and members of the Lokpal, the Human Rights Commission and the Central Vigilance Commissioner.

Even the argument is flawed because the absence of the LOP will not affect the appointments process vis-a-vis the CVC and the CIC because both these Acts provide for the leader of the largest parliamentary group to stand in for the LOP—if there is no LOP.

Even in regard to selection of the chairperson and members of the Lokpal and the National Human Rights Commission, the absence of a LOP will not hinder the process, Both these Acts unequivocally declare that no appointment will be invalid "merely by reason of any vacancy in the Selection Committee." If need be, these Acts can be amended to allow the leader of the largest parliamentary group to be in these selection committee, But, even without the amendment, the appointments can be made. In any case, the Narendra Modi government made Mr. Mallikarjun Kharge, the leader of the Congress Party in the House as a Special Invitee to the committee to select the Lokpal. Sadly, Mr. Kharge refused to participate in the process.

The history of Lok Sabha elections shows that whenever the Congress won the Parliament elections handsomely, the opposition was decimated and no opposition party secured even 10 per cent of the seats to be entitled to the status of LOP. Even in the days of the Jawaharlal Nehru, who was said to be a great democrat the Congress showed no magnanimity to relax the rules and designate and opposition leader as the leader of Opposition in all these Lok Sabhas.

On the other hand, whenever the Congress was defeated, as in 1977, 1989, 1996, 1998 and 1999, it won enough seats for its leader to be designated the LOP. However, the Narendra Modi-wave has blotched the Congress's copybook both in and 2019.

Now, if any one says "democracy will be in peril" if the Congress does not get the status of LOP in the Lok Sabha, those who know the history of Parliament will say that this puerile nonsense.

www.asuryaprakash.com, 29 May, 2019

□

Stopping the Evil of Defections

The decision of Venkaiah Naidu, the vice president and Chairman of the Rajya Sabha to disqualify two members of his House—Sharad Yadav and Ali Anwar Ansari—and the reasoning provided by him have added a new dimension to the anti-defection law while strengthening its provisions and reinforcing the original intent of the lawmakers.

This decision of the chairman will have a significant bearing on how presiding officers will henceforth consider what constitutes "voluntarily giving up" of membership of a House. It will also, hopefully, push presiding officers to complete inquiries under this law within three months and stop needless procrastination.

The issue of defection of these two members arose following the decision of the Bihar Chief Minister Nitish Kumar to break away from a pre-poll alliance known as the Mahagathbandhan with some parties including Lalu Yadav's RJD and strike an alliance with the BJP. Both Yadav and Ansari opposed Nitish's decision, joined forces with Lalu and publicly denounced the new alignment. However, Nitish commanded the support of an overwhelming majority of the lawmakers and office-bearers of his party—the JD(U). Consequently, the JD(U) lost no time in dislodging Sharad Yadav from the post of leader of the JD(U) in the Upper House and initiated proceedings against Yadav and Ansari.

Under paragraph 2(a) of the anti-defection law, which is placed in the Tenth Schedule of the Constitution, a member can be disqualified if he "voluntarily gives up" the membership of the party to which he belongs or when he votes or abstains from voting in the House, contrary to the directions issued by the political party to which he belongs. The critical question that arose in these two cases was whether the conduct of the two MPs amounted to them "voluntarily giving up" the membership of their party, the JD(U).

The two MPs argued that they had not voluntarily given up membership of the party. In fact it was Nitish who had done so by violating the aims laid down in the party constitution and "by acting against the principles on which the party was founded", they claimed. They also contended that the decision of Nitish to break away from the Mahagathbandhan and to align himself with the BJP had resulted in a split in the JD(U) and that their faction commanded majority support after the split.

The MPs tried to argue that the sanctity of a pre-poll alliance cannot be violated. But their attempt to equate the Mahagathbandhan to a political party does not hold water. In fact, the Second Administrative Reforms Commission has recommended that the anti-defection law be amended to protect the sanctity of pre-poll alliances. It has said that coalitions are now the norm and there is a need to legally bind pre-poll coalition partners to their alliances.

However, the Parliament has not extended the anti-defection law to pre-poll alliances. So, as the law stands today, it revolves round just political parties. The National Commission to Review the Working of the Constitution also emphasised the need for legislators defecting from one party to another to contest elections afresh.

The chairman set aside their objections to the party electing a new leader in the Rajya Sabha. He said, "I have to go by the dictum that in a democracy, it is the rule of the majority and the voice of the majority that will have to be accepted." In this case he said the two MPs had failed to provide evidence that their group commanded a majority in the legislature party. Further, the public denouncement of Nitish for withdrawing from the Mahagathbandhan by the two MPs and their decision to share public platforms with the JD(U)'s rivals "are enough to establish beyond doubt" that they had indulged in anti-party activities.

The central point to be determined in this case is whether

the two MPs had "voluntarily given up" membership of the party. The chairman relied on two significant judgments of the Supreme Court in support of the contention that these words had a much wider connotation than just the formal resignation from a party. In Ram Naik *vs.* Union of India, the Supreme Court observed that the words "voluntarily given up his membership" are not synonymous with resignation and have a wider connotation. Even in the absence of a formal resignation, an inference can be drawn from the conduct of a member that he has voluntarily given up his membership of the political party to which he belongs.

In another case, the Supreme Court observed that "the act of voluntarily giving up the membership of the political party may be either express or implied". Prior to the Supreme Court's judgment in the Ram Naik Case, the Committee of Privileges of the Eighth Lok Sabha examined the question as to what constituted "voluntarily giving up membership".

The committee felt that one should not place a narrow interpretation of the constitutional provision.

"The intention of the lawmakers is quite clear; that it is not only the overt act of tendering resignation but also by his conduct that a member may give up the membership of his political party. The committee are of the view that if a member by his conduct makes it manifestly clear that he is not bound by party discipline and is prepared even to wreck it by his conduct, he should be prepared to pay the price of losing his seat".

Venkaiah Naidu also referred to the widespread criticism of some presiding officers for the inordinate delay in deciding such cases and said that all cases should be decided within three months. Only then can the evil of defections be effectively thwarted.

The New Indian Express, 22 December, 2017

□

Chapter-3

OUR DEMOCRACY

Democracy Defined

A full-fledged democracy must have the following eight elements:

1. *An inviolable commitment to freedom of expression; freedom of conscience and other Fundamental Rights*
2. *An unambiguous constitutional commitment to secularism*
3. *Separation of Religion and State*
4. *Republican form of government*
5. *Constitutional right to equality before law and equal protection of the laws*
6. *Right to life and personal liberty*
7. *Gender Equality*
8. *Universal Adult Suffrage*

All these eight essentials exist in India

www.asuryaprakash.com

□

Measuring Democracy–Stench of Racism!

A Swedish Institute which claims to study democracies around the world has downgraded India and put it far below several nations, many of whom lack the essentials of democracy like secularism, separation of state and religion and equality before law, which are firmly embedded in India's constitution.

The report is called Democracy Report 2020 and is produced by 'Varieties of Democracy' (V-Dem), a research institute based in the University of Gothenburg, Sweden. The institute claims that "it has a nuanced approach to measuring democracy–historical, multidimensional, nuanced, and disaggregated -employing state-of-the-art methodology". Each of these claims need to be tested.

The report makes a startling claim that India "is on the verge of losing its status as a democracy due to the severely shrinking space for the media, civil society, and the opposition under Prime Minister Modi's government". On the other hand, the best democracies are supposedly Denmark, Estonia, Sweden, Switzerland, Norway etc. India is at a lowly number 90. This report must be denounced lock, stock and barrel for the following reasons:

Let us examine the claim that media space is "severely shrinking" in India after Mr. Modi became Prime Minister. You will find this laughable in the light of the reports of the Registrar General of Newspapers in India and other agencies which track media growth. India has witnessed a media boom over the last decade and the figures for the last six years should make anyone's jaw drop. The circulation of daily newspapers in India in 2014 was 150 million copies. By the year 2018, it had jumped to 240 million copies. There are about 250 million households in the country and of them as many as 160 million households had television sets in 2014. By the year 2018, this figure was closer to 200 million. But the media growth story extends beyond mainstream media. There has been an exponential growth in the social media in recent years and this is reflected in the number of internet connections, which has spiralled from 150 million in the year 2014 to over 500 million five years hence.

Further, just take a look at the shrill debates that are on in Indian news television programmes every evening and the talking heads representing different political and social voices trying to outshout each other and you will realise that our democracy has become too argumentative and even bordering on chaos. So, where is this decline of democracy?

Finally, let us look at the social media. Not a week passes without the anti-Modi lobby running hashtags like "Narendra Modi Worst Prime Minister" on Twitter regularly and thousands of followers of political parties opposed to him endorsing this line and adding their own abusive comments or cartoons. Therefore, the charge that freedom of expression is under severe threat in the country is ridiculous and smacks of uninformed opinion. Also, in view of all this evidence, anyone who says that "media space is shrinking" in India and that civil society and the "opposition" are stifled, needs to get his head examined.

The second defect in the report is that it attributes whatever deficiencies it has found vis a vis freedom of expression to Mr. Modi. This is downright irresponsible for the reasons that have been cited above and also from a constitutional point of view. Obviously, the report is written by individuals who are totally oblivious of India's constitutional scheme. India is a federal republic in the sense that the legislative and executive powers are shared between the Union and the governments in the states and the constitution itself spells out the subjects that are allotted to the Union Government and the state governments. Further, neither

Mr. Modi nor his party or the coalition to which it belongs, govern all the 28 states and eight union territories in the country. About half of these states are ruled by political parties and coalitions which are opposed to Mr. Modi's party. At last count, there were 42 political parties governing these states.

Also, a significant responsibility given to the states by the constitution is maintenance of "law and order", which means states are responsible for the administration of the criminal justice system. Therefore, when a state government registers a case against a journalist for defamation etc, the Union has nothing to do with it. In recent times there have been challenges to media freedom in some states, several of whom are run by trenchant critics of Mr. Modi.

Having examined the constitutions of dozens of nations, this writer is of the view that a pristine democracy must contain the following eight fundamentals: An inviolable commitment to freedom of expression and freedom of conscience; an unambiguous commitment to secularism–separation of religion and State; Republican form of government; Constitutional right to equality before law; Right to life and personal liberty; and universal adult suffrage. All these eight essentials exist in the Indian Constitution. Now let us look at the V. Dem report and the countries ahead of India. Denmark is the best democracy according to this report. But, is it? Its constitution says that the Evangelical Lutheran Church which is based on the Holy Bible "shall be the established church of Denmark". Further, "the State has a duty to support the Church of Denmark financially and in other ways". Sweden is Number 3, but it is not a republic. Its constitution says the head of State "shall be a king or queen". More importantly, the constitution says the king or queen cannot be prosecuted for his or her actions, which means equality before law (Art 14 in our Constitution) has no place in Sweden. Further, the constitution says the king "shall always profess the pure evangelical faith". It also does not allow the prince or princess to marry at will. They need government permission to do so! Therefore, Sweden is not a republic, it is not a secular State as its head of State is wedded to a church. Equality before law is also absent because the king cannot be censured or accused.

Other nations which have been put ahead of India include Papua New Guinea, a nation based on Christian principles; Argentina, where the federal government supports the Roman Catholic Apostolic Religion, India is not only a secular, democratic nation but also the most vibrant and diverse nation in the world. It has the 'secular" ideal embedded in the Preamble of its constitution. It is home to all the religions and its population is ethnically diverse and its people speak 122 languages and 170 dialects.

Therefore, those who seek to run down India are actually running down democracy itself. These Western notions of "democracy", where the authors propound theories convenient to them, need to be challenged. Indians need to now stand up and say "Don't lecture us–your theories have a strong stench of racism and Christian communalism."

www.asuryaprakash.com, 28 March, 2021

□

Stop Lecturing India about Democracy

India is the largest and most vibrant democracy in the world. Why do we allow small nations, often incomplete democracies, to define the concept and lecture us on these values?

While laying the foundation stone for the new Parliament building in the national capital last week, Prime Minister Narendra Modi spoke of India's tryst with democracy long before the Magna Carta was signed in England in 1215 offering liberty and freedom to the people. He referred to Anubhava Mantapa—a peoples' Parliament open to all sections of society—established by the philosopher-saint Basaveshwara in Karnataka a century earlier.

The egalitarian principles laid down by the saint were later incorporated in the composition of democratic assemblies in many countries. Modi also referred to the prevailing electoral rules during the Chola period in the 10th century, as seen in inscriptions found in Uthiramerur, a village in Kanchipuram district, Tamil Nadu. The inscription said every kudumbam (community) would be represented in the peoples' assembly. It also listed out the rules for eligibility of candidates and said persons who do not declare their assets would be barred from contesting elections. He also referred to the sanghas and sabhas that existed in different parts of ancient India.

These were extremely progressive democratic traditions. Further, Indians have a great comfort level with democracy, as evidenced by the steady increase in the voter turnout, whereas people are/were losing interest in democracy in many other nations. Finally, of course, India is the largest and most vibrant democracy in the world. It is, therefore, the "Mother of Democracy". In the light of all this evidence, he wondered why India's democracy should be viewed through Western eyes.

This brings us to the question as to why the citizens of the largest democracy allow small nations across the Western world, which are often incomplete democracies, to define the concept and lecture India on these values. A case in point is the annual exercise undertaken by some NGOs and academic institutions in the West to weigh nations on the democracy scale. For example, a recent report on democracy, produced by a Swedish Institute called Varieties of Democracy (V-Dem), has downgraded India and put it far below several nations, many of whom lack the essentials of democracy like secularism, separation of state and religion, and equality before law, which are firmly embedded in India's Constitution.

The report places India at a lowly 90, while the best democracies are supposedly Denmark, Estonia, Sweden, Switzerland, Norway, etc. This needs to be challenged. Having examined the constitutions of dozens of nations, this writer is of the view that a pristine democracy must contain the following eight fundamentals: An inviolable commitment to freedom of expression and of conscience; an unambiguous commitment to secularism; separation of religion and state; republican form of government; constitutional right to equality before law; gender equality; right to life and personal liberty; and universal adult suffrage. All these eight essentials exist in the Indian Constitution.

Now let us look at the V-Dem report and the countries ahead of India. Denmark is the best democracy according to this report. But is it? Its Constitution says that the Evangelical Lutheran Church, which is based on the Holy Bible, "shall be the established church of Denmark". Further, "the State has a duty to support the Church of Denmark financially and in other ways". Sweden is number 3, but it is not a republic. Its constitution says the head of state "shall be a king or queen".

More importantly, the Constitution says the king or queen

cannot be prosecuted for his or her actions, which means equality before law (Article 14 in our Constitution) has no place in Sweden. Further, the constitution says the king "shall always profess the pure evangelical faith". It also does not allow the prince or princess to marry at will. They need government permission to do so! Therefore, Sweden is not a republic, it is not a secular nation, its head of state is wedded to a church and members of the royal family do not have freedom of conscience. Equality before law is also absent because the king cannot be censured or accused. Yet, V-Dem wants us to accept Sweden as a model democracy. India will never accept it.

Finally, coming back to what the prime minister said last week, we need to shake off the reticence of the Nehru era and take charge of the discourse on democracy. Henceforth, the Indian story will have to revolve around this central theme and the Ministry of External Affairs will have to make this India's USP, beginning by ticking off non-secular, non-republican nations and countries that do not have the equivalent of Article 14 (equality before laws) and Article 27 (state shall not fund any particular religion) when they comment on India. Only then will Modi's vision to see India being recognised as the 'Mother of Democracy' be realised.

The New Indian Express, 15 December, 2020

□

Time to Challenge this False Narrative

The Swedish agency V-Dem, attached to the University of Gothenburg that produces a democracy report every year, has once again downgraded India in its 2021 report. According to this institution, India was an "electoral democracy" in 2010 and it has now turned into an "electoral autocracy". This report makes some sweeping accusations against India. It questions the integrity of the electoral system in the country and says "freedom and fairness of elections was hard hit" when the Lok Sabha election was held in 2019, leading to downgrading of the country to an electoral autocracy.

This institute now says India is as autocratic as Pakistan, even though it is an Islamic Republic that constitutionally bars non-Muslims from holding the office of president and prime minister. Further, this report says India is worse than Bangladesh, which has Islam as the state religion. The most objectionable part of this report is the question it has raised about the integrity of elections in India, with specific reference to the 2019 Lok Sabha election. Every Indian who values the country's Constitution and electoral history must condemn this conclusion because of the following reasons: one, this institute presumes that India is run by one party; two, that other parties do not matter.

This is totally absurd because as many as 44 political parties are in power in 31 states and Union territories in the country, excluding the BJP. Parties like the Trinamool Congress (TMC), the

Telangana Rashtra Samithi (TRS), the Biju Janata Dal (BJD) and the YSR Congress in Andhra Pradesh won a majority of the seats in their states in that election in 2019. The TMC and the BJD won 22 Lok Sabha seats each while the DMK picked up 23 and the TRS got 9.

Further, after Narendra Modi became the prime minister in 2014, the Aam Aadmi Party (AAP) won 67 of the 70 seats in the Delhi Assembly, the Marxists won in Kerala, Mamata Bannerjee's TMC registered a massive victory in West Bengal and the Congress won the state Assembly elections convincingly in Rajasthan and Chhattisgarh, to name just a few of the states that voted against the BJP. Therefore, when someone questions the integrity of our election system, Indians must question the integrity of the institutions that are saying this.

Strangely, the V-Dem report claims that "freedom of association" is another thing that is slipping out of the hands of Indian citizens. The Freedom House Report on "Freedom in the World 2021" is also singing a similar tune. It says political rights and civil liberties are eroding in India. How can dozens of political parties, including Muslim parties that are opposed to the ruling BJP at the Centre, win handsome seats in state Assemblies and in Parliament if political rights are curbed? If you need further proof of how false this claim is, please visit the Ghazipur border near Delhi, where our farmers are asserting their political rights and civil liberties, and have blocked a major national highway for several months. This year too, as in 2020, nations such as Denmark, Sweden and Norway are on top of the democracy index of V-Dem. So, the time has come to study the constitutions of these nations and see how they compare with India.

The Constitution of Denmark says the Evangelical Lutheran Church "shall be the established Church of Denmark" and supported by the state. Sweden's constitution ordains that the King shall always profess the pure evangelical faith and the prince or princess would need government permission to marry! Norway's constitution says the King "shall at all times profess the Evangelical-Lutheran Religion".

On the other hand, India, which has civilisationally been a

secular nation and even has secularism embedded in the Preamble of its Constitution, is hardly a democracy according to this agency and is placed at number 97.Apart from secularism, separation of religion and state and equality before law are all absent in the constitutions of these three nations. Also, they are not republics like India where the head of state is elected.

You can imagine the absurdity of the rating by this organisation when you find Maldives placed way ahead of India. The Constitution of Maldives says only a Muslim can be a citizen of that country. So, here again, there is no separation of religion and state (in fact, the state is wedded to religion) and there is no sign of secularism. Yet, it is supposedly a much better democracy than India!

Having examined the constitutions of nations that are supposedly better democracies than India, this writer is of the view that only those nations that have all the eight fundamentals listed below can be classified as full-fledged democracies. They are: an inviolable commitment to freedom of expression and freedom of conscience; an unambiguous commitment to secularism; separation of religion and state; republican form of government; right to equality before law (as in Article 14 of the Indian Constitution); right to life and personal liberty (as in Article 21 of the Indian Constitution); gender equality; and universal adult suffrage. We have all the eight elements, but many of the so-called "democracies" placed above India in these reports do not.

India is the world's largest and most vibrant democracy. India is also the most liberal and diverse society in the world. Therefore, the time has come for the citizens to become aware of their own constitutional strengths and treat these reports with the contempt that they deserve!

The New Indian Express, 10 April, 2021

□

Elections Cannot be a Luxury in Democracy

Although there have been howls of protest over Gujarat's path-breaking law to make voting compulsory in elections to local bodies, this is certainly a move that is worthy of serious examination. Those familiar with the behaviour of electors in the country over the last sixty years and the bizarre nature of electoral outcomes consequent to the emergence of dozens of regional and caste-based parties across the country over the last quarter of a century will vouch for the fact that all is not well with the present system of elections.

In the absence of compulsory voting, the first-past-the-post system, that is currently in vogue, has thrown up extraordinary results that completely negate the basic principle of representation of the people, namely that the representative chosen commands the support of a majority of the electors in his or constituency.

The FPTP has proved to be inadequate for a number of reasons. The first of these is that close to 40 per cent of the electors choose not to exercise their franchise, resulting in a direct impact on the outcome of an election. The next problem is the multiplicity of political parties and the perpetual splintering of existing parties, especially at the regional level. This has resulted in quadrangular if not five-cornered contests in every assembly and parliamentary constituency among serious contenders, thereby resulting in a four or five-way split of the already depleted number of votes in the box. Such fragmentation of the votes polled leads to lowering of threshold for victory.

Election data show that such fragmentation of the vote results in MLAs and MPs winning their seats with the support of just 20 per cent of the electors in their constituencies. As a result, we do not have the foggiest idea of what actually is the mandate of the majority of the electors in a given constituency. This remains a mystery forever. What we have before us is actually the preference of a minority.

However, despite mounting evidence that most legislators in India today enter democratic bodies riding on a minority vote, politicians, who are the major beneficiaries of this systemic defect, are unwilling to address the issue and search for remedies.

There could be a variety of reasons for the prevailing inertia within the political class. It could be fear of change or plain selfinterest that has prevented the political class from acknowledging this issue and undertaking an honest audit of the electoral system. To an extent, the in action of politicians is understandable but what is inexplicable is the attitude of the Election Commission of India.

Despite mounting evidence of the failure of FPTP to ensure the representativeness of individuals voted to power in each constituency and the representativeness of the parties voted to power in the States and at the Centre, the Election Commission has made no effort to start a debate on the failings of the current system or to come up with a prescription to apply correctives.

Instead, what we see is wild reactions from one Election Commissioner, Mr. Harishankar Brahma, who asks if crores of electors who fail to vote will be put in jail! Mr Brahma obviously is not acquainted with the prevailing practices in other countries in this regard. The law in this regard need not be so stringent as to send someone to jail. For Mr Brahma's benefit, here are some examples of how other countries ensure maximum voting in elections:

According to the Institute of Democracy and Electoral Assistance, as many as 33 countries across the world have made voting compulsory. Prominent among them are Belgium, Switzerland, Australia, Singapore, Argentina, Austria, Cyprus, Peru, Greece and Bolivia. Belgium set the ball rolling with the introduction of compulsory voting in 1892. Australia introduced it in 1924. We need to look at the laws pertaining to compulsory voting in all these countries and draft a law that suits our genius. The penalty that is imposed on violators of this law varies from nation to nation.

For example, in Australia, those who fail to turn up for voting are fined \$20 to \$50. Switzerland, Austria, Cyprus and Peru also impose fines on absentee voters.

In Belgium, repeated abstention by a voter can lead to disenfranchisement. In Singapore a citizen who does not vote is removed from the list of electors. Getting back on the voters' list can be cumbersome. In Bolivia, the penalty for not voting in an election is a salary cut whereas in Greece, the penalty could be harsher conditions for securing a passport or a driving licence.

So, the Gujarat law is the first of its kind in the world. But, certainly, it's the first such initiative within the country. We also need to incorporate this in Article 51A of the Constitution which deals with Fundamental Duties. Voting in elections must be made a fundamental duty. The right to vote must also become a duty to vote.

The National Commission to Review the Working of the Constitution too has recommended something on these lines. It has said in its report that "duty to vote at elections" and active participation in the democratic process of governance "should be included in Article-51A".

As regards to penalties for not voting, no body needs to go to the jail. The authorities can insist on proof of voting in the last election when renewing cards given to persons below the poverty line or at the time of renewing ration cards, driving licences or passports.

Those who fail to provide proof can be made to pay a fine. A poor citizen seeking renewal of his or her below the poverty line card can be asked to pay a small fine while those who come for renewal of passports can be made to cough up a bigger fine.

As this writer had said on an earlier occasion, the atomisation of the polity and the low turn-out of voters have reduced the democratic process to a complete sham. We can lend some authenticity to India's democratic march by taking the difficult but inevitable decision to make voting compulsory.

In India, Gujarat has shown the way. If we fail to do so and allow the citizens the luxury of treating elections with contempt, the day may not be far off when forces inimical to democracy will use these very arguments to put an end to the charade that is currently on and snuff out what little is left of representative democracy in India.

The Pioneer, 25 November, 2014

□

Time to End the Vicious Cycle of Elections

A Committee of Parliament which recently examined the vexed issue of frequent polls in the country has come up with what could be the most practical way to end the vicious cycle of elections, which not only takes a heavy toll of governance, but also destabilises duly-elected governments and imposes a heavy burden on the exechequer.

After the Constitution came into being in 1950, elections to the Lok Sabha and all state assemblies were held simultaneously in 1952, 1957, 1962 and 1967 and all the newly elected legislative bodies were constituted between March and April in each of these years. In the first three elections, it was virtually one-party rule with the Congress Party holding sway over the voters almost everywhere. However in 1967, the electorate dislodged the Congress in a few states and voted in unstable coalitions. A couple of these governments collapsed ahead of time in the late 1960s, thus marginally disrupting the arrangement of simultaneous elections to the Lok Sabha and all the state assemblies. However, the real damage was done by Prime Minister Indira Gandhi, who recommended early dissolution of the Fourth Lok Sabha and a fresh election one year ahead of schedule in 1971.

Since then, the arrangement of simultaneous elections has come to an end and over a period of time, the country has got into a vicious cycle of elections which has begun to hurt governance in a big way. We are now saddled with elections in a bunch of states every year leading to disruption of normal life, a phenomenal flow of black money into the electoral arenas and intense national debates on the meaning of the mandate in each state. For example, if the party or coalition in power at the Centre is defeated in a state, all other parties see it as a mandate against that party or coalition (example: the defeat of the BJP in the Bihar Assembly election last November). Similarly, if a party or coalition which is running the federal government wins a state assembly election, it wastes no time in declaring that the victory signifies a renewed voter confidence in it and in its leader (example: the victory of the BJP in Haryana, Maharashtra in October 2014). The truth is that barring exceptions, both these propositions are untrue. Time and again we have seen electorates in the states clearly distinguishing a state election from a national election, yet, no party lets go of the opportunity to confuse one mandate with another. The same holds true when a party in power in the state gets a drubbing in a Lok Sabha election (example the Samajwadi Party's performance in Uttar Pradesh in 2014). But the political slugfest that follows an election erodes the confidence of those who have been chosen to rule for a five-year term at the Centre and in the states and needlessly injects instability within the ruling parties and coalitions at both levels.

Apart from political instability, this cycle of elections takes a toll on governance and leads to some other problems as well. All this has been examined in detail by the department-related Parliamentary Standing Committee on Personnel, Public Services, Law and Justice in its report on the feasibility of holding simultaneous elections to the Lok Sabha and state legislative assemblies, which was tabled in Parliament last December.

On the governance front, the Parliamentary committee has noted that whenever elections are announced, the Model Code of Conduct comes into play in the states in question, and this results in the stalling of development programmes of both the Central and state governments. Therefore, if a bunch of states go to the polls every year, governance takes a hit for one quarter of each year when the code is in force. The committee has therefore rightly noted that "this often leads to policy paralysis and governance deficit". The committee is also of the view that frequent elections disrupt normal life and the functioning of essential services. "If simultaneous elections are held, this period of disruption would be limited to a certain pre-determined period of time". The third issue is the cost of elections. If the Lok Sabha and state assembly elections are held simultaneously, it would reduce the massive expenditure incurred for conduct of separate elections every year. The committee noted that the Election Commission has estimated that the cost of holding elections to the Lok Sabha and state assemblies in the current disaggregated form was `4500 crore. Lastly, it said that when elections are not held together, crucial manpower has to be deployed for prolonged periods on election duty. For example, in 2014, when the Lok Sabha election was held along with elections in four states, polling was conducted over nine phases and as many as 1,077 in situ companies and 1,349 mobile companies of central forces had to be deployed, apart from the huge contingent of polling staff drawn from central and state services.

There has been sufficient debate on the ill-effects of frequent elections on administration, governance, the cost of holding elections, phenomenal election spending by political parties and its links to the generation and use of black money and disruption of normal life. However, no one had really come up with a workable solution that would fit into the constitutional scheme of things. It seemed as if there was no way in which Humpty-Dumpty could be put together ever again. This Parliamentary committee, however, seems to have a solution to the problem. It has suggested that to begin with, states can be divided into two groups "one group of states going to the polls in November 2016 and another group in June 2019 in conjunction with the next Lok Sabha election. This way, there will be just two rounds of elections in the country in a five-year period. In order to achieve this, the tenure of the existing state assemblies will have to be curtailed or extended by some months. In any case, the Election Commission is empowered by the Representation of the People Act, 1951 to call an election six months prior to the end of the normal term of the Lok Sabha or any state assembly. This is the first concrete idea that has emerged to reduce the frequency of elections and save the people and the administration from election fatigue. All political parties need to seriously ponder over this if they wish to ensure that India's democratic process does not become a hindrance to development and governance.

The New Indian Express, 19 January, 2016

□

When the People Vote you out, Blame EVMs

The controversy raised by Bahujan Samaj Party leader Mayawati and Delhi Chief Minister Arvind Kejriwal about the credibility of electronic voting machines (EVMs) following the massive victory of the Bharatiya Janata Party (BJP) in the recently held Uttar Pradesh Assembly election has once again raised the question as to whether these machines are tamper-proof. These doubts and accusations are not new. They had been raised over the last decade by many political parties including the BJP, but some significant developments in recent years have weakened the arguments against the deployment of these voting machines.

Among them are: Successful deployment of these machines in several national elections during this period without any serious challenge to their efficacy and credibility; the remarkable end to booth-capturing after these machines were introduced; judicial pronouncements that do not support a return to paper ballots, but encourage introduction of Voter Verifiable Paper Audit Trail (VVPAT) to put an end to all controversies; and the Election Commission of India's (ECI) determined efforts to introduce the paper trail in national elections at the earliest.

But, before we address the substantive issues vis-à-vis voting machines, we also need to ask why there was no ruckus about deployment of voting machines after the election to the Delhi Assembly in February 2015. In that election, Kejriwal's Aam Aadmi Party won a mind-boggling 67 of the 70 seats in the Assembly. The

BJP bagged the remaining three. Kejriwal's party secured 54.34 per cent of the votes, but 95.71 per cent of the seats, whereas the BJP secured 32.19 per cent of the votes but just four per cent of the seats. These results showed a complete disjunction between vote-share and seat-share and would surely have merited a protest, because one rarely sees such a one-sided election. But, strangely, there were no Doubting Thomases at that time! Therefore, those who feel nothing was amiss in Delhi in 2015 have a rather weak case vis-à-vis Uttar Pradesh 2017.

The ECI thought of a more efficient method of voting via EVMs way back in the 1980s because of rampant booth-capturing, violence and destruction of ballot papers etc. in elections. The commission first thought of this revolutionary idea when S.L. Shakdhar was the Chief Election Commissioner and KGanesan, the Secretary of the ECI. They decided to take the risk of introducing the machines on an experimental basis, even though the election law did not provide for the use of machines to record votes. Some polling booths in Parur Assembly constituency in Kerala were chosen for the experiment in 1982.

This legal infirmity was corrected with an amendment to the Representation of the People Act, 1951, in March 1989. Prior to this amendment, the election law only spoke of ballot papers. Consequent to this amendment, Section 61A incorporated the idea of a voting machine and explained that "voting machine" means any machine or apparatus, whether operated electronically or otherwise, used for giving or recording of votes; and any reference to a ballot box or ballot paper in this Act or the rules made there under shall, save as otherwise provided, be construed as including a reference to such voting machine wherever such voting machine is used at any election.

Following controversies and accusations that EVMs could be manipulated, the election Commission agreed in principle in 2010 to introduce the Voter Verifiable Paper Audit Trail (VVPAT). This results in the generation of a paper slip bearing the name and symbol of the candidate for whom the vote is cast, apart from the recording of the vote in the control unit in the machine. This system ensures greater transparency in that it enables the voter to see that his or her vote has gone to the candidate of his or her choice.

It also provides an alternate system to count the votes polled, in case of a dispute. In other words, one need not rely wholly on the numbers dished out by the control unit in the machine. A printer is attached to the balloting unit and kept in the voting compartment. It is visible to the voter for seven seconds through a transparent window. The Election Commission used VVPAT for the first time in a by- election in Nagaland in 2013.

The use of EVMs has been challenged before many High Courts and even before the Supreme Court in recent years. But the judiciary is not convinced that the machines can be manipulated. On the other hand, many High Courts have given the EVMs the thumbs-up. The ECI has summed up some of the judiciary observations on its website. For example, the Karnataka High Court has said this invention was undoubtedly "a great achievement... and a national pride". The Madras High Court ruled out any possibility of tampering of the machines. It said the EVMs cannot be compared to personal computers. The programming of computers had no bearing with the EVMs. The Delhi High Court asked the ECI to consult all parties and develop a VVPAT system that would put a final end to all doubt.

The Supreme Court has also directed ECI to introduce VVPAT in phases and asked the Government to provide funds for the purpose. The commission is keen to introduce the paper trail in all constituencies during the next Lok Sabha election in 2019. It has asked the Government to allocate Rs. 3,174 crore for the purpose. The commission told the Supreme Court recently that it could get the required number of VVPAT units manufactured in 30 months from the date of sanction of funds.

While the ECI has reaffirmed its complete faith in the "infallibility" of the EVMs, it has also initiated steps to introduce the paper trail as directed by the apex court. In the last round of elections to five State Assemblies in February-March 2017, the ECI deployed 52,000 VVPATs. In Goa, for instance, it deployed the paper trail in all the 40 State Assembly constituencies.

Given these firm judicial pronouncements and the move

towards full deployment of VVPAT—which will ensure that the machine is credible—the arguments against EVMs must end. The paper trail will bring in much needed transparency and also offer a fall-back in case of disputes. let us not go back to the era of paper ballots and booth-capturing!

The Pioneer, 11 April, 2017

□

Money Power Damaging our Democracy

Although the use of muscle power to capture booths and intimidate voters belonging to vulnerable social groups has drastically come down in recent years, the percentage of candidates with criminal records still remains a matter of concern. But the bigger worry is money power. During a recent tour of some constituencies in Karnataka, this writer heard from political leaders and those in the know that in most constituencies, candidates have to spend upwards of `20 crore to be in the reckoning. There was also near unanimity that some candidates in the old Mysore area had spent over `100 crore! With top contenders in every Lok Sabha seat spending phenomenal sums of money, the democratic process is now out-of-bounds for the average citizen.

National Election watch (NEW) and Association for Democratic Rights (ADR) have been providing detailed analysis of the information provided by candidates in their sworn affidavits while filing their nominations. Their analysis of the 521 members of the outgoing Lok Sabha based on their affidavits should be a matter of deep concern.

The NEW-ADR analysis found that 174 of the 521 MPs had declared that criminal cases were pending against them, constituting one-third of the Lok Sabha. Further, among them, 106 MPs (20 per cent) were facing serious criminal cases like murder, attempt to murder, kidnapping, communal disharmony etc. Thirty five per cent of the MPs belonging to the BJP and 16 per cent of the Congress and AIADMK MPs in the outgoing Lok Sabha have criminal backgrounds. However, the Shiv Sena topped the list. About 83 per cent of this party's MPs have criminal records.

As regards the financial muscle of candidates, the survey showed that of the 521 sitting MPs, 430 (83 per cent) were crorepatis in 2014 and they had average assets of `14.72 crore. About 87 per cent of the BJP MPs are crorepatis, as against 82 per cent in the Congress and 78 per cent in the AIADMK. The average assets of BJP MPs was `12 crore, while that of Congress MPs was `15.47 crore.

A recent report by NEW-ADR after examining the affidavits of candidates in the fray in the first two phases of the current Lok Sabha election is also revealing. Of the 2,923 candidates, the NEW-ADR analysis of 2,856 affidavits shows that 464 have criminal records constituting 16 per cent of the total. Of them 313 candidates have serious criminal cases.

As regards the net worth of candidates, 824 of them—29 per cent—are crorepatis and they have, on an average, assets of over `5 crore. However, this is the average of 2,856 candidates. The net worth of successful candidates will be much, much higher when you look at the amount of money being spent in each constituency.

A comparison of criminal records of outgoing MPs and candidates in this election shows that the new House will have its share of such individuals. What do we do with the fact that one-third of our MPs have criminal records and 20 per cent of them are facing serious criminal cases like murder, attempt to murder and kidnapping?

This needs to be reversed and the best way to do it is to bar all those against whom serious criminal charges have been framed in a court of law from contesting elections until they are acquitted. In order to prevent vindictive prosecution, the courts must dispose of these cases on a priority basis as recommended by the National Commission to Review the Working of the Constitution which was headed by former CJI, M.N. Venkatachalaiah.

Five decades ago, there would be large-scale violence during elections in the country. States like Bihar and Uttar Pradesh were notorious for booth capturing. Prominent candidates in the fray would have their own armed gangs to disrupt polling in booths which were not favourable to them. The gangs would open fire, chase away officials, capture booths and burn the paper ballots. This is now a thing of the past.

But the other big issue—money power—has reached monstrous proportions. Although muscle power has been brought under control, spending in elections has gone completely out of control and the Election Commission appears to be totally helpless despite huge deployment of observers and seizure of cash, gold, liquor and drugs meant for bribing voters. In the first two phases of this election, the Election Commission has already seized close to `700 crore in cash, liquor worth `218 crore and drugs and narcotics worth `1,152 crore. They have also seized gold and precious metals worth over `500 crore. Although this is unprecedented, this is still the tip of the iceberg.

Having travelled in some states and heard reports of voter bribing, one can safely say that although the EC has raised the permissible expenditure in a Lok Sabha constituency in the larger states to `70 lakh, the spending is upwards of `20 crore per candidate. Thus, if we have two main contenders for each of the 543 elected seats in the Lok Sabha, the candidates and their parties would have splurged over `20,000 crore, mostly to bribe voters, in this election.

With feudal, caste-based political families loaded with such huge, ill-gotten resources playing the game, democracy is becoming a no-entry zone for the average citizen. The EC must come face-to-face with this reality and find ways to stop the bribing of voters. Failing which, democracy will be reduced to an absolute farce.

The New Indian Express, 23 April, 2019

□

Nepotism Everywhere

The sudden and tragic demise of Sushant Singh Rajput in rather mysterious circumstances has triggered a huge debate on all that is wrong with Bollywood, especially the incestuous relationship that exists within the film fraternity and the discouragement, if not hostility, with which it greets "outsiders." While the Mumbai police is still probing the cause of his death, Sushant's colleague, Kangana Ranaut, another "outsider" who has had to struggle to find her place in the industry, has stirred the hornet's nest by talking about a "movie mafia" that exists in Mumbai and the nepotistic tendencies that it promotes. Her detailed interview to a private television channel recently has dredged up a lot of muck and brought the issue of nepotism to the centrestage.

One of the allegations against the "Bollywood mafia" after Sushant's tragic death is that it drives talented "outsiders" out of the business while promoting mediocrity among "nepo-kids" (children of film stars). This is not to say that star kids are not talented. Many of them have blossomed as excellent actors. But there is no denying the fact that they have a safety net. Interestingly, what is true of the cinema world in Mumbai is also true of the world of politics in Lutyens' Delhi and elsewhere in the country. Nepotism is so well entrenched that it is now central to our way of life. However, even if it is a bit late in the day, one must identify this trend and call it out because it militates against the democratic dharma, which demands a level-playing field for everyone.

Producer-director Karan Johar, who has been at the receiving end of Kangana's accusations, has not, in fact, denied the part played by nepotism in the film industry. He has stated publicly that when a producer launches the son of a movie star, he is actually wanting to be in a "comfort zone" because eventually, it's also a commercial decision. "A big movie star's son is going to get the eye balls...you don't want to take a chance...it's money." In other words, he says, producers feel "protected" when they are in that (nepotism) zone.

Is this not true of politics as well? Just look at the way party tickets are distributed during a parliamentary election and you realise that "being connected" matters a lot—or so it did for much of the seven decades that have gone by after independence. In fact, nepotism is so well entrenched that the children and grandchildren of individuals, who held public offices at the national level in India many decades ago, almost deem it their right to represent the constituencies which their grandfathers or grandmothers represented and live in the very houses which their forefathers occupied in Lutyens' Delhi. They get so attached to these houses that after a while they even forget that these dwellings are public properties. And in case they are not living in those houses, the second and third generation politicians demand that they be converted into memorials or mausoleums.

The Nehru-Gandhis are the real initiators of this trend in our national politics and in Lutyens' Delhi. It began in the days of our first Prime Minister Jawaharlal Nehru, when he ensured the appointment of his daughter, Indira Gandhi, as the president of the Indian National Congress in 1959. What happened thereafter is fairly well-known to the people of the country. As one member of this family succeeded another as the country's Prime Minister, the family's familiarity with our republican Constitution grew weaker and weaker and it began to imagine that India was indeed a monarchy.

As this family entrenched itself and started promoting its relatives and friends, the Nehruvian School became dominant and ambitious bureaucrats, academicians, thought leaders, artists, media professionals and businessmen became part of it. All of them realised that only those who were part of this caravan, could climb the ladder in bureaucracy, academia, media and so on.

Barring honourable exceptions, all the Governors, Vice Chancellors, newspaper editors, TV anchors and Padma Award winners were members of this school. There was no such thing as respect for diversity or other points of view. In politics, those who made it to the Lok Sabha and the Rajya Sabha in the days of the Congress's complete dominance, had to be part of this ideological "biraadri" of their fellow travellers. So the whims and fancies of this family became the law and its nepotistic attitude was dignified and universalised when it promoted the children and grandchildren of its loyalists and hangers-on.

All this went on unchallenged until Narendra Modi became the Prime Minister in May 2014. He has emerged as the arch disruptor and has substantially worked towards creation of a level-playing field in Lutyens' Delhi. Kangana is doing the same in Bollywood—fearlessly calling out those who shamelessly promote nepotism in the Hindi film industry and even launch vicious attacks on talented "outsiders" who dare to find a place for themselves in Bollywood.

For example, it appears to be common practice to crack jokes in television shows and public events at the expense of newcomers like what Shah Rukh Khan and Shahid Kapoor did to Sushant during an IIFA awards event. Kangana also talks about some extremely worrying situations, like when a noted Bollywood director told Sushant that he was not drifting but drowning.

Further, Sushant began life in Maldiha in Purnia district, Bihar. He was a National Olympiad winner in physics. A rank holder in an entrance exam for a top-of-the-line engineering college. He had eclectic interests, ranging from reading to mathematics and astronomy to dance, music and cinema. Was he too much of an intellectual for Bollywood because many "stars" have publicly gloated over their poor academic record? In fact, Karan Johar has confessed that he was told at a young age that if he wanted to make Hindi movies, "you don't need to be qualified....and this doesn't speak highly of the fraternity I come from."

This writer is not a movie buff but he got to see some of Sushant's work—his lead roles in Chichchore and in the biopic on MS Dhoni, for example. His sensitive portrayals in both these movies is there for all to see. So how come Bollywood, instead of embracing and promoting such talent, chose to drive him into a corner? If there is a "mafia" or to put it more accurately, a cosy club of nepotists, it must be identified and called out. The issues raised by Kangana call for some serious debate and cleaning up.

Further, if Sushant's death is not to go in vain, the democratisation of Bollywood is essential and a level-playing field is absolutely essential. But this can happen only if the current national indignation at the treatment meted out to Sushant is turned into a national movement to encourage the work of talented "outsiders" and, more importantly, gets reflected at the box office.

The Pioneer, 28 July, 2020

□

Too Many Parties Spoil India's Political Broth

For long years, it has been recognised that a major lacuna in our democratic process is the haphazard growth of political parties and the absence of a basic law to govern them. Strange as it may seem, although we are the largest and most vibrant democracy in the world with a staggering 814 million electors, barring exceptions, there is hardly any internal democracy within political parties and a majority of them virtually function like private limited companies owned and tightly controlled by political families.

The absence of internal democracy within political parties is, therefore, the greatest irony in democratic India and many jurists and thinkers and national commissions have repeatedly drawn the attention of the political class to set this right, but because of the mushroom growth of regional parties and their impact on the composition of the two Houses of Parliament, there has not been much movement on this front.

For example, in 1999, the law Commission suggested regulation of political parties to ensure inner party democracy, transparency in regard to flow of funds etc. It said the Representation of the People Act should be amended to deal with these issues. Significantly, it observed that a political party "cannot be a dictatorship internally, and democratic in its functioning outside". The National Commission to Review the Working of the Constitution, headed by former Chief Justice M.N. Venkatachaliah had noted that unless the political party system was reformed, there could be no electoral reforms worth the name. This commission said there was a need for a comprehensive legislation to regulate political parties and to deal with issues such as registration of political parties as national and State parties and their de-recognition. It said there was need to pay attention to inner party democracy, ensure regular party elections, training of party cadres etc. Further, it said political parties should be instruments of good governance.

The law Commission analysed the laws governing political parties in Germany, Portugal and Spain in its 255th Report on Electoral Reforms. It had the following observations to make: In Germany, Article 21 of the Constitution deals with regulation of political parties. It says that political parties shall participate in the formation of the political will of the people and that they may be freely established. However, their internal organisation must conform tc democratic principles and they must publicly account for their assets and for the sources of their funds. Significantly, because of Germany's tryst with dictatorship in the first half of the 20th century, the second part of this Article says that parties which "by reason of their aims or the behavior of their adherents, seek to undermine or abolish the free democratic basic order or to endanger the existence of the Federal Republic of Germany shall be unconstitutional. The Federal Constitutional Court shall rule on the question of unconstitutionality". These provisions have been backed up by a law to regulate political parties.

Analysing the laws governing political parties, the law Commission said that Germany regulates parties both for its unconstitutional actions and unconstitutional aims which have not been put to action. The Constitutional Court has exercised its power to declare parties unconstitutional on two occasions when it banned the neo-Nazi Socialist Imperial Party in 1952 and the German Communist Party in 1956. Banning the Communist party, the court had said that it could deny the advancement of an idea that violated the principle of individual dignity, "even if such an idea had popular support". It said those who are called upon to participate in the formation of the political will "must be unanimous in their affirmation of the basic values of the Constitution".

In Portugal too, political parties are regulated by the Constitution. Here the Constitution prohibits political parties which have a regional or religious objective. It also expects political parties to have internal democracy. The Constitution says that democratic parties must be governed by the principles of democratic transparency, organisation and management, and participation of all members. Here too the courts can abolish political parties that violate these Constitutional principles.

The law Commission has noted that unlike Germany and Portugal, "Spain only regulates the action of its political parties, not their aims or intentions. The Constitution says the creation and activities of political parties are free in so far as they respect the Constitution and the law. "Their internal structure and their functioning must be democratic". The law dealing with political parties States that elections to governing bodies of political parties must be by secret ballot and democratically controlled.

India's Constitution makers did not take cognisance of political parties. They made arrangements for the superintendence, direction and control of elections by the Election Commission of India, establishment of the two Houses of Parliament and the legislative Assemblies in the State and stipulated the qualifications and disqualifications for entering these legislative bodies. They did not foresee the need to put in constitutional provisions to regulate political parties. Therefore, the only provision for regulation of political parties is in a section in the Representation of the People Act, which empowers the Election Commission to register political parties. All that is needed is for the political party to say in its party memorandum that it bears true faith and allegiance to the Constitution of India. The ECI, in turn, has asked applicant parties to provide information in regard to party organs, office-bearers and it must state that it will hold periodic internal elections.

The law Commission has noted that these provisions do not empower the ECI to enforce internal democracy in political parties because there are no penal provisions. Further, its power to intervene in these matters stands further weakened by the Supreme Court's judgement in Indian National Congress (I) versus Institute of Social Welfare, wherein the court said that existing provisions in the RP Act and the Election Symbols (Reservation and Allotment) Order, 1968 do not empower the ECI to de-register political parties on the grounds of violating the Constitution or breaching the undertaking given to it at the time of registration. Therefore, the law Commission has concluded that there is no mechanism to review a party's practices which militate against the principles enshrined in the Constitution or against the requirements of the ECI's guidelines.

The law Commission has, therefore, recommended several amendments to the RP Act to regulate political parties and to ensure internal democracy. It wants unambiguous provisions in the law to enable the ECI to de-register parties which fail to adhere to these tenets. These are sound proposals and long overdue. The Government must come up with suitable legislative measures to implement them. Only then will the weaknesses in the inner core of our democratic system be tackled.

The Pioneer, 9 June, 2015

□

End is Near for India's Communists

Friedrich Engels had said that one of the principal outcomes of the proletarian revolution would be the withering away of the state. In India, post-2019, the state has emerged stronger than ever before and it is the Communist parties which are actually withering away! While much of the focus after the recent Lok Sabha election has been on the disastrous performance of the Congress, the real big story is the declining fortunes of the two Communist parties in India.

The Left parties had a decent presence in several states in the early decades after Independence. The undivided Communist Party of India (CPI) won 16 seats in the first Lok Sabha election in 1951-52. It rose to 29 seats in 1962; the party got around 9 per cent of the votes polled. After the party split, the CPI and the CPI(M) bagged 42 seats in 1967, but their vote share hovered around 9 per cent. This trend continued for three decades.

The two parties put up their best performance in 2004 when they together secured 53 seats in the Lok Sabha. Thereafter, their fortunes crashed. In 2014, the two could win just ten seats and their national vote share dropped to 4 per cent. This time, they are well below the danger mark having secured just five seats and about 2 per cent of the national vote.

While most political parties around the world, including Communist parties, re-invent themselves to stay afloat and win popular support, the CPI and the CPI(M) have stubbornly stuck to the theories and slogans that defined them decades ago. Their ideas about the working class, organised labour and the capitalist-proletariat binary remains unchanged, even though the world has moved on. This writer found examples of this during the Lok Sabha poll in West Bengal, where, during the road shows, CPI(M) cadres kept chanting "Inquilab Zindabad" while waving their red hammer and sickle flags.

Which revolution were they talking about in this day and age when the market economy rules the roost! The best example of how these two parties are completely out of sync with today's reality is their refusal to acknowledge the advantages accruing to the poorest of the poor through many innovative schemes like the 'Pradhan Mantri Mudra Yojana', the 'Pradhan Mantri Ujjwala Yojana', the 'Jan Dhan Yojana' and the direct benefit transfer scheme.

Mudra is an innovative programme launched by Prime Minister Narendra Modi to kindle the entrepreneurial spirit among the poorer sections of society. The idea is to "fund the unfunded". The applicants get loans ranging from `50,000 to `10 lakh. These small entrepreneurs in turn employ five to ten people to run their enterprise, be it a small eatery, a bakery, a garment or leather-goods making micro unit or a tea stall.

This writer met many beneficiaries during his travels to several states recently. The available data on the Mudra scheme is indeed heartening. Women entrepreneurs are the major beneficiaries of Mudra loans across sectors and constitute 70 per cent of those who have taken advantage of this scheme. Earlier this year, the government announced that it had disbursed loans worth `7.23 lakh crore.

Under the Ujjwala programme, the government provides a free cooking gas connection to families below the poverty line. Over 70 million families have benefited from the scheme. Another such programme with far-reaching impact is the scheme to build houses for the poor and toilets in every home. Though some of these schemes were initiated by the previous governments, the implementation was sluggish in the absence of motivation and commitment. These schemes picked up pace after Modi became prime minister in 2014.

All these schemes are aimed at ensuring the dignity of

women and children. One would have thought that programmes of this kind would be hailed by the Communists, but that has not happened. The spokespersons of these two parties have been consistently running down these schemes meant exclusively to better the lives of the poorer classes, simply because these schemes were launched by Modi and since he is the driving force to ensure their completion within the shortest possible time. The election results show that this kind of negativity has not gone down well with the people.

There are many other factors which have rendered the two Communist parties unpopular. The first of these is their approach to secularism. The two parties have moved far away from the Shah Bano days when Somnath Chatterjee, Saifuddin Choudhury and several others took on the Muslim clergy and strongly opposed the Rajiv Gandhi government's decision to bring in a law to prevent Muslim women from taking benefit of a civil law and a Supreme Court judgment providing maintenance to divorced women. That was in 1986.

However, over the last three decades the Left has become the standard bearer of the pseudo-secular brigade, become hostile to the Hindu majority and is pretending as if radical Islam is not an issue at all. The most recent example of its contempt for Hindu sentiment is the way it handled the Sabarimala issue and encouraged individuals to deride Hindus, their customs and their way of life.Where will they go from here? Will they do what the British Labour Party did some decades ago and change the way they think and work itself? If they again turn left, it's a dead-end. If they turn right, they will cease to be left! Where are they headed? The nation wants to know!

The New Indian Express, 18 June, 2019

□

Chapter-4

OUR COURTS

Remembering Justice Khanna—The Real Hero

The news of the demise of Justice H.R. Khanna, one of the greatest heroes of the second freedom struggle that India's citizens were called upon to wage after Indira Gandhi imposed the infamous Emergency, brings back memories of the sacrifices that this judge made in order to preserve core constitutional values and to uphold the democratic rights of citizens. As students of constitutional law are well aware, a tribute to this great judge will necessarily revolve around his valiant defence of the citizen's right to life and personal liberty even as his brother judges bartered away this right in that forgettable majority-decision of the Supreme Court in what is known as the Habeas Corpus Case.

In that case, the Supreme Court was called upon to determine whether citizens could move courts to safeguard their right under Article 21 of the Constitution, when the Emergency was on force. While four of his colleagues on the Bench said "No", Justice Khanna dissented and said "...the Constitution and the laws of India do not permit life and liberty to be at the mercy of the absolute power of the Executive."

While all Articles in Chapter III of the Constitution dealing with Fundamental Rights are important, Article 21 is rather special. It says "No person shall be deprived of his life and personal liberty except according to procedure established by law". This is a kind of constitutional provision that highlights the distinction between democracy and dictatorship, between rule of law and the law of the jungle. Such is the importance of this fundamental right that no nation that does not have such a provision in its Constitution can ever claim to be a democracy. Yet, the first thing that Indira Gandhi did after she imposed the Emergency was to get the President to rubber stamp an order suspending all fundamental rights including the right to life and personal liberty.

Once this order was passed, thousands of political workers, journalists and social activists who were jailed by the government moved the High Courts challenging this order and claiming that Article 21 cannot be suspended. Many political leaders like Lal Krishna Advani and Madhu Dandvate were among the petitioners. The Supreme Court directed the transfer of these cases to itself. A five-judge Bench comprising the Chief Justice Mr. A.N. Ray and Justices H.R. Khanna, M.H. Beg, Y.V. Chandrachud and P.N. Bhagawati heard these petitions. During the hearing Mr. Niren De, the Attorney-General contended that so long as the Emergency was in force, no citizen could knock on the doors of a court to seek enforcement of the right to life and personal liberty.

Any democrat would have been aghast to hear such an argument. But most of the judges heard the Attorney-General in silence. Justice Khanna notes in his autobiography `Neither Roses Nor Thorns' that he found some of his colleagues, who used to be very vocal about human rights and civil liberties, "were sitting tongue tied" and "their silence seemed rather ominous." Justice Khanna therefore decided to confront the Attorney-General. He asked him whether, in view of his submissions, there would be any remedy "if a police officer because of personal enmity killed another man?" Justice Khanna says the Attorney-General's answer was unequivocal. Consistent with his argument, he said "there would be no judicial remedy in such a case so long as the Emergency lasts." Mr. De further said "It may shock your conscience, it shocks mine, but consistent with my submissions, no proceedings can be taken in a court of law on that score."

Although it "shocked" the conscience of the Attorney-General, it did not stir the conscience of the majority on the Bench. Chief Justice Ray and Justices Beg, Chandrachud and Bhagwati upheld the government's contention that it had the right to suspend the right to life and personal liberty. Justice Khanna dissented. The case raised questions which impact the basic values affecting life, liberty and the rule of law he said while rejecting the government's contention.

Even as he did so, he knew the consequences that would follow. This judgement was delivered in the last week of April, 1976. Nine months hence, Chief Justice Ray was to retire and Justice Khanna, as the senior-most judge in the court, was in line for the office of Chief Justice. But, Justice Khanna knew that the Congress Party wanted "committed judges" and had therefore superseded Justices Hegde, Shelat and Grover soon after the court delivered the judgement in the Keshavananda Bharati Case on 24 April, 1973. Justice Khanna was also on this Bench and was a key player in formulating the doctrine of "basic structure" propounded by the majority. Now, in this case too Justice Khanna had displeased the government. The consequences were as anticipated. The government superseded him and appointed Justice Beg as Chief Justice in January, 1977. Soon after Justice Beg's appointment was announced, Justice Khanna sent in his resignation to the President. But even before his super-session, the Congress government did everything possible to tell Justice Khanna that he was persona non grata. It struck his name off the list of invitees for official functions and Congress ministers and government officials shunned him like the plague. Justice Khanna bore all this humiliation with utmost dignity. However, what really gave him solace in those trying months were the congratulations conveyed clandestinely to him by some persons in government, for his "bold" judgement. But the biggest irony was that the Attorney-General, who had argued that the citizen had no right to life during the Emergency, drew him aside at a judge's party and said "Judge, may I express my admiration and congratulations to you for that great judgement."

Granville Austin, the author of the most definitive book on India's constitutional history.

'Working a Democratic Constitution—The Indian Experience'-offers an explanation for the Attorney-General's apparent dishonesty. He says "the Attorney-General feared he and his foreign-born wife might be harassed if the government and the coterie became aware of his doubts about the Emergency and its Constitution Amendments. His friends noticed his tension and heavy smoking."

Justice Khanna's sacrifice for the sake of democracy and constitutional principles is best exemplified by the fact that after Justice Beg, the other two judges who concurred with the government in this case- Justices Chandrachud and Bhagawati– also went on to become Chief Justices of the Supreme Court. Justice Khanna's sacrifice will never be in vain if we disseminate the story of his judgeship to every new generation because his heroic virtues are certain to inspire many citizens in different walks of life to stand up and be counted when there is a threat to democracy and the rule of law.

The Pioneer, 4 March, 2008

□

The Swamiji who Protected our Constitutional Rights

The news of the demise of Shri Kesavananda Bharati Sripadagalvaru, head of the Edaneer Mutt in Kasargod, Kerala, earlier this month brings back memories of one of the most memorable cases in India's legal history. This resulted in a landmark judgment of the Supreme Court that fortified the essential features of our Constitution and shielded them from potential parliamentary attack.

The court propounded the basic structure doctrine to erect these fortifications in this case, which was triggered by the Swamiji's petition in 1972 challenging a couple of land enactments in Kerala and three amendments to the Constitution, which, among others, deprived him of his fundamental right to practise his religion and manage his religious affairs (Articles-25 and 26).

The case—His Holiness Kesavananda Bharati Sripadagalvaru vs State of Kerala (1973)—and the consequences of the apex court's judgment for our constitutional well-being are so immense that it must be told and retold for the benefit of every generation, so that they may understand the importance of fundamental rights and independent institutions for them to breathe the free air of democracy.

This case had many firsts. It was heard by a 13-judge Bench, the largest constituted in the apex court's history; the court heard the arguments for 315 hours over 70 days; Nani Palkhivala, the legendary lawyer, argued the case for the Swamiji for 33 of those

70 days; and, finally, the court delivered its historic verdict and said that while Parliament had the power to amend any part of the Constitution, it cannot abrogate its "basic structure".

This decision of the court has provided the citizenry with a vajra kavach (a protective armour), which will enable them to experience and cherish the core values in our Constitution, irrespective of electoral outcomes and political upheavals. It is also a decision that has blessed the country's supreme text, which was sought to be mutilated by the Indira Gandhi government during the dreaded Emergency, with longevity and shielded it from forces inimical to the values embedded in it.

The basic structure doctrine and its inviolability was propounded by seven of the 13 judges on the Bench headed by the then Chief Justice S.M. Sikri. The court held that the following elements constitute the basic structure: supremacy of the Constituti n; republican and democratic form of government; secular character of the Constitution; separation of powers between the legislature, executive and judiciary; and the federal character of the Constitution.

The Chief Justice and the other judges in majority dwelt at length on the meaning of the word "amendment" in Article-368. They held that Parliament had the power to amend the Constitution, "but not so as to result in damaging or destroying (its) structure and identity". A creature of the Constitution cannot devour the Constitution itself.

The Supreme Court reiterated the Doctrine of Basic Structure in several cases after Kesavananda Bharati and thereby etched these principles in stone, as it were, never to be tampered or trifled with. These cases include Indira Nehru Gandhi vs Shri Raj Narain (1975) and Minerva Mills Ltd vs Union of India (1980). With the passage of time, many other elements have been added to the definition of basic structure including the objectives prescribed in the Preamble, the balance between fundamental rights and directive principles, and judicial review, to name a few.

The value of this judgment for the citizenry is immense because supremacy of the Constitution means no individual, institution or ism can get a perch above it and the egalitarian and democratic values enshrined in it gain permanency; republican form of government means the right of citizens to have an elected head of state like President Ram Nath Kovind and not a monarch or a scion of any particular family; secularism ensures that the state has no religion; separation of powers is a guarantee against aggregation of powers of all three estates into one entity; and finally, the preservation of the federal features protects the rights of states outlined in the Constitution.

Later during the Emergency in 1975, a sinister attempt was made by the Indira Gandhi government to overturn Kesavananda Bharati when it got Chief Justice A.N. Ray to constitute another 13-judge Bench to reconsider this judgement. Once again, Palkhivala rose to the occasion and argued so eloquently and vehemently against Justice Ray's move that the latter dismantled the Bench and abandoned the move within two days. M.V. Kamath, Nani Palkhivala's biographer, quotes one of the judges as saying "never before in the history of the court has there been a performance like this". Another judge said: "It was not Nani who spoke.

It was divinity speaking through him." In his autobiography, Justice H.R. Khanna says "my feeling and that of some of my colleagues was that the height of eloquence to which Palkhivala rose on that day had seldom been equalled and never surpassed in the history of the Supreme Court". Kamath and Granville Austin, the most authentic chronicler of independent India's constitutional history, record many uncomfortable truths about the Kesavananda Bharati case and after, which tell us how perilously close we were to losing the most precious gift given to us by the founding fathers.

One wonders whether there can be a judgment more important than this for the preservation of our democratic traditions. This is therefore a moment to pay tribute to the Swamiji for his decision to move the apex court to protect his constitutional rights, and, willy-nilly, the basic rights of 1,350 million Indians. This is also a moment to salute his lawyer, Nani Palkhivala, who propounded the basic structure theory in his arguments and convinced the court to adopt it in Kesavananda and thereafter.

The New Indian Express, 25 September, 2020

□

NOTA not Insignificant Anymore

The outcome of the recently held Gujarat Assembly election has for the first time clearly established the power of the NOTA (None of the Above) option and provided evidence that it can play a significant role in a major election in the country.

India entered the 'NOTA Age' as it were, in 2013 after the Supreme Court's judgment in the PUCL & Anr vs. Union of India & Anr in which it directed the Election Commission to add the NOTA button to electronic voting machines. The apex court held that giving the voter the right not to vote for any candidate was extremely important in a democracy. The Law Commission and the Election Commission were also in favour of giving the voter the right to reject all candidates.

The Supreme Court cited the example of 13 nations where NOTA is in vogue and said, "Such an option gives the voter the right to express his disapproval with the kind of candidates that are being put up by the political parties. When the political parties will realise that a large number of people are expressing their disapproval with the candidates being put up by them, gradually there will be a systemic change and the political parties will be forced to accept the will of the people and field candidates who are known for their integrity". Since then NOTA has come into vogue in elections in the country, but its impact was significant in Gujarat.

In the Gujarat elections, there were 21 seats in which the votes polled by NOTA were more than the margin between the first two candidates. Of these, there were 12 seats where the BJP's margin of de feat was less than NOTA. There is a view that most of those who voted NOTA were those who were registering their protest with the BJP without wanting to translate their cynicism into a positive vote for the Congress. They wanted to inflict a kind of mild punishment on the party which has been in power for 22 years, without ever wanting to provide an advantage to the Grand Old Party

Which means that in the absence of such discontentment, the BJP would have bagged all or most of these seats. This is the most credible hypothesis because the Congress has been out of power for over two decades in the state and has also been dislodged from power at the federal level. Secondly, throughout the Gujarat campaign it thought the electorate was hostile towards the BJP and tried to whip up a frenzy against demonetisation and GST. It can therefore take credit for rise in the number of NOTA votes—but nothing more. In this election at least the Congress lacked the qualification to be worthy of the votes that went into NOTA.

A look at the outcomes in the 12 seats where NOTA dam aged the BJP is revealing. In Chhota Udaipur, Congress won barely with about 1,100 votes and there were 5,870 NOTA votes. In Dangs, the Congress' victory margin was just about 800, but 2,184 voters pressed the NOTA button. In Deodar, the Congress margin of victory was less than 1,000, but the number of NOTA votes was 2,988. However, Kaprada would be the most obvious as also Mansa and Jetpur: In Kaprada, the Congress defeated the BJP by a mere 170 votes, but the number of NOTA votes counted was 3.868. The BJP lost the Mansa seat by just 524 votes when as many as 3,000 voters made NOTA their choice. In Jetpur, the BJP's margin of defeat was 3,052 votes but NOTA had more than double of it—6,155.

Morva Hadaf, Sojitra, Wankaner, Jamjhodpur, Dhanera and Talaja were some other seats which slipped out of the BJP's hands. In Talaja, the Congress won the seat by 1,779 votes but NOTA notched up 2,918. In Wankaner, the BJP lost by 1,361 votes while 3,170 voters opted for NOTA.

As stated earlier, there were some seats where the Congress' margin of defeat was less than NOTA. Among them were Vagra,

Vijaipur, Prantij and Porbandar. But as the party was not suffering from anti incumbency, it may not be correct to put these votes in the party's kitty. At best, it can be argued that but for NOTA, the BJP's margin of victory would have been better.

Apart from NOTA, it can be seen that the electoral outcome in Gujarat is different from other states. Usually when the difference in vote share between the first two parties is 10 percent or thereabouts, the winning party inflicts a crushing defeat on the second party and takes away 75 to 80 per cent of the seats in an Assembly. But, this has never happened in the Gujarat Assembly elections. For example, in the last Assembly election in Rajasthan held in 2013, the BJP secured 45 per cent of the vote against the Congress' 33 per cent and won 163 of the 200 seats (81.5 per cent) in the Assembly. The Congress ended up with just 21 seats. In Madhya Pradesh in 2013, the BJP secured 45 per cent of the vote and a 8.5 per cent advantage over the Congress. This translated to 165 of the 230 seats for the BJP (71.7 per cent) and 58 seats for the Congress. More recently in Himachal Pradesh, the BJP's 7 per cent advantage helped it bag 44 of the 68 seats.

Therefore, it can be said that Gujarat follows a different trajectory. This time, despite a seven per cent advantage in vote share, NOTA made the contest tighter. This is some thing which all political par ties will now have to take note of. It could well add a new dimension to our electoral politics.

The New Indian Express, 2 January, 2018

□

A Thick Hide is a Must

The recent judgment of the Allahabad High Court upholding the freedom of expression guaranteed under Article 19(1)(a) and chiding the State of Uttar Pradesh (UP) for malicious prosecution of a person who had criticised the Chief Minister for "poor handling of law and order in his State", should hopefully have a salutary effect on the State Governments which have been recklessly using penal provisions in our laws against those who express dissent.

The case pertained to a First Information Report (FIR) lodged in August 2020 against Yashwant Singh, who put out a tweet criticising the Chief Minister for transforming the State "into a jungle raj in which no law and order prevails". The tweet also made reference to various incidents of abduction, demand of ransom and murders. He was accused of violating two provisions in the law—Section 500 of the Indian Penal Code (IPC) pertaining to defamation and Section 66D of the Information Technology (IT) Act, 2008, which pertains to personation, or what is commonly understood as impersonation. Yashwant Singh petitioned the High Court and sought the quashing of the FIR.

The petitioner's counsel contended that the right to comment on the affairs of the State was well within Yashwant Singh's constitutional right envisaged under Article 19 of the Constitution of India and that "mere dissent does not amount to criminality". Hence, the FIR registered against him was mala fide "and was meant only to coerce him to stop expressing his dissent against the State Government". He also contended that no offence had been made out and that the FIR should be quashed.

A Division Bench, comprising Justices Pankaj Naqvi and Vivek Agarwal of the Allahabad High Court, has made a succinct but significant observation while quashing the FIR and other proceedings against the petitioner. Referring to the charge of "defamation" under Section 500 of the IPC, the judges said that no case had been made out "as the alleged tweet cannot be said to fall within the mischief of defamation". The judges struck a blow for democracy when they said that "expressing dissent on the law and order situation in the State is a hallmark of a constitutional liberal democracy like ours, constitutionally protected under Article 19 of the Constitution".

The second charge against the petitioner pertained to violation of Section 66D of the IT Act, 2008, which states: "Whoever, by means of any communication device or computer resource, cheats by personation, shall be punished with imprisonment of either description for a term which may extend to three years and shall also be liable to a fine which may extend to Rs 1 lakh." The judges analysed these provisions vis-à-vis the allegation made in the FIR and said that they did not find "even remotely" a commission of offence under Section 66D, as the said provision relates to cheating by personation and it is not the case of prosecution that while committing the overt act, the petitioner tweeted using somebody else's twitter handle nor was there any allegation of cheating. Hence, the court concluded that no offence had been made out under this Section as well.

As far as the State is concerned, this is indeed a damning indictment of the Government and the police. To prosecute a citizen for criminal defamation—which can entail a fine or a jail term which can extend up to two years—because he is disappointed with the Chief Minister's handling of the law and order situation is something unheard of in this country, and the judges have rightly ticked off the State for doing so.

But this scenario is not confined to UP only. Several other Chief Ministers and State Governments have begun challenging the basic freedoms given to all citizens by the Constitution. The State of West Bengal would head this list, not only for the sheer number of such cases but also for starting this trend of jailing its critics. It all started with the Mamata Banerjee Government arresting Prof. Ambikesh Mahapatra of Jadavpur University and his friend in 2012 and charging them with offences under the IT Act for circulating cartoons lampooning the Chief Minister. Following his arrest, Prof. Mahapatra moved the State Human Rights Commission, which criticised their arrest and directed the State Government to pay each of them a compensation of Rs. 50,000. The State did not comply with the directions of the commission, compelling the Professor to move the Calcutta High Court. The court upheld the rights commission's order and enhanced the amount of compensation payable to Prof. Mahapatra and his friend to Rs. 75,000 each.

Even more absurd was the sedition charge slapped on a folk singer in Tamil Nadu in 2015 for criticising the then Chief Minister J Jayalalithaa's policy on the issue of prohibition.

The Communist Party of India (Marxist)-led Kerala Government was unhappy with the State Lalithakala Akademi's decision to select a cartoon, which mocked a Bishop accused of rape, for its annual awards. Several Christian outfits and the State Government wanted the autonomous body to re-consider its decision. The Akademi, however, did not relent.

Those of us who are senior citizens, have lived and thrived in a healthy democratic environment in this country in which we have said much harsher things against the persons in power. At the height of the controversy over the kickbacks paid by Bofors, the Swedish arms manufacturer, to Indian politicians and others, the Indian Express ran Ram Jethmalani's famous 10 questions to Prime Minister Rajiv Gandhi every day. Reading those questions, Rajiv must have squirmed every morning but he had to grin and bear it!

In fact, many of these Chief Ministers must look at how Prime Minister Narendra Modi deals with those who abuse him on the social media. The Modi-baiters constantly upload cartoons and memes seeking to ridicule him on Twitter and Facebook. They often generate hashtags like "#Worst Prime-Minister" or some such and begin a trend along with their camp followers. On his last birthday, they created a hashtag, "#National Unemployment Day", and kept it going the whole day. He is probably the most trolled Indian. Often, his political enemies cross the limits of decency. As Modi himself said at a public meeting during the last Lok Sabha elections, a Congress leader called him "gandi naali ka keeda" (a gutter insect) while another said that he was a "mad dog". Can there be anything more defamatory and abusive than this? If the Prime Minister's Office were to prosecute all these people, Modi would need to create a full-fledged department to handle these prosecutions.

In fact, this is one of the professional hazards of being in public life in a democracy and, over the years, and especially in the age of social media, the politicians across democratic countries—including India—have learnt to develop a thick hide. Some of our Chief Ministers must follow suit.

The Pioneer, 5 January, 2021

□

Rajiv, Modi and Muslim Women

Even though the Lok Sabha passed The Muslim Women (Protection of Rights of Marriage) Bill, 2018 last week, the political slugfest over it is likely to continue with the opposition parties threatening to gang up and stall the legislation that seeks to address a critical issue of gender disparity among Muslims—the right of Muslim men to divorce their wives on a whim, despite a clear verdict from the Supreme Court against such a practice.

When the apex court delivered its judgment in Shayara Bano vs Union of India in August 2017, it set aside the practice of *talaq-e-biddat* (three pronouncements of *talaq* at one and the same time), used by some Muslim men to divorce their wives. This practice had been challenged before the Supreme Court on the grounds that it was discriminatory and against the dignity of women.

While disposing of this case, the court, in its 3-2 judgment, made certain observations fundamental to this issue. It said the law that governed Muslims in matters such as marriage, divorce, inheritance, etc., was the Muslim Personal Law (Shariat) Application Act, 1937. The court relied on an important judgment delivered by it in 2002 which touched upon the matters at hand, namely Shamim Ara vs State of UP. The court had noted: "....The correct law of *talaq* as ordained by the Holy Quran is that *talaq* must be for a reasonable cause and be preceded by attempts at reconciliation between the husband and the wife by two arbiters—one of them from the wife's family and the other from the husband's; if the attempts fail, *talaq* may be effected."

The SC's judgment in the recent case gave a fillip to the

Centre's desire to fill the gap in regard to legislation in this area of law. A legislative measure also became imperative when the government found that despite the SC's judgment, cases of triple *talaq* were still being reported from various parts of the country. This compelled the government to bring in an ordinance and to later come up with a Bill to replace the ordinance. Although the Lok Sabha has passed the Bill with the huge support of MPs, parties opposed to the BJP are unwilling to bite the bullet.

Sadly, parties that nurture the Muslim vote bank have generally blocked progressive laws vis-a-vis the Muslims. These parties believe any initiative seeking to align Muslim Personal Law to the grand constitutional scheme will be rejected by the Muslims and will cost them at the hustings. This has been the narrative since the days of Jawaharlal Nehru. The Congress has been at the forefront of this approach, leading to terrible imbalance in the enforcement of constitutional and legal provisions across the land and across communities.

The current legislative effort by the Modi government to restore the constitutional rights of Muslim women comes in the wake of some telling observations of the SC in the Shayara Bano Case. Given that it is instant and irrevocable, Justices R.F. Nariman and U.U. Lalit said it is "obvious that any attempt at reconciliation between the husband and wife by two arbiters from their families, which is essential to save the marital tie, cannot ever take place." So, this "form of *talaq* is manifestly arbitrary in the sense that the marital tie can be broken capriciously and whimsically by a Muslim man without any attempt at reconciliation so as to save it. This form of *talaq* must be held to be violative of the fundamental right contained under Article 14 of the Constitution." The judges also held Section 2 of the 1937 Act to be void. They said it must be struck down as being void to the extent that it recognises and enforces triple *talaq*.

This is where we get to see the distinct approach of the Rajiv Gandhi government in the 1980s and the Modi government now to significant judgments of the SC. In the 1980s, when the apex court held that a divorced Muslim woman was entitled to maintenance from her husband, despite a massive majority of over 410 MPs in the Lok Sabha, the then PM Rajiv lost the historic opportunity to stamp out pseudo-secularism, practiced by his party since Nehru's days. He succumbed to pressure from Muslim clerics and brought in a legislation to undo the SC's verdict. This single decision of the Congress has wrought havoc on the secular, democratic traditions of the country, and electoral data shows the party has never recovered from it. The Shah Bano case also compelled the people to turn towards the BJP, in the hope that this party would usher in genuine secularism as ordained by the Constitution. The difference between the two parties is now well established with the Modi government, unlike the Rajiv government, taking legislative measures to enforce the SC's judgment on triple *talaq*.

Whatever the fate of this Bill in the Rajya Sabha in the coming week, all political parties, and especially the Congress, will be tested. The Congress, despite its recent successes in Assembly elections, is still seen as a party reluctant to enforce the constitutional scheme across communities. Many other parties too are toeing this line, hoping to get minority votes in 2019. And in order to achieve this, they have no qualms in displaying contempt for the SC as well. This approach has contributed significantly to the rise of the BJP. If the party remains the sole opponent of pseudo-secularism, it will have the field entirely to itself. Its opponents will emerge as a *mahagathbandhan* of pseudo-secularism, which the people have begun to abhor.

History will hold the Congress, which succumbed to the mullahs and used its brute majority in the Houses of Parliament to annul a historic SC judgment granting maintenance to divorced Muslim women in the famous Shah Bano Case, as singularly responsible for selective deployment of constitutional provisions and weakening the constitutional scheme, merely to get Muslim votes.

The New Indian Express, 1 January, 2019

□

The Minority, Majority Debate

What should be the unit—the nation or a State—to determine a "linguistic" or "religious" minority. Though this question has been categorically settled by an 11-judge Bench of the Supreme Court in the TMA Pai Foundation case, it keeps cropping up again and again in one form of the other and is once again before the Supreme Court following an appeal by the State of Punjab against a Punjab and Haryana High Court judgement that Sikhs are not a 'minority' in Punjab.

The issue came up for judicial determination before the Punjab and Haryana High Court some years ago when the Punjab Government's notification of 13 April, 2001, which enabled Sikh educational institutions to enjoy minority benefits and reserve seats for members of that community was challenged. The court set aside the notification and declared that the Sikhs do not constitute a minority in that State (as per the 2001 census, the Sikhs constituted 59.90 per cent of the population of the State).

Apart from other issues that may be raised in this case, two issues which could have a bearing on the outcome of this case is the law as it stands today consequent to the TMA Pai Foundation case in October 2002 and the latest data available on religious demography.

In the TMA Pai case, the court discussed the issue as to what should be the unit—the State or the country as a whole—to determine the existence of a religious or linguistic minority? It said: Article 30(1) deals with religious minorities and linguistic minorities. The opening words of Article 30(1) make it clear that religious and linguistic minorities have been put at par, in so far as that article is concerned.

Therefore, whatever the unit—whether a State or the whole of India—for determining a linguistic minority, it would be the same in relation to a religious minority. India is divided into different linguistic States. The States have been carved out on the basis of the language of the majority of persons of that region.

For example, Andhra Pradesh was established on the basis of the language of that region, viz, Telugu. 'linguistic minority' can, therefore, logically only be in relation to a particular State. If the determination of 'linguistic minority' for the purpose of Article 30 is to be in relation to the whole of India, then within the State of Andhra Pradesh, Telugu speakers will have to be regarded as a 'linguistic minority'.

This will clearly be contrary to the concept of linguistic States. If, therefore, the State has to be regarded as the unit for determining 'linguistic minority' vis-à-vis Article 30, then with "religious minority" being on the same footing, it is the State in relation to which the majority or minority status will have to be determined."

The court also discussed some other related Supreme Court judgements including the Kerala Education Bill case and two cases pertaining to DAV colleges. In the second DAV Case, "the Supreme Court rejected the contention that since Hindus were a majority in India, they could not be a religious minority in the State of Punjab, as it took the State as the unit to determine whether the Hindus were a minority community".

The TMA Pai judgement further said that "there can, therefore, be little doubt that this court has consistently held that, with regard to the State law, the unit to determine a religious or linguistic minority can only be the State".

Thereafter, the court took note of the 42 Amendment which included education in the Concurrent list under Entry 25, consequent to which Parliament can also legislate in relation to education, which was earlier only a State subject. Would this in any way change the position in regard to determination of 'linguistic' and 'religious' minority for the purposes of Article 30.

The court answered this question in the most unambiguous terms and said: "The minority for the purpose of Article 30 cannot have different meanings depending upon who is legislating. Language being the basis for the establishment of different states for the purpose of Article 30, a 'linguistic minority' will have to be determined in relation to the State in which the educational institution is sought to be established. The position in regard to the religious minority is similar, since both religious and linguistic minorities have been put at par in Article 30."

The other crucial factor that the court will have to take note of is the demographic changes that have taken place in India since independence. As per the religion data collected during the 2011 census, although the Hindus constitute the religious majority in the country, the percentage of Hindus in the country has dropped from 83.40 per cent in 1961 to 79.80 per cent in 2011. Hindus are now in a minority in seven States and one Union Territory.

Their share of the population in these States in percentage terms is as follows: Jammu & Kashmir (28.40), Punjab (38.50), Nagaland (8.70), Mizoram (2.70), Meghalaya (11.50), Arunachal Pradesh (29.00) and Manipur (41.40). In lakshadweep, it is just 2.80 per cent. On the other hand, the Christians are in an overwhelming majority in three States—Nagaland, Mizoram and Meghalaya while the Muslims are a majority in the State of Jammu & Kashmir and in lakshadweep. The Sikhs constitute the majority in Punjab.

Nagaland is among the States which have seen dramatic demographic change. Census data shows that Christians constituted just 52.98 per cent of the population of the State in 1951. Since then it has been a hop, step and jump for the Christian community in this State. For example between 1981 and 2001, the Hindu population in Nagaland dropped from 14.36 to 7.70 per cent, while the Christian population jumped from 80.21 to 90.00 per cent. With the Hindus falling way behind the half-way mark in seven States and one Union Territory, they have emerged as a significant minority in a quarter of India's States.

During the preliminary hearing a fortnight ago, the court seemed aware of the demographic reality in different States as it signaled that the issue at hand could have a bearing on other States where the Christians and Muslims are in a majority.

One can only bow in reverence to the extraordinary foresight displayed by our Constitution-makers while drafting Article 30 and to the interpretation of this Article by the judges on the Bench which settled the TMA Pai case. One must await the apex court's opinion on this issue yet again, especially in the light of fresh evidence of demographic change and the complex mosaic of majority-minority which is now a reality in the country.

The Pioneer, 2 February, 2016

□

Chapter-5

OUR MEDIA

Press Freedom Index by RSF—Biased, Subjective, Non-transparent

Burkina Faso way Ahead of India!

The Paris-based NGO, Reporters Without Borders (RSF), has come out with its latest Press Freedom Index to judge the degree of freedom available to journalists in different countries of the world. This index places India, the world's largest, the most vibrant and liberal democracy and arguably the most plural society, down below at number 142 among 180 countries assessed for this evaluation. This is two notches below 140, the position occupied by India a year ago.

Why, according to RSF, does India perform so poorly vis-à-vis other nations, when it comes to press freedom? This calls for some serious analysis of the RSF's understanding of democracy and the methodology that it employs.

The RSF website says the degree of freedom available to journalists is determined by pooling responses of experts to an elaborate questionnaire devised by it. The quantitative data is combined with qualitative analysis on abuses and acts of violence against journalists during the period evaluated. The criteria evaluated in the questionnaire, which has 87 questions, are pluralism, media independence, media environment and self-censorship, legislative framework, transparency, and the quality of the infrastructure that supports the production of news and information. This on-line questionnaire is sent by RSF to 18 NGOs across the world and a network of 150 correspondents and to researchers, jurists, human rights activists chosen by these correspondents. About ten per cent of the respondents are foreign correspondents working in the country being evaluated.But, here is the catch. The sample size for the survey for a country like India, which has 1330 million citizens, is too small and little is known of the respondents chosen. We shall deal with this a little later.

First of all, one would presume that a good democratic environment is sine qua non for a free press, but, strangely, there is little or no weight age in this index for fundamentals of democracy like a republican government; an inviolable commitment to freedom of speech and expression in a country's constitution; an unambiguous constitutional commitment to pursuit of secular values; separation of religion and State; the fundamental right to equality before law and the equal protection of the laws; gender equality; and the fundamental right to life and personal liberty. It appears as if RSF does not see the need for any of this while judging whether there is press freedom in a country, and this is its biggest flaw.

This becomes obvious when one sees the ranking of certain nations, which cannot even qualify as democracies, way ahead of India. Here are some samples:

While the RSF Index places India at 142, Burkina Faso is over a hundred points ahead at number 36. This is the country which was identified by the State Department of the U.S. sometime ago in its Trafficking in Persons Report saying that slavery continued to exist in Burkina Faso and that Burkinabè children were often the victims. It said slavery is an entrenched institution with a long history that dates back to the Arab slave trade. In 2018, an estimated 82,000 people in the country were living under "modern slavery" according to the Global Slavery Index. The Republic of Maldives is placed at number 79 in the CSF Index. Its constitution states that Islam is the religion of the State of Maldives and "no law contrary to the tenets of Islam shall be enacted in the Maldives". Article 9 (d) of the Constitution declares that "a non-Muslim may not become a citizen of the Maldives".

The Sultanate of Oman, which is at 135 in the Index, is an Arab, Islamic nation. Article 2 of the constitution of Oman says the religion of the State is Islam and Islamic Sharia is the basis for legislation. The system of governance is Sultani, hereditary in the male descendants of Sayyid Turki bin Said bin Sultan, provided that whomever is to be chosen from amongst them as successor "shall be a Muslim, mature, rational and the legitimate son of Omani Muslim parents".

In other words, it is neither a secular state nor a republic and there is no gender equality because the constitution ordains that the head of state shall be a Muslim male.

The Index places Comoros at number 75. The constitution says the Comorian people solemnly affirm their will "to draw from Islam, the religion of the state, the permanent inspiration of the principles and rules that govern the union........".

Now, let us look at some nations where the State is unabashedly wedded to Christianity. Argentina is at number 64. Its Constitution declares that the federal government supports the Roman Catholic Apostolic religion. The Constitution of Malta, which is at number 81 in the RSF Index declares that "the religion of Malta is the Roman Catholic Apostolic Religion". It says the authorities of the Roman Catholic Apostolic Church "have the duty and the right to teach which principles are right and which are wrong" and that religious teaching of the Roman Catholic Apostolic Faith shall be provided in all State schools as part of compulsory education.

The Kingdom of Norway tops the RSF list and is declared the nation with the maximum press freedom. Its constitution describes its form of government as a limited and hereditary monarchy and says "Our values will remain our Christian and humanistic heritage". Laying down the eligibility criteria to be head of State in Norway, it says "The King shall at all times profess the Evangelical-Lutheran religion". It also grants immunity to the head of state—"the King's person is sacred; he cannot be censured or accused". In other words, it is not a secular state; it is not republican; and one of the basic fundamentals of democracy–equality before the law and the equal application of the laws (Art 14 in the Indian Constitution) – has no place in Norway.

The constitution of Denmark, which is number 3 in the CSF list declares that the Evangelical Lutheran Church shall be the established Church of Denmark, "and as such will be supported by the State". This means that "it is based on the Holy Bible, various ecclesiastical symbolic books, and the teachings of the German theologian Martin Luther........". Today, the State has a duty to support the Church of Denmark financially and in other ways".

Greece is at number 65 in this Index. Article 3 of its constitution declares that "the prevailing religion in Greece is that of the Eastern Orthodox Church of Christ. The orthodox Church of Greece, acknowledging our Lord Jesus Christ as its head, is inseparably united in doctrine with the Great Church of Christ in Constantinople and with every other Church of Christ of the same doctrine".

Is not separation of church and State and religion and State central to democracy? This is one of the problematic issues with the RSF Index, but there are many more.

www.asuryaprakash.com, 22 May, 2020

Why India Should Reject the Press Freedom Index Lock, Stock and Barrel

How can India, which has secularism embedded in the preamble of its constitution and which has no state religion, and which elects its head of state in the best traditions of egalitarianism lag behind hereditary monarchies wedded to churches and gender inequality? Further, how can theocracies and religion-based states which cannot even be classified as democracies, have press freedom better than a secular democracy like India? These are questions that first come to mind when one looks at the RSF's laboured effort at producing a Press Freedom Index.

The RSF Website claims that press freedom in countries is judged under six categories On the touchstone of pluralism, it measures the degree to which opinions are represented in the media. If that be so, RSF wants us to believe that there is greater pluralism in media in theocracies and Islamic states and states where even citizenship is denied to non-Muslims than in India, the most pluralistic society in the world!

The second touchstone is media independence–to measure the degree to which media is able to function independent of politics, government, religious power and influence. And, if we go by the RSF Index, "religious power and influence" on the media in Argentina, Malta, Denmark etc where the State is wedded to the Church and in Maldives, the Sultanate of Oman, Comoros etc where the State is wedded to Islam, is far less than in secular, democratic India!

The third criterion is "media environment and self-censorship". Liberal India has been witnessing a media boom over the last few decades, so much so, that the total print order of publications in the country has crossed 430 million copies in dozens of languages and the nation boasts of over 800 television channels of which a quarter deal with news and current affairs. The respondents are expected to analyse the environment in which journalists work. Can there be another nation which boasts of such media diversity? Also, when it comes to self-censorship, I hope RSF is aware of the consequences of non-compliance with self-censorship in Islamic States and theocracies. I hope it also has some idea of self- censorship that is de rigueur in the U.K vis-à-vis the Queen and in nations like Belgium, the Netherlands, Norway, Denmark etc regarding their royalty. Self-censorship is anathema to a diverse, vibrant democracy like India.

As regards the "legislative framework" that governs media, starting with the Indian Constitution and a plethora of laws made by parliament, the media is provided with adequate insulation to enable it to work freely and fearlessly.

"Transparency" is another criteria on which India scores high. There is a great deal of divergence of political opinion in the editorial positions taken by Indian media houses, just as in the USA and other democracies and no media house ever hides its stripes. One can see all the colours of the rainbow in the media bouquet including those committed to communism, socialism, centrism, the right wing etc. Also, to those who complain of lack of transparency, one must say that the boot is on the other leg. The media was non-transparent in the past because of its excessive left-wing lilt. This stands corrected now because all shades of opinion find their place. In fact, it is this plurality which ensures free flow of information and opinion and it must be said without fear of contradiction that this kind of plurality is simply not available elsewhere.

This can also be seen on the social media as well, where there is a virtual free-for-all with the worst abuses hurled at political leaders including with the Prime Minister. If you are looking for "transparency", you will get it in abundance on these platforms, but if you are looking for decency, this is not the place to go!

Finally, the index examined the quality of infrastructure that supports the production of news and information. India is technologically advanced and offers state-of-the-art infrastructure for those who want it. Also, because of its leadership in Information Technology, Indian media companies are building robust social media platforms to take their businesses to new platforms.

Apart from all this, the methodology adopted by RSF is highly questionable. It must name its correspondents in each nation; provide the list of respondents along with their social, political, economic background, place of residence etc. Unless the sample is credible, the inferences will be suspect. There are other drawbacks: The core team based in Paris determines the questions and the weightage given to each answer – not a satisfactory situation; RSF does not explain the definition of press freedom. Instead uses terms like press freedom, freedom of information etc loosely; and finally, the questionnaire is so long and exhaustive, that it would leave most respondents exhausted even before the process is over.

Finally, it must be said that the work of RSF is subjective, biased and non- transparent the biggest flaw is the RSF's complete disrespect for the foundational principles of democracy. It seems to delude itself into believing that press freedom.

www.asuryaprakash.com, 22 May, 2020

□

Some Home Truths for Western Media

Most Western media outlets, for reasons best known to them, have been generally hostile to India. They have never acknowledged the strengths of our country, the most important of which is that it is the most democratic, diverse and resilient nation in the world with the most progressive laws and policies. But nobody would have expected that this hostility towards India would be on such full display when the nation was taking decisive measures to combat the novel coronavirus. Even as I write this piece, more than 18.5 lakh people are afflicted with the coronavirus, of which the US accounts for over 5.57 lakh cases and over 20,500 deaths, surpassing China, where the trouble began, many times over. The virus has claimed over 19,900 lives in Italy and 17,200 in Spain.

However, US President Donald Trump and leaders in many American states are still humming and hawing about imposing a complete lockdown— something that seems necessary in order to contain the disease. It is generally believed that things have got out of hand in the US because of laxity in enforcing social distancing and contact tracing. India, on the other hand, thanks to the decisive action of the government, launched a massive campaign to test passengers arriving on international flights, identify those with Covid-19 symptoms and quarantine them, and educate people on social distancing. Further, when cases were detected, contact tracing was done so vigorously and systematically that it became central to the plan to contain the epidemic.

Those flying in from corona hotspots like Italy, Iran, etc., were taken straight to camps manned by paramilitary forces for quarantine. Later, the prime minister called for a mock drill on March 22 and a complete lockdown of the country from the night of March 24. Indians had never experienced anything like this, also because social distancing is anathema to us for both demographic and cultural reasons. Yet, the nation responded to PM Modi's call in a jiffy and ensured that the lockdown was an overwhelming success, barring some pockets of resistance. That is why the total cases in India, with a population of 1.3 billion, which is four times that of the US, currently stands at around 9,000 with about 300 fatalities. Yet, India has over 1,00,000 Covid beds right now and is converting a mind-boggling 20,000 railway coaches into Covid wards.

This is not to say that we are over the hump. The next three to four weeks are crucial, but whatever the trajectory of India's corona graph, nobody dare say that India was lax, ill-prepared or irresponsible— the adjectives that are now being used to describe the response of the most "developed" nations in the world. Further, despite the fractious nature of our politics, the nation has come together in a remarkable show of unity to fight the deadly virus. This is quite in contrast to the finger-pointing and name-calling that is currently on in the US between the federal government and the states, something that is clearly avoidable when the nation is facing a deadly epidemic. Given this background, one is amazed to see the kind of reporting that is emanating from India in Western news outlets. The New York Times, which, as the name suggests is based in the city where Covid-19 has simply got out of control, is finding fault with India's decision to go in for a 21-day lockdown, saying that the country's "already fragile economy will collapse". The newspaper quotes a professor from, where else, the JNU, to say that this decision will "devastate" 50% of the workers in the informal sector.

Shall we then go by this mindless advisory, lift the lockdown and allow 10 million Indians to die? In fact, the anti-India sentiment that prevails across Western media platforms is so strong that there is not even grudging acknowledgement of the aggressive efforts initiated by the federal and state governments and institutions to contain the epidemic. For example, contact tracing in a country like India that has 1,300 million people, is like looking for a pin in a haystack, but our law enforcement and health authorities have been doing this with such meticulousness that it should be a model for other societies. Western media outlets have been reporting that the lockdown has rendered thousands of migrant workers hungry and shelterless. The picture that is being painted is that they will all die of hunger. This is utter rubbish. India today has the resilience to withstand a crisis of this nature, governments that are proactive, and a middleclass with disposable incomes and the humanitarian spirit. In fact, this is the big India story— phenomenal unity amidst diversity, caring, sharing, foresight, discipline and confidence.

But this story is missing in the Western media. What do you attribute this to? Shame over their own failures; racism; or is there something else? In fact, apart from The New York Times, many other Western media platforms including The Washington Post and news agencies have deliberately shut themselves off these facts. Sadly, there are some media establishments in India as well, who have peddled this nonsense because of their visceral hatred of the current prime minister. In fact, many of them are secretly hoping that India will fail, so that they may point fingers at PM Modi, whom they dislike. But let us make no mistake, India's political leadership at the federal level and in the states, and India's health administrators know what is best for India— not correspondents of New York Times, et al., who are peddling their political wares from their safe homes in Delhi. Americans must thank their stars that these journalists and writers are not advising their government. We must all remember the hard truth conveyed by the PM some days ago: "If you can't handle these 21 days, this country will go back 21 years." This writer's advice to correspondents of the New York Times and other western media: India is in strong hands. You take care!

The New Indian Express, 14 April, 2020

□

The Centre's New IT Rules

Balancing the need for regulation to keep out obnoxious online content that promotes violence and vulgarity with the need to preserve our constitutional values and freedom of expression is at the core of the new rules which have been formulated by the Union government to address concerns regarding new media.

The policy has tried to create the much-needed level-playing field between online news platforms and print media on the one hand and online and television news media on the other. It has also tried to bring online news portals within the ambit of the code of ethics that governs print media. These include the norms of journalistic conduct drawn up by the Press Council Act and the Cable Television Networks (Regulation) Rules, 1994. This was long overdue because of the recklessness and irresponsibility that is on display on some of these platforms.

Similarly, while the cinema industry has a film certification agency with oversight responsibilities, OTT platforms have none. However, in order to ensure artistic freedom, the government has proposed self-regulation and has said that the OTT entities should get together, evolve a code and come up with content classification so that a mechanism is evolved to preclude non-adults from viewing adult content. They must get down to do it. The grievance redressal mechanism thought of is three-tier, with the publishers and self-regulating bodies being the first two. The third tier is the central government oversight committee. The policy proposed requires publishers to appoint grievance redressal officers and ensure a time-bound acknowledgement and disposal of grievances. Then, there can be a self-regulating body headed by a retired judge.

Online platforms are wary of rules that seek verification of accounts, access control etc., but these issues need to be resolved within the framework of India's laws. For example, while mainstream media is conscious of provisions in the Indian Penal Code (IPC) that deal with the promotion of violence, enmity among communities, defamation etc., the content on online platforms seems to be oblivious of all this. The vulgar comments posted on social media about women professionals in media or other fields and the inability of the Indian state to deal with such behaviour makes one wonder whether the IPC is even applicable in cyberspace.

The Indian digital and OTT players can draw lessons from the concerted action taken by digital companies in Australia, which have come together and drawn up a code to deal with fake news and disinformation. This is called the Australian Code of Practice on Disinformation and Misinformation and was released only recently by the Digital Industry Group.

The Australian Communications and Media Authority (ACMA) has welcomed the initiative and said that more than two-thirds of Australians were concerned about "what is real or fake on the internet". In response, the ACMA says that digital platforms agreed to a self-regulatory code "to provide safeguards against serious harms arising from the spread of dis-and misinformation". Some of the actions promised by the digital platforms include disabling accounts and removal of content.

In the UK, the government is all set to bring in a law to make online companies responsible for harmful content and also to punish companies that fail to remove such content. The aim of the proposed "Online Safety Bill" is to protect internet users and deal firmly with platforms that promote violence, terrorist material, child abuse, cyber bullying, etc. Digital Secretary Oliver Dowden was quoted as saying, "I'm unabashedly pro-tech but that can't mean a tech free-for-all". This, in a sense, sums up the current mood on this issue across democracies. In the UK, self-regulation governs print media and private television and radio are regulated by the Independent Television Commission and the Radio Authority as provided by a statute.

As regards the two ministers who announced the government's guidelines—Ravi Shankar Prasad and Prakash Javadekar—it should not be forgotten that both of them are the heroes of what is called the "Second Freedom Struggle". They fought against the dreaded Emergency imposed by Prime Minister Indira Gandhi in the mid-1970s and suffered incarceration so that the people got back their Constitution and democracy. Obviously, their commitment to basic democratic values has and will continue to influence their policy formulations vis-à-vis media regulation.

Finally, a word about the framework within which companies should operate in India. As the Union Minister for Information Technology, Prasad said they must function within the laws of the land. This is non-negotiable. In recent times, Twitter has tried to define freedom of expression and even claimed that it seeks to protect the freedom of expression of Indians. "Freedom of expression" is embedded in the chapter on fundamental rights in our Constitution and it is circumscribed by what are called "reasonable restrictions". These are in place because India is a vibrant democracy and the most diverse society in the world with many social, political and economic complexities. That is why India's founding fathers had, with great intuition and foresight, introduced a caveat vis-à-vis freedom of expression, so that constitutional rights promote internal peace and harmony. What these freedoms are and what these restrictions are have been defined by our Supreme Court in innumerable cases and the law as laid down by India's apex court is the law of the land. We do not want some private international companies to assume the role of some supra courts and put their own spin on our Constitution.

The New Indian Express, 27 February, 2021

□

Sorry, there can be no Twitter Republic

While the social-media platform, Twitter, is dragging its feet in regard to compliance with the provisions of the Information Technology (Intermediary Guidelines and Digital Ethics Code) Rules, 2021, there is growing evidence of this company's double standards and what one would regard as direct interference in the internal affairs of our country.

Being a global giant with a net worth far bigger than the GDP of many nations, the company has begun to imagine itself as bigger than the Indian Republic. Before we do anything else, we need to help the company overcome this conflict with reality.

Hopefully, the recent Delhi High Court order directing it to comply with the new rules will have a sobering effect, because its public posturing in recent times smacks of an affront to the Constitution and the laws of India.

Twitter claimed recently that it had proved to be vital "for public conversation and a source of support for people during the pandemic" and that consequently, it is concerned about "the potential threat to freedom of expression for the people we serve".

The usefulness of social media platforms such as Twitter and Facebook for human conversations is undeniable, just as many other technological advances in various fields such as motor transport, aviation, telephony, robotics, the internet, etc., over the last two centuries have promoted human communication, mobility, health care, etc., and have contributed to human advancement. All these developments have also contributed to the advancement of democracy and fundamental rights like freedom of expression, movement, trade and profession. But that cannot make any motor or aviation company the sole arbiter when it comes to freedom of movement. Nor does it give a telecom company the right to adjudicate on freedom of communication.

Twitter has responded to the new IT regulations by saying that it is "deeply committed to the people of India" and that along with civil society in India and around the world, it has "concerns" about "core elements of the new IT Rules". It claims that some aspects of these regulations "inhibit free, open public conversation".

Ravishankar Prasad, the Union Minister for IT, has called out Twitter and exposed its hollowness. The government has said that while it respects privacy, the only instance of scuttling free speech on Twitter has been done by the company itself through its opaque policies "as a result of which people's accounts are suspended and tweets deleted arbitrarily without recourse".

The international news channel Wion has also called out the micro-blogging site and provided an exemplary example of Twitter's opacity and double standards.

The channel's popular anchor Palki Upadhyay reported that Wion's weekend edition of Grativas Plus on May 30 on women's reproductive freedom, women's rights and the right to abortion, broadcast only on digital media, was "filtered" out by Twitter.

The ten-minute video, which was based on research and data, argued for repeal of regressive laws and giving women a choice. Twitter branded this "sensitive material", filtered it out and restricted the channel's access to conversation on the video.

As a result, the channel's social media team could not see viewers responses. Does a conversation on abortion qualify as "sensitive material"?

The channel quoted one expert, Jitin Jain, who said, "Twitter is today attempting to control global content discourse from a corporate board room. Its decisions on content are often opaque and smack of policy contradictions and double standards, often guided by the political atmosphere rather than long-term policy and principles."

This is indeed a sharp indictment of Twitter and the site, which is given to so much of grand-standing, will have to clean up its act. Also, the company must certainly resist the temptation to deliver sermons. It claimed, "It is the collective responsibility of elected officials, industry, and civil society to safeguard the interests of the public."

By doing so, it seeks to place itself on par with elected officials (persons chosen by the people to head the executive branch of government) and Indian civil society. This is clearly out of line. No company, Indian or international, can claim parity with an elected government that has been given the mandate by the people. Nor can it say that it is in the same league as India's civil society.

In fact, by its obstinacy, Twitter has provoked a razor-sharp response from the Union government, which has said, "Twitter needs to stop beating around the bush and comply with the laws of the land. Lawmaking and policy formulations are the sole prerogative of the sovereign. Twitter is just a social media platform and it has no locus in dictating what India's legal policy framework should be." One wonders whether any government in India has had to be so blunt with any other corporation.

With regards to safeguarding the interests of citizens, Twitter must be told in unequivocal terms that neither the Constitution nor the people of India have outsourced this responsibility to any individual or corporation. Under the Constitution, the executive, the legislature and the judiciary share this responsibility. Therefore, no citizen or institution will allow Twitter to become a supra entity that will legislate, execute and adjudicate and, above all, become the supreme dispenser of fundamental freedoms in our country.

One hopes Twitter will contain itself while dealing with the world's largest and most vibrant democracy. It would be delusionary for it to think that a Republic of Twitter can supplant the Republic of India. If it does not understand this basic truth, it will learn it the hard way!

The New Indian Express, 7 June, 2021

□

Why the Media Missed the 'tsuNAMO'

The Bharatiya Janata Party's spectacular victory in Uttar Pradesh and its impressive performance in three other states has stunned commentators and psephologists alike. The eventual outcome in this unforgettable electoral battle was nowhere near what most political pundits were churning out as considered analysis or what pollsters were predicting in their pre-poll surveys and even exit polls. It seemed as if mainstream media—both print and television—had lost the capacity to step back and dispassionately view the electoral drama as it unfolded. One of the prime reasons for this is the deep-seated prejudice and even hatred for Prime Minister Narendra Modi and the BJP among commentators and the unwillingness to go beyond the moth-eaten script that sees everything through the prism of so-called secularism and Hindu communalism. As per this narrative—largely pushed by Nehruvians and their Marxist friends—the Nehruvians are the good guys in Indian politics. The Marxists, who ride piggyback on the Nehruvians are also, by association, good guys. Those who have a nationalist bent of mind are the bad guys and those who represent regional political forces are to be tolerated and manipulated whenever necessary.

The Nehruvian and Marxist schools have permeated the media, specially the English media, the academia and the bureaucracy over the last seventy years and ensured that much of the discourse is along the lines scripted by them. Therefore, it is fashionable to be Nehruvian or left-leaning. Those who do not conform to these two schools are to be treated as pariahs and generally kept away from the upper echelons of the editorial departments.

Coming back to UP 2017, since the media, dominated by these two schools, views everything through this prism, they were unwilling to go beyond this template of the electoral battle being a Maha Yuddh between "secular" forces and Hindu Communalists! As the results show, they went horribly wrong because the people did not perceive their so-called secular parties as "secular". Nor did they perceive Modi and his party as a bunch of Hindu communalists! In reality, it was a battle between retrograde forces like the Congress Party, the Samajwadi Party (SP) and Bahujan Samaj Party (BSP)—who were bombarding the people with divisive, decrepit slogans of an old India—and Prime Minister Modi, who was offering the youth and the aspirational classes a new India in which the mool mantra would be equal opportunities for everyone. This media also got it completely wrong when it came to demonetisation.

Although the poorest of the poor, who stood in long queues for hours, backed Modi to the hilt on this, influential sections of the media never saw this. It also did not see that Modi had through his fair implementation of policies such as Ujjwal (providing cooking gas connections free to women from BPL households), the Jan-Dhan Yojana and the low-premium insurance scheme for the poor, had over the last two years, quietly entered the hearts and hearths of the poor.

It is here that one can draw a comparison between him and Indira Gandhi. She too caught the imagination of the poor and spoke ad nauseum about banishing poverty (Garibi Hatao), but had no plan to execute it. The comparison must end here, because Modi's ability to execute his ideas is of a different level altogether. While she nationalised banks and squandered public money on bogus loan melas in which the beneficiaries were often Congress workers, Modi got a mind-boggling 250 million poor citizens to open bank accounts.

The media also lost track of the fact that Modi never played the communal card in this election. He only spoke of development policies that would embrace everyone. Since the media is used to a staple diet of communal or caste conflict in electoral politics, it refused to believe that the prime minister was seeking votes on the most secular agenda of them all—development! In any case, the media believed that development is not "sexy" enough to garner votes!

There are several messages emanating from Uttar Pradesh, Uttarakhand and Manipur and from Orissa and Maharastra, which witnessed panchayat and municipal elections recently. It is now obvious that the people see Modi as a decisive leader who can take tough decisions and re-build a strong and united India. They are worried about the fissiparous tendencies that are growing in the country and the overt and covert support that the Congress Party and left-leaning elements in our polity are lending to those who are trying to weaken the unity and integrity of India. The strange developments in university campuses in New Delhi and West Bengal, where students, supported by the Left, are heard shouting Bharat ko Tudke, Tukde Karenge (We will break-up India) has unnerved the average Indian. Further, he is unable to understand how leaders of many national and regional parties could support Kashmiri militants and others who are raising secessionist slogans. The vulgar appeasement of religious minorities and the divisive politics of many regional and caste-based parties has also become a matter of concern.

Finally, the country is yet to recover from the wobbly coalition that Manmohan Singh headed for ten years, which enfeebled the country and raised serious doubts about our ability to govern ourselves. Overall, after a lapse of three decades, there is a national mood building up in favour of a robust, over-arching national party headed by a strong leader who can take tough decisions and keep the country together. The mood is against unstable coalitions, parties which play denominational politics and parties like the two communist parties playing the treacherous game of encouraging centrifugal forces. And, who can fix all this? Modi, of course!

The New Indian Express, 14 March, 2017

□

Chapter-6

THE SECULAR & THE PSEUDO-SECULAR

Law may be Personal, Constitution is for all

After 70 years of pussyfooting on an issue that militates against the core values of our Constitution, the Union Government has made a series of unambiguous assertions in its affidavit before the Supreme Court in the Shayara Bano case, which will go a long way in strengthening our secular, democratic traditions. The main prayer in this case by a divorced Muslim woman is that the fundamental rights guaranteed to every citizen by the Constitution must prevail over personal laws and that religious practices cannot override constitutional provisions. It is heartening to see that the Government has backed this prayer and said constitutional provisions ought to supersede everything else. Never before has the Union Government expressed itself in such a forthright manner on this issue. Not only has it opposed triple *talaq*, but it has said that gender equality is "non-negotiable".

Muslim personal law in India permits the practice of *talaq-e-bidat* or *talaq-e-badai*, which includes a Muslim man divorcing his wife by pronouncing more than one *talaq* in a single *tuhr* (the period between two menstruations) or pronouncing an irrevocable instantaneous divorce at one go. The petitioner has told the court that *Talaq-e-bidat* (unilateral triple *talaq*) "which practically treats women like chattel, is neither harmonious with the modern principles of human rights and gender equality, nor is it an integral part of the Islamic faith". She said Muslim women had been given *talaq* over Skype, Facebook or even text messages, and there was no protection against such arbitrary divorces. But, there is something even more repugnant than this, and that is called *Nikah halala*. As per this tenet or practice, should a Muslim husband pronounce *talaq* in a fit of anger or under the influence of an intoxicant and later repent, he cannot take back his wife and restore the marriage. The woman will have to undergo *Nikah halala* (meaning marriage to another man) and then secure a divorce from that man. Only then can she re-marry her former husband.

Shayara Bano has challenged these practices and appealed to the court to declare the Muslim Personal Law (Shariat) Application Act, 1937, as unconstitutional in so far as it validates *Talaq-e-bidat*, *Nikah halala* and polygamy. The petitioner argues that it violates her fundamental rights enshrined in Articles 14, 15, 21 and 25.

The Narendra Modi Government's views in this matter are in contrast to the Rajiv Gandhi Government's response to the issue of safeguarding the fundamental rights of Muslim women. Buckling under the Muslim clergy's pressure, that Government overturned a progressive judgement of the Supreme Court in the Shah Bano case, which declared that a divorced Muslim woman was entitled to maintenance under the country's secular law. Rajiv Gandhi brought in a legislation in Parliament to upturn the apex court's verdict and to virtually uphold the primacy of the Muslim Personal Law over fundamental rights guaranteed by the Constitution. This was nothing but petty pursuit of a Muslim vote-bank at the altar of our constitutional well-being. The Modi Government's affidavit seeks to correct this monstrous folly and restore the primacy of the Constitution over everything else.

The present case rises following the divorce of Shayara Bano by her husband via triple *talaq* a year ago. Shayara Bano has since moved the Supreme Court and the petitions of several Muslim women's groups and scholars have been clubbed with this petition. The court asked the Union Government to respond to the petitioner's plea.

Shayara Bano has cited several judgements of the Supreme Court to back her petition. She has said that in Sarla Mudgal's case, the court had observed that bigamous marriage had been made punishable amongst Christians by the Christian Marriage Act,

1872; amongst Parsis by the Parsi Marriage and Divorce Act, 1936; and amongst Hindus, Buddhists, Sikhs and Jains by the Hindu Marriage Act, 1955. However, the Dissolution of Muslim Marriages Act, 1939, does not protect Muslim women from bigamy. It means that all women except Muslim women are legally protected from the ill effects of bigamous marriages.

There is another celebrated and much-cited verdict of the Bombay High Court by two of India's eminent judges—Chief Justice MC Chagla and Justice PB Gajendragadkar. In the State of Bombay versus Narasu Appa Mali, delivered in 1952, wherein the constitutional validity of the Bombay Prevention of Hindu Bigamous Marriages Act, 1946, was challenged, the two judges tackled the core issue vis-à-vis personal laws. They held that a sharp distinction must be drawn between religious faith and belief and religious practices. Since the state only protects religious faith and belief, religious practices that run counter to public order, morality or health or a policy of social welfare must give way to the good of the people of the state.

The central question which Shayara Bano has raised is that, while religious faith and belief is protected by the Constitution, religious practices fall in another category, specially those that run counter to basic human and fundamental rights. Therefore, a complete ban on polygamy, *Nikah halala* and unilateral triple *talaq* is the need of the hour.

The Union Government's affidavit states that "gender equality and the dignity of women are non-negotiable, over-arching constitutional values", and raises the question as to whether "in a secular democracy, religion can be a reason to deny equal status and dignity, available to women under the Constitution of India". Second, whether women who profess a certain religion, can be relegated to a status which is significantly more vulnerable than their counterparts who profess any other faith.

Next, the Government has said that the underlying idea behind the preservation of personal laws is the preservation of plurality and diversity among the people. But, can this be a pretext for denying women the status and gender equality they are entitled to under the Constitution, as citizens of India? Gender justice is a constitutional goal of overwhelming importance and magnitude. If this is not accomplished, half the country's citizenry will be unable to enjoy to the fullest, the rights available under the Constitution of India.

Unlike the humming and hawing that one saw in the past, the Union Government has come out forcefully in defence of the fundamental rights of all citizens. The bottom line is that the Constitution is supreme. There can be no text above it! So, it's now over to the Supreme Court.

The Pioneer, 25 October, 2016

□

Rubbing Salt into Sikhs' Wounds

Congress President Rahul Gandhi's assertion that the Grand Old Party was not involved in the barbarous assault on the Sikh community after Indira Gandhi's assassination in 1984 flies in the face of truckloads of evidence—placed before several commissions and committees of inquiry that probed the violence. The testimonies of thousands of witnesses not only established instigation of frenzied mobs by Congress politicians but also the unpardonable paralysis of the administration and police in the national capital and many other cities in North India while the mobs were running amok.

The anti-Sikh pogrom began almost immediately after the government announced on the evening of 31 October 1984 that Indira Gandhi had succumbed to the bullets of her assassins. As news of her assassination spread, Congress cadres became belligerent, raised slogans like "Khoon Ka Badla Khoon Se Lenge" (we will avenge blood with blood) and roamed the national capital and cities in the North torching Sikh places of worship, establishments and property.

Rajiv Gandhi was sworn in as PM immediately after the assassination and, technically speaking, a new government was in place. But there was no government. The state had withered away. In all 2,732 Sikhs were killed in those riots—2,146 in Delhi and 586 in some other towns in northern region. The Sikhs suffered loss of homes and property on an unprecedented scale.

The Justice Nanavati Commission of Inquiry that probed the riots found shocking evidence of the complicity of the police in the riots in Delhi. Although the violence was spread all over the national capital, the police had registered only 587 FIRs against the mobsters and even among these, the police declared over 240 cases as "untraced" and around 250 cases ended in acquittals. Further, 11 FIRs were quashed and in another 11 cases, the accused were discharged.

After weighing the evidence that came before it, the commission came to the following conclusions: "Rumours were circulated which had the effect of inciting people against the Sikhs and prompted them to take revenge ... At some places the mobs indulging in violent attacks had come in DTC buses or vehicles.

They either came armed with weapons and inflammable materials like kerosene, petrol ... or were supplied with such materials soon after they were taken to the localities where the Sikhs were to be attacked ... Persons who could organise attacks were contacted and given instructions to kill Sikhs ... The attacks were made in a systematic manner and without much fear of the police, almost suggesting they were assured that they would not be harmed while committing those acts and even thereafter. Male members of the Sikh community were taken out of their houses and burnt alive. In some cases, tyres were put round their necks and then they were set on fire by pouring kerosene or petrol on them."

This is a brief account of the graphic description of the cruelty perpetrated by Congress goons that the Commission took note of. As regards those who instigated the murderous mobs, the commission said: "Large number of affidavits indicate that local Congress(I) leaders and workers had either incited or helped the mobs in attacking the Sikhs. But for the backing and help of influential and resourceful persons, killing of Sikhs so swiftly and in large numbers could not have happened.

In many places the mobs consisted of outsiders ... Bringing them from outside required an organised effort. There is evidence to show that outsiders were shown the houses of the Sikhs." Further, when Sikhs collected at a gurudwara to defend themselves, the police persuaded them to return to their homes on the assurance they would be protected. But the mobs took over and the police looked the other way, it added.

The Commission said affidavits filed before it state that Congress leaders and workers were behind the riots: "No other person or organisation ... is alleged to have taken part in those incidents. The slogans raised during the riots also indicate that some of the persons who constituted the mobs were Congress workers or sympathisers." Some material was also put before the commission which said Rajiv told one of his officials that "the Sikhs should be taught a lesson". The Commission did not pursue this because the evidence available was vague. However, it indicted the government for the complicity of the police and administration with the rioters and for the inordinate delay in calling in the Army.

The Indian state was in a state of paralysis after Indira's assassination and this is explained by the shocking non-response of the then President Giani Zail Singh to pleas for protection from the Sikhs. The noted writer Patwant Singh told the Commission that he was part of a delegation of eminent citizens which called on the president on the morning of November 1.

They told him he had a moral and constitutional obligation to end the violence. The president said he "did not have the power" to intervene. The delegation asked Zail Singh if he was saying he had no power to stop anarchy and bloodshed? "The president remained silent." But the delegation persisted and urged the president to speak forcefully to the PM. Zail Singh said, "I will do so in three or four days time"! That was the three or four days in which the mass murder of Sikhs took place.

There is sufficient evidence to indict the Congress on two counts—for unleashing brutality of the worst kind on members of a religious minority and for the government's collaboration with the perpetrators of violence. Rahul is only rubbing salt on the wounds of the Sikhs by now claiming that his party was not involved. He must read the Nanavati Commission reports and the affidavits filed before it.

The Pioneer, 11 September, 2018

□

Babri and Rao: Spurious Tomes Stand Exposed

The bane of modern Indian history is the unconscionable distortions injected into it by historians owing allegiance to the Marxist and Nehruvian schools. This has resulted in a string of untruths being bandied about for decades about personalities and events both in the pre and post-independence eras.

Such is the grip of these two schools over academia that even after free-thinking historians, who are not prisoners of ideology, exhumed many truths that negated the mythologies palmed of by these palace historians, misrepresentations continue to permeate the textbooks and lectures in schools and colleges.

Subhas Chandra Bose, Sardar Patel, BR Ambedkar, Syama Prasad Mukherjee and Rajendra Prasad are some of the names that immediately come to mind, the national leaders whose contributions have been deliberately ignored and who have been victims of the falsification of history. In more recent times, a prominent victim of the machinations of these two schools is PV Narasimha Rao, one of India's most cerebral and successful prime ministers who saved India's unity and integrity and pulled the country out of an economic rut during 1991-96 and put it on the high road to growth.

The purpose of the so-called scholarship by entrenched academics from these two schools has been three-fold: one, to present members of the Nehru-Gandhi family as near faultless individuals who were deeply wedded to the core values of the constitution and who sacrificed everything for the country; two, to present all their contemporaries as petty individuals with petty goals and with questionable commitment to constitutional values; and, three, credit all national achievements to members of this family and all failures to others.

This shameless and continuous glorification of one political family makes one wonder whether our academia secretly pines for a return to monarchy. Seen in the context of this fraudulent output by these historians, specially in the capital's universities, Vinay Sitapati's Half Lion—How P.V. Narasimha Rao Transformed India—comes as a breath of fresh air.

Narasimha Rao became Prime Minister at a critical moment in the nation's history. India was standing at the door of the International Monetary Fund with a begging bowl and its foreign exchange reserves had slipped to such an alarming low that there was danger of default on loans.

Rao picked up Manmohan Singh as his Finance Minister and began the noble task of dismantling the socialist economy that Jawaharlal Nehru and Indira Gandhi had thrust on the country. He opened up the economy, liberated it from the licence-permit raj, unshackled the entrepreneurial instincts of millions of Indians and invited foreign investments into various sectors. These decisions brought about a spectacular turn around in the economy, restored hope among Indians and gave them the confidence to take on the world. He also pulled Punjab, which was engulfed by secessionist forces, from the brink and saved the unity and integrity of India.

Instead of acknowledging the man's phenomenal contribution, the Nehru-Gandhis and academics and writers hovering around this family, have falsely accused him of damaging India's secular fabric and of being complicit in the fall of the Babri Masjid in Ayodhya. Having pinned this monstrous charge on him, they hope this will wipe out his phenomenal contribution to the country.

One scholar even spread the story that Rao was napping while the masjid was being demolished. Another said he was "doing puja" while the demolition was on.

Sitapati's scholarly book covers a whole range of issues from Rao's early days to his tenure as a union minister, his prime ministership, the challenge on the economic front, the crisis in Punjab and elsewhere, the nuclear policy and the fall of the Babri

Masjid. For want of space, this column will confine itself to just the Babri Masjid issue.

The author throws up enough evidence to demolish the false accusations made against Rao regarding his conduct on 6 December, 1992. He shows how Rajiv Gandhi succumbed to Muslim fundamentalism and then swung to appease Hindu sentiment. He opened the locks of the Ram Temple and even blessed the Shilanyas ceremony for the temple.

Sitapati shows how the Union Cabinet was unwilling to impose President's Rule in Uttar Pradesh prior to December 6, merely on the suspicion that the BJP government in the state would not protect the structure. Article 356 of the Constitution cannot be invoked on assumptions. The Cabinet Committee on Political Affairs (CCPA), that considers such issues, met five times in November alone. The state's governor too sent a report saying the law and order situation, specially on the communal front "is satisfactory". Yet, Rao ensured massive deployment of central forces near the disputed structure prior to December 6. The situation that prevailed just prior to the demolition was that "the Supreme Court, the state governor and law ministry officials, all seemed against central rule".

That is why after the demolition, Mr. Pranab Mukherjee told partymen, "All decisions were taken in the meetings of the Cabinet and CCPA. Responsibility is collective; the onus cannot only be on the prime minister or home minister." Sitapati, who had access to Rao's personal papers, takes us through this narrative that presents facts that negate the spurious theories that have been in circulation. There is lots more to this book, but that will have to wait till later.

Half Lion is the first scholarly effort to correct the distortions that have crept into our understanding of social and political developments in India over the last three decades. It also seeks to restore Narasimha Rao's well deserved place in the pantheon of great Indian leaders.

The New Indian Express, 19 July, 2016

□

Need to Re-write History

For over six decades after independence, "the Establishment" in Lutyens' Delhi comprised people belonging to the Nehruvian-Marxist, pseudo-secular consensus. These ideological brothers-in-arms influenced everything—from school curriculum to public policy to history writing—and built up a false narrative that systematically debunked and condemned India's civilisational journey.

Such was the influence of this consensus that it successfully managed to draw away three generations of Indians born after independence from the country's great heritage and also inject a sense of shame among citizens about their own past. Much of this damage was done by Left-leaning politicians, bureaucrats and academics, who ensured through educational material—from primary school text books to major tomes on history, government policy and legislative measures—that the populace developed an allergy to its own culture and traditions.

Further, since the overwhelming majority of the people in the country were Hindus and since India's civilisational experience for millennia was Hindu, the grand scheme of this pseudo-secular establishment became anti-Hindu. It encouraged people to negate anything associated with Hinduism and to eulogise everything that was non-Hindu. This extended to various fields and included condemnation of the Vedas, treating the great epics—the *Ramayana* and the *Mahabharata*—with derision, pooh-poohing yoga and ayurveda and pouring ridicule on Sanskrit, the mother of Indian languages.

I wonder if there is another example of this kind where a miniscule minority of people launched an enterprise with such success to get the people living in a land to invalidate their own civilisation and culture.

They worked this consensus successfully for 67 years—and this included the six years during which the National Democratic Alliance (NDA) coalition was in power between 1998 and 2004—until they met their nemesis in Narendra Modi. Finally, the people of India decided that enough was enough and knocked down the Nehruvian-Marxist brigade from its perch in 2014. People reiterated their position in the 2019 Lok Sabha election and with this, the process of changing the narrative and getting the people to own, appreciate and applaud the phenomenal contribution of the oldest civilisation in the world has begun.

Now that the people of India have ensured the marginalisation of the Nehruvian-Marxist pseudo-secular school, work must begin to restore national pride. It is in this context that one must see Union Home Minister Amit Shah's recent call for re-writing history. Shah cited many examples and said that but for Veer Savarkar, who described the events of 1857 as the "first war of independence", historians would have written it off as a mere revolt against the British.

Shah is right when he says we must write history that is faithful to facts, in other words, re-write history. For example, let us take the case of Aurangzeb. He asked his Governors in 1669 to destroy Hindu temples, including the most revered Kashi Vishwanath temple, the Somnath temple in Gujarat and the Krishna temple in Mathura. He built a huge mosque after destroying the Mathura temple and had the idols of the Krishna mandir buried under the steps of a mosque in Agra.

Aurangzeb is also the emperor who offered Government jobs to Hindus who converted to Islam. Computation of prison terms was another incentive. He also imposed higher customs duty on Hindus, who imported goods into his territory and imposed a tax on the Hindus (jizya) who wished to practise their faith. Finally, let us not forget that it was Aurangzeb who destroyed Sikh gurdwaras, imprisoned and tortured Guru Tegh Bahadur and eventually beheaded him when the latter refused to convert to Islam. He continued his assault on Sikhism during the tenure of Guru Gobind Singh and killed his sons as well.

This is the story of Aurangzeb. Yet, historians of the variety named above have tried to bury these facts and even paint him as person who was "secular." If ever there was a prize for fraudulent history, this would get it. Will someone from the pseudo-secular, Nehru-Marxist combine tell us as to what was the rationale in naming a key arterial road in New Delhi after this tyrant?

Similarly, many towns and key roads and suburbs in other cities have been named after him—all because the Hindu-hating Nehru-Marxists controlled the levers of power in this country for over six decades. Similarly, Babar, Humayun and Jehangir have been accorded pride of place in the national capital and elsewhere in the country.

How can India remain a secular, democratic nation so long as it perpetuates the memory of such invaders? If we are to preserve our Constitution and our secular, democratic tradition, our history books must mirror these truths and our public policy must get attuned to the core values in our Constitution—meaning thereby that the last vestiges of these dreadful memories must be wiped out forever.

Fortunately, the name of Aurangzeb has been obliterated from that road in New Delhi and it has been named after the most honourable former President, APJ Abdul Kalam. Others, who fall in Aurangzeb's category, deserve similar treatment. Also, the truth about their empires and their bigotry must be part of the school curriculum, if only to emphasise that India's future lies not in such bigotry but in genuine democracy where the mantra is equality and equity. François Gautier, the French journalist who has made India his home, and Koenraad Elst, the Belgian scholar, have both alerted the people of the country to the humongous fraud that has been perpetrated by Left-leaning politicians, academics and bureaucrats since independence.

Gautier's book, A History of India as it Happened: Not as it Has Been Written, which was first published six years ago, is one of those books which compels the nation to re-write history.

Elst is another scholar who has focussed on the phenomenal damage done by Marxist historians, who have tried to erase from Hindu memory "the history of their persecution by the swordsmen of Islam." Elst says in his book, Negationism in India: Concealing the record of Islam, says India has its own "full-fledged brand of negationism" and "this movement is led by Islamic apologists and Marxist academics and followed by all the politicians, journalists and intellectuals, who call themselves secularists."

Also, this has been promoted by the Indian State. He says the English-educated class has turned the negation of India's civilisational greatness into a fashion statement. The Home Minister is also saying very much the same.

The Pioneer, 22 October, 2019

□

Why Sangh Parivar Must Frequent Nehru Memorial

Barring historians, scholars and serious students of modern Indian history who are regular visitors to Teen Murti House and who have a fair idea of what is on offer, everyone else, including the aam aadmi is certain to be utterly confused about the activities of The Nehru Memorial Museum and Library (NMML) Society that runs the place. The cacophonous debate over the future of this Society and its plans for development have drowned out saner voices and resulted in needless controversies and disinformation with regard to the activities of this institution, which will celebrate its golden jubilee next year. At the heart of this political wrangle is propaganda that the NMML Society's remit is confined to Nehru, his papers, his thoughts, his family and nothing else. Second, that the key personalities of the so-called Right can have no place in the NMML premises.

Some facts about how this institution was conceived and run over the last 49 years should not only set the record straight but also help the general public wade through the disinformation and get closer to the truth. As decided by its founders, the NMML Society has three main constituents: a Nehru memorial museum; a library on modern India; and a centre for research in modern Indian history. These are the three main functions of the institution. The NMML's Memorandum of Association mandates the institution to acquire, maintain and preserve papers of nationalist leaders of modern India and other eminent Indians who distinguished themselves in any field. It is also called upon to organise lectures and seminars to encourage the study of modern Indian history. Further, it has the responsibility to maintain a library of books, pamphlets among other things and other materials bearing on the history of modern India, with special reference to the freedom movement. In addition, the society has to institute fellowships and maintain records of non-official organisations and associations.

As the society's remit covers such a wide range of activities specific to modern Indian history, it has, despite the resistance from some individuals claiming proprietorial rights over the institution, carried on its task as ordained by the society's founders. Since modern Indian history is central to the institution's work, the NMML Library has diligently gone about collecting manuscripts, personal papers and published works of individuals and documents pertaining to institutions. Notwithstanding the myopic view, intellectual dishonesty and pressures from leftist academicians and some members of the Nehruvian school, the society has had curators who have remained loyal to the Memorandum of Association. That is why the library boasts of material pertaining to icons of the so-called Right. These include personal papers and letters written by Dr. Hedgewar, the founder of the Rashtriya Swayamsevak Sangh (RSS); Madhav Sadashiv Golwalkar (Guru Golwalkar), who succeeded Hedgewar as Sarsanghchalak of the RSS in 1940 and headed the organisation for over three decades; Dr. B.S. Moonje, who was the President of the Hindu Mahasabhaand; Dr. Syama Prasad Mookerjee, the leader of the Hindu Mahasabha and founder of the Jana Sangh.

The institution papers in the possession of the library include that of the All India Hindu Mahasabha. The library has published works of Mr. Deendayal Upadhyaya, the co-founder of the Jana Sangh and its chief ideologue. The material available in the library is documented in the publication NMML Manuscripts: An Introduction, brought out by the institution.

Some excerpts from this publication are listed below: The library has 949 letters written by Dr. Hedgewar to various individuals in Marathi and English between 1903-37. These documents, which were donated by the Shri Guruji Smriti-Sankalan Samithi, are valuable because of Dr. Hedgewar's political activities during that period, including his participation in the Home Rule campaign in 1918. He organised the volunteer corps at the Nagpur Session of the Congress and was jailed for his involvement in the non-cooperation movement in 1921. He founded the RSS in 1925. Dr. Moonje's papers include his diaries between 1926-36, his correspondence with various personalities prior to 1936 with considerable material on the affairs of the Hindu Mahasabha. Dr. Moonje lived with Mahatma Gandhi in Durban, took part in the Home Rule Movement and was a member of the Central Legislative Assembly. He also headed the Hindu Mahasabha.

On Guru Golwalkar, the material available includes his correspondence with Hedgewar, Jawaharlal Nehru, Sardar Patel, Govinda Menon, Babasaheb Apte and many others. The letters deal chiefly with the activities and organisational work of the RSS. Interestingly, the Golwalkar Papers were handed over to the library by the person in-charge of the RSS office in New Delhi.

The library boasts of a huge collection of papers pertaining to Dr. Syama Prasad Mookerjee, running to 70,000 pages. These papers, which include over 3,000 letters, speeches and writings and press clippings, were gifted to the library by Justice Rama Prasad Mookerjee and Mr. Uma Prasad Mookerjee. It has the exchange of correspondence between Dr Mookerjee and Jawaharlal Nehru, Sardar Patel, Sir M. Visveswaraya and many others. The library states that a bulk of these papers pertain to the Bengal Legislative Assembly, the Constituent Assembly, Hindu Mahasabha, the Wavell Plan, the partition of Bengal, Mahatma Gandhi's assassination, and the formation of the Jana Sangh. It also includes his diaries between 1939-46. These papers are of immense value to students of modern Indian history because of Dr. Mookerjee's extraordinary life and achievements. He became Vice-Chancellor of the Calcutta University at the age of 33; was Member of the Bengal Legislative Council, the Constituent Assembly and the first Lok Sabha. He was Finance Minister in Bengal and later, the Union Minister for Industry and Supply. He resigned from the Nehru Cabinet over the Nehru-Liaqat Pact in 1950 and went on to launch the Bharatiya Jana Sangh (BJS), which in later years became the Bharatiya Janata Party (BJP).

Given these facts, the controversy whipped up in some quarters over an exhibition at the NMML outlining the life and work of Deendayal Upadhyaya, seems rather silly. Mr. Upadhyaya joined Dr. Mookerjee to launch the Bharatiya Jana Sangh, became the party's first General Secretary and chief ideologue. His mantra of Integral Humanism and his concept of Antyodayais at the core of the policies pursued by India's largest political party—the BJP—today and his imprint is already there in many socio-economic programmes launched by the Narendra Modi Government at the Centre.

So, the question really is not why the Sangh Parivar is now visible in these precincts. We need to ask why members of this political family stayed away from the NMML all these years when the library had such a wealth of original material on their icons?

The New Indian Express, 13 October, 2015

□

Exit Aurangzeb, enter APJ Abdul Kalam

One would have thought that the renaming of Aurangzeb Road, an arterial avenue in the heart of New Delhi, as Dr. APJ Abdul Kalam Road, after the most loved and respected national icon in recent times would have been universally hailed. But, sadly, that is not to be. Sections of the political class, including those who often swear by the core values in our Constitution have taken umbrage at this decision and have sprung to the defence of one of the biggest despots in the country's history. While doing so, they have hurt the sentiments of millions of Indians who loved the simple, secular Kalam, who ignited the minds of the nation's youth.

Those who oppose the renaming of Aurangzeb Road, argue that history should not be tampered with and that this is an attempt to obliterate history. This is a specious argument on two counts. First, no such argument was ever advanced when dozens of roads and landmarks in Delhi were renamed over the last 50 years. Second, how can history be erased if a road is renamed.

Indians have been obsessed with renaming roads all across the country since independence. In fact, it was considered de rigueur to make such changes and as a result, most arterial roads in New Delhi have been renamed since 1947, and most of them have been named after icons of one political party—The Congress. Here is a small sample:

Kingsway is now Rajpath and Queen's Way is Janpath. York Road has become Motilal Nehru Marg and poor Sir Arthur, the Duke of Connaught, after whom Delhi's centerpiece—the upmarket circular shopping mall—was named, was officially knocked out in the 1990s. Now Connaught Circus and Connaught Place stand renamed as Indira Chowk and Rajiv Chowk. It is another matter that Delhiites have rejected the change. No commuter or autowallah ever refers to Connaught Circus as Indira Chowk.

Apart from Motilal Nehru, Indira Gandhi and Rajiv Gandhi, many more leaders of the Congress have dislodged icons of the British Empire on Delhi's streets. For example, Queen Victoria Road became Rajendra Prasad Road and King Edward Road was renamed Maulana Azad Road; Curzon Road is now Kasturba Gandhi Marg; Hardinge Avenue is now Tilak Marg. Old Mill Road stands renamed as Rafi Marg, after Rafi Ahmed Kidwai; Hastings Road was renamed Krishna Menon Marg; Dupleix Road became K. Kamraj Marg; Canning Road is now Shrimant Madhavrao Scindia Marg; Wellesley Road became Dr. Zakir Hussain Marg and Willingdon Crescent, Mother Teresa Crescent.

The bleeding hearts for Aurangzeb had no tears to shed for the noble Duke of Connaught, when he was given the short shrift two decades ago. After all, it was the Duke of Connaught who inaugurated the Central legislative Assembly, the precursor to today's Lok Sabha in 1921.

The Assembly, which was the lower House in the bicameral Parliament, was constituted following the Government of India Act, 1919. Is it fair to obliterate the name of the man who inaugurated the apex legislative body in IndiaIJ What sin had he committed to warrant such ill-treatmentIJ And what about Cornwallis, Dupleix or Canning. What crimes did they commit.

Another argument that is repeated ad nauseam is that this is an attempt to obliterate history. Nothing can be farther from the truth. How can one wipe out the cruelty and violence unleashed by Aurangzeb on his Hindu subjects merely by removing his name from an arterial road in Delhi.

For example, who will forget that Aurangzeb issued an order to his Governors on 8 April, 1669, to demolish the schools and temples of the Hindus leading to the destruction of hundreds of temples including the Kashi Vishwanath temple at Benaras, the Krishna temple at Mathura and the Somnath temple. Following the destruction of the temple at Mathura, he built a lofty mosque at that site. The idols were brought to Agra and buried under the steps of the mosque of Begum Sahib "in order to be continually trodden upon".

Ten years later, on 2 April, 1679, he imposed jizya—a tax that the Hindus had to pay in order to continue to practice their faith. The list is endless, but here are a few more nuggets from the life of this man who is a darling of Marxist historians: He offered Government jobs and commutation of prison terms for those who converted to Islam; in April, 1665, he fixed different rates of customs duty for imported goods for Muslim (2.5 per cent) and Hindu merchants (five per cent); in 1668, he prohibited all Hindu fairs; in 1671, he dismissed all Hindu head-clerks and accountants and hired Muslims in their place.

Aurangzeb was most vengeful when he dealt with the Sikhs. He ordered the destruction of Sikh places of worship, imprisoned Guru Tegh Bahadur and beheaded him after torturing him for many days because he refused to convert to Islam. He continued the assault on Sikhism during the tenure of Guru Gobind Singh and killed four of his sons.

This is just a glimpse of the life and crimes of Aurangzeb culled out from the monumental work of some of India's greatest historians like Jadunath Sarkar and R.C. Majumdar, who had an unblinkered approach to history.

Will this history of the abominable Aurangzeb be expunged by altering the name of a road in New Delhi. Far from destroying history, this will serve a very noble cause. The names of British monarchs and viceroys were removed from our roads to wipe out obvious daily reminders of our colonial past and to reinforce the idea of independence. Similarly, now, roads bearing the names of persons like Aurangzeb must be renamed to reinforce the ideas of secularism and democracy.

The question, therefore, is not why Aurangzeb Road is now named after Kalam. We must ask: Why the Indian state glorify Aurangzeb all these years. Who was behind this horrendous idea and why was this atrocity, committed on the nation's secular, democratic fabric, allowed to continue for six decades after the adoption of a Constitution with the most cherished secular and democratic values.

Actually, the name change represents the advance of a nation from the vestiges of medieval barbarism to the most secular, democratic and modern ideas that someone like Kalam stood for. But, those who steered the Indian state all these years and permitted the glorification of one of the most dreadful characters in India's history, seem to be still voting for Aurangzeb!

They have a lot of answering to do!

The Pioneer, 15 September, 2015

□

Mullahs Cannot Have Veto Power

The campaign launched by the radical Muslim clergy and phony liberals against the Law Commission of India's well-intentioned and long overdue exercise to undertake a revision and reform of family laws in line with the constitutional mandate in Article 44 to bring in a Uniform Civil Code (UCC), is yet another example of the maladjustment of some sections of the citizenry to the core values in our Constitution. The Law Commission has put out a questionnaire and asked citizens, irrespective of denomination, to respond to the issues raised in it. It has said that the objective behind the endeavour is "to address discrimination against vulnerable groups and harmonise the various cultural practices" and to start a "healthy conversation" about the viability of a common civil code. The aim of the exercise is to examine family laws of all religions and to tackle social injustice.

How can any citizen of democratic India take exception to this? The Muslim clergy, which seeks to block constitutional rights of Muslim women in the name of religious freedom, has taken exception to the Law Commission's efforts and also tried to portray the commission's effort as an attempt to target Muslims. Anyone who examines the work of the commission since its inception will realise that this is utter rubbish. While the commission has rarely, if ever, discussed Muslim Personal Law, it has examined and opined on Hindu and Christian laws. In fact, there is a pattern to this. In the view of the Muslim clergy and their pseudo-secular cohorts, every institution in the country has a right to interfere with religious practices of the Hindus, Christians and others, but the Muslims are a class apart.

Similarly, when it comes to re-location of places of worship and some such measure to be undertaken by the state for the public good, the state can do so with respect of every place of worship except those belonging to the Muslims. The attitude of the clergy to such issues has not only disturbed communal harmony but also deprived Muslim women of their constitutional rights. It is therefore heartening to see Muslim women like Sharaya Bano and several Muslim women's groups demanding their rights. The question therefore is not why the Law Commission has launched this initiative now, but why this commission, which has such an important remit, allowed Muslim women to suffer such deprivation in terms of their fundamental rights for 66 years after our Constitution came into being. For those who spread the canard that the commission is targeting Muslims, here is a glimpse of the commission's interventions in respect of Hindu customs and laws since its inception. The 59th report dwelt on the amendments to the Hindu Marriage Act, 1955 and the Special Marriage Act, 1954. The 71st report re-visited this issue and the commission took the view that irretrievable breakdown of marriage constituted a ground for divorce. The 73rd report discussed criminal liability of husband for non-payment of maintenance.

The 74th and 83rd reports reviewed the Hindu Widows Remarriage Act and the Guardians and Wards Act and the Hindu Minority and Guardianship Act. The 1980s saw a huge jump in reporting of dowry deaths leading to a nation-wide campaign for stricter laws to deal with a husbands, in-laws and other relatives who harass a woman for dowry and indulge in barbaric acts like bride burning when her parents failed to meet their demands. The commission turned its focus on this issue in its 91st report. It recommended amendments to the Hindu Marriage Act, 1955; the Indian Penal Code, 1860 and the Indian Evidence Act, 1872. The commission returned to the provisions of the Hindu Marriage Act in its 98th report. The commission examined property rights of women and proposed reforms in Hindu Law for this purpose in its 174th report, returned to irretrievable breakdown of marriage as another ground of divorce in its 217th report. The right of a Hindu wife to maintenance was examined in the 252nd report.

The commission has dealt with many customary and personal laws pertaining to Christians also. The 15th and 90th reports examined marriage laws and the grounds of divorce amongst Christians, whereas the 224th discussed changes to enable non-domiciled estranged Christian wives to seek divorce. In light of this evidence, how can anyone say that the commission is targeting Muslims? The opposition to the commission's questionnaire is thus beyond comprehension. In its questionnaire, the commission asks respondents whether they are aware of Article 44 of the Constitution and whether a UCC includes subjects such as marriage, divorce, adoption, guardianship and child custody, maintenance, succession and inheritance. It has many questions pertaining specifically to Hindus and Christians. Question number 6 asks whether polygamy, polyandry and customary practices such as Maitri-karar (friendship deed) should be banned or regulated while question number 7 asks whether the practice of triple talaq be abolished in toto, retained or retained with amendments. The Muslim clergy has reacted adversely to the questionnaire itself, but in particular to these two questions. While triple talaq is entirely an Islamic affair, polygamy stands on a different footing. Polygamy is not exclusive to Muslims, yet whenever polygamy is questioned, the Muslim clergy presumes that it is a campaign against adherents of Islam. In the light of all this facts, should we allow a few Mullahs to derail or disrupt our march towards equality and fraternity? The Nehruvians and their Marxists cohorts have allowed the Mullahs to trample on our constitutional rights since independence and given them the veto power on everything. This must end.

The New Indian Express, 8 November, 2016

□

Beheadings in France

The decision of the French President Emmanuel Macron to defend freedom of speech in his country, following the barbaric beheading of a school teacher and some others by radicalised Muslims, has led to violent protests across Islamic nations. The perpetrators of these violent acts in France, it is believed, were seeking to avenge the caricaturing of Prophet Mohammed in a French magazine. So it has become a blasphemy versus free speech issue in a nation that rests on the foundation of liberty, equality and fraternity.

Most of the protesters in the Islamic world are justifying the beheadings and baying for the blood of the French President. The biggest culprit is the former Malaysian Prime Minister, Mahathir Bin Mohamad, who said that Muslims have the right "to be angry and to kill millions of French people for the massacres of the past". This is an open encouragement to bloodshed and must easily be the most outrageous and irresponsible statement made by a person who has held an important public office in a big nation. It is surprising that Twitter has only deleted Mohamad's tweet and restrained itself from taking more severe action.

While all this is on in the Islamic world, how should citizens of India respond to the developments in France? Several Indian cities have seen angry protests by Muslim citizens against the caricaturing of the Prophet. There is legitimacy for these protests so long as they are peaceful and non-violent and do not cause any disturbance to the normal run of life. That is why the conduct of Farhan Zuberi, a student leader from Aligarh Muslim University

(AMU), who has justified the beheadings in France and held out an open threat to behead anyone speaking against Islam, deserves to be condemned.

India, given its democratic credentials, has taken the right stand against this kind of violence. The Foreign Ministry condemned the beheading of the school teacher in Paris and said there can be no justification for terrorism "for any reason or under any circumstances". For once, the Ministry put aside its weakness for prevarication and "strongly deplored" the personal attack on the French President and said it is a violation of the most basic standards of international discourse. Prime Minister Narendra Modi has also taken a firm stand. In a tweet, he strongly condemned the terrorist attacks, including the heinous attack in Nice inside a church. "India stands with France in the fight against terrorism", he tweeted.

This is where all Indians have to draw the line. They cannot behave like the citizens in the Islamic States where everything revolves around religion and the space for public discourse is severely constricted.

For the moment, it can be said that the violent outbursts of the AMU student leader are an aberration. It is not the rule. All those who value democracy speak a different language. That is why the statement of one hundred Indian personalities, who "unequivocally and unconditionally" condemned the recent killings in France by fanatics in the name of faith, is important. The signatories to this statement, who included actor Naseeruddin Shah, former Indian Police Service Officer, Julio Ribeiro and lyricist Hussain Haidri, said: "We are deeply disturbed by the convoluted logic of some self-appointed guardians of Indian Muslims in rationalising cold-blooded murder and deplore the outrageous remarks of some heads of state." The signatories attacked whataboutery and condemned attempts to rationalise crimes by comparing them with other similar crimes. They said this was irrational and absurd. "No god, gods, goddesses, prophets or saints may be invoked to justify the killing and/or terrorising of fellow human beings."

India is the world's largest, secular, liberal, democratic

republic and all of us who care for the free air we breathe must unite against individuals who defend such brutality.

As citizens of the most democratic and diverse nation in the world, our future lies in the preservation of the core values in our Constitution and our democratic way of life. Secular, liberal democracies cannot survive, let alone flourish, if any section of the population offers justification for violence in order to assert the correctness of its stand. This applies to all Indian citizens and, in the present context, especially to citizens who are adherents of Islam. No citizen of India can take lessons from Islamic nations which have no respect for plurality and equality. We are different. In fact, we are unique, and we must assert our uniqueness and the exalted status that our Constitution has given us.

Co-existence within a plural society demands a high degree of tolerance. Our Constitution makers recognised this and it is here that our constitutional arrangement is slightly different from that of France. Our "freedom of expression" is subject to "reasonable restrictions." We cannot use it to disturb, among other things, "public order, decency, morality" or resort to "defamation or incitement to an offence." This is further reinforced by provisions in the Indian Penal Code, such as Section 153 A, 295 and 295 A, which prohibit any activity which promotes enmity between different groups or amounts to "deliberate and malicious acts intended to outrage the religious feelings of any class by insulting its religion or the religious beliefs". Therefore, we are distinct and we should completely stay clear of the violence that is being promoted by the Islamic nations against France.

As the campaign for a separate Muslim nation started building up in the 1940s, Dr. B.R. Ambedkar, after much deliberation, came to the conclusion that the creation of Pakistan was inevitable. In his book, Thoughts on Pakistan, he said, "The allegiance of a Muslim does not rest on his domicile in the country which is his, but on the faith to which he belongs. To the Muslim Ubi Bene Ibi Patria is unthinkable. Wherever there is the rule of Islam, there is his own country. In other words, Islam can never allow a true Muslim to adopt India as his motherland and regard a Hindu as his kith and kin." Dr. Ambedkar said this 75 years ago and in a certain context—when Muslims in India said that they constituted a separate nation—and established Pakistan. About 35 million Muslims stayed back in India after Pakistan was born because they believed that life in a liberal, democratic environment was far better than in an Islamic State. In these Muslim families, the third generation is growing up with the protection and safeguards offered by India's Constitution.

These citizens, like all others belonging to other faiths, who have grown up under this secular, democratic umbrella, can see that Pakistan is a failed State that is weighed down by its own failures and has cross-border terrorism as a single-point national agenda. The issues that prompted the creation of Pakistan are no longer relevant. That being the case, they need to prove Dr. Ambedkar wrong. The times have changed and peaceful co-existence offers all of us the best chance. As Indians, we all need to stand by France and all other democracies and wage a united war against terrorism and against all those who are opposed to secular, democratic values.

The Pioneer, 3 November, 2020

□

Chapter-7

NATIONAL–ANTI-NATIONAL

So, It's Fashionable to be Anti-national?

There may indeed be a case for a fresh look at Section-124 A of the Indian Penal Code (IPC) dealing with sedition, but one must not allow this academic debate on the validity of such a provision to cloud the core issue that is before us, namely, the shameful assault on our Constitution and the challenge posed to India's unity and integrity by a bunch of students at the Jawaharlal Nehru University (JNU) in New Delhi and in the Jadavpur University campus in West Bengal.

Just read the contents of the poster put up in JNU for the controversial event held on February 9 last and you will realise that centrifugal forces have begun to exert pressure on the nation's core. The poster said it was a "cultural evening of protest" (whatever that means) with poets, artists and singers. It said this event was "Against the judicial killing of Afzal Guru & Maqbool Bhat; in solidarity with the struggle of the Kashmiri people for their democratic right to self-determination."

Further, it said there would be an art exhibition & a photo exhibition portraying "the history of the occupation of Kashmir & the people's struggle against it". It invited everyone "to join us in protest, in rage against the occupation and in solidarity with the valiant people of Kashmir." A recent Delhi High Court order on a bail application moved by a student arrested in this connection, quoted the slogans that the students were raising at this alleged cultural evening. Just read them and decide for yourself whether any Indian citizen who stands committed to the unity and integrity of India; who has any respect for our Constitution, and for the soldiers defending our borders would ever raise such slogans? Here they are:

Afzal Guru, Maqbool Bhat Zindabad; Bharat Ki Barbadi Tak Jung Rahegi, Jung Rahegi; Go India, Go Back; Indian Army Murdabad; Bharat Tere Tukkde Honge I Inshaallah, Inshaallah; Afzal Ki Hatya Nahi Sahenge, Nahi Sahenge; and finally, Bandook Ki Dum Par Lenge Azadi.

The High Court Judge was apprised of the sequence of events leading to the controversial incident on February 9. A group of students initially sought and secured permission for "a cultural evening" at the Sabarmati Dhaba on the JNU campus. Later, JNU authorities realised that some mischief was afoot when they saw the posters put up in all the hostels. These posters referred to 'the judicial killing' of Afzal Guru and Maqbool Bhat. Apprehending trouble, the university authorities cancelled the permission given to the organsiers and also called in the police. That evening "the shouting of anti-national slogans continued unabated".

The High Court was also given a set of photographs which showed students holding posters with photographs of Afzal Guru, who was one of the masterminds behind the attack on India's Parliament in December, 2001. In other words, in the name of "democracy" and "free speech", they were espousing the cause of a terrorist who planned the assault on our temple of democracy! The posters put up in Jadavpur University went even further. One poster said: Hum Kya Chahe—AZADI: Kashmir Ki Azadi; Nagaland Ki Azadi; Manipur Ki Azadi.

Shockingly, there are professors in JNU and elsewhere who claim that these slogans fall within the ambit of "Freedom of Expression" guaranteed under Article-19(1)(a) of the Constitution! Referring to the slogans raised in JNU, Justice Pratibha Rani of the Delhi High Court said: "Suffice it to note that such persons enjoy the freedom to raise such slogans in the comfort of the university campus but without realising that they are in this safe environment because our forces are there at the battle field situated at the highest altitude in the world where even oxygen is so scarce that those who are shouting anti-national slogans holding posters of Afzal Guru and Maqbool Bhat close to their chest honouring their martyrdom, may not be even able to withstand such conditions for an hour ..."

Further, the judge observed that such slogans may have a demoralising effect on the family of martyrs who return home in coffins draped in the tricolour. The judge was even more trenchant when dealing with anti-national slogans raised in the university campus. She said those shouting such slogans cannot claim protection of the fundamental right to freedom of speech and expression. Whenever there is an infection in a limb, the first effort is to cure it through antibiotics, followed by a second line of treatment. "Sometimes, it may require surgical intervention also. However, if the infection results in infecting the limb to the extent that it becomes gangrene, amputation is the only treatment".

Many pseudo-secularists, who are now doubling up as pseudo-nationalists, are unable to stomach the rapier-like thrust of the Learned Judge's observations and are trying to belittle her by saying that she had delivered a sermon when called upon to pass an order on a bail application. Some others have been even more uncharitable, but their objections need to be brushed aside, because they are unwilling to address the primary issue and punish the original sinners who were mocking at India's Constitution and the country's unity and integrity.

Frustrated by the drubbing that their parties received in the Lok Sabha poll of 2014 (total vote share—4 per cent), the two main communist parties have been orchestrating many campaigns against the Narendra Modi government ever since it came to power in May, 2014. Such is their desperation that they have now begun to support groups espousing fissiparous ideas. As a result, the Hate-Modi Campaign is now slowly turning into a Hate-India campaign.

An "eminent jurist", while stating the legal position, has gone on record to say that it is not a criminal offence to be anti-national. Similarly, it can be argued that no citizen is legally bound to remain committed to the unity and integrity of India. If the provision relating to sedition is out-dated, how come none of those supporting these students, has suggested legislative measures to enforce loyalty to the Constitution?

Are there no limits to tolerance? Is it too much to ask a citizen to remain loyal to the country's Constitution, its flag, its unity and integrity? Can India, which is such a diverse society, survive this kind of permissiveness? We are all aware that there is a lunatic fringe towards the left of our political spectrum. Should we allow it to occupy centre-stage and gnaw at the vitals of the most liberal, democratic and plural nation in the world?

The New Indian Express, 15 March, 2016

□

A Shameless Brigade that Mocks at Our Tricolour

The last fortnight has seen an intense debate over the unfortunate happenings in some university campuses, including Jawaharlal Nehru University (JNU) and Jadavpur University, where some students raised anti-national slogans, challenged the unity and integrity of India and mocked at the Union Government's decision to hoist the national flag in all central universities.

Many of those participating in this shrill debate on television channels and campuses displayed a visceral hatred for a duly elected government at the Centre and in order to spite it, took the Pakistani line on the Kashmir issue and even went to the absurd extent of describing the national tricolour as a "Hindu Flag".

Though these are fringe elements, which are electorally irrelevant, they need to be challenged because of the disproportionate media space they occupy and the distorted image of India that they are peddling outside the country. Tragically, these so-called "Professors", who peddle such gibberish about the national flag, need to be educated on the history of the flag, almost seven decades after we won our independence and adopted it. The observations of Dr. S. Radhakrishnan, philosopher and former president and a great mind that guided India during the traumatic phase of partition and freedom, on the national flag should be compulsory reading for these malcontents in our politics and academia. Dr. Radhakrishnan's opening remarks in the Constituent Assembly in July 1947 at the time of adoption of the flag were indeed prophetic.

It was as if he was addressing the nation after listening to the recent cacophonous debate on nationalism and the national flag and desperately trying to instil some sense into those who were questioning the need for the tricolour in our universities. He said: "What is essential today is to equip ourselves with new strength and new character... if the country is to achieve the great ideal of unity and liberty which it fought for... times are hard. Everywhere we are consumed by phantasies. Our minds are haunted by myths. The world is full of misunderstandings, suspicions and distrusts. In these difficult days, it depends on us under what banner we fight." He then went on to explain the deep meaning that every aspect of India's flag carried. He said the white band at the centre represented the path of light... the ideal light, the light of truth, of transparent simplicity. The Ashoka Chakra in the middle represented the wheel of Dharma. "The wheel is perpetually revolving... there is life in movement. Our Dharma is Sanatana, eternal. Its uninterrupted continuity is its Sanatana character."

The Bhagwa or saffron band at the top represents the spirit of renunciation. "All forms of renunciation are to be embodied in Raja Dharma. Philosophers must be kings. Our leaders must be... people who are imbued with the spirit of renunciation which that saffron colour has transmitted to us from the beginning of our history... It stands for the fact that the world belongs not to the wealthy... but to the weak and the humble, the dedicated and the detached." The green band, he said, reminded us of our relation to the earth and plant life. We must build our paradise here on green earth and in order to do so, "we must be guided by truth (white), practice virtue (the wheel), adopt the method of self-control and renunciation (saffron)," he explained. In conclusion, he said, the flag tells us, "Be alert, be ever on the move, go forward, work for a free, flexible compassionate, decent, democratic society in which the Christians, Sikhs, Muslims, Hindus and Buddhists will all find a safe shelter." The entire assembly responded with loud cheers when Dr. Radhakrishnan concluded his speech.

Jawaharlal Nehru, who moved the resolution for adoption of the national flag, said: "It is a Flag which has been variously described. Some people, having misunderstood its significance, have thought of it in communal terms and believe that some part of it represents this community or that. We thought of a design for a Flag... which would represent the spirit of the nation, the tradition of the nation... through thousands of years. So, we devised this flag. A nation, and especially a nation like India with an immemorial past, lives by other things also, the things of the spirit. If India had not been associated with these ideals and things of the spirit during these thousands of years, what would India have been?" Nehru also spoke of how the Congress Party's flag formed the basis for designing the national flag.

The Charka in the Congress Party's flag had been replaced by the Ashoka Chakra. Several other members of the Constituent hailed the flag. Mohammed Sheriff said that the white, saffron and green in the flag signified purity, renunciation and sacrifice, had great spiritual significance and these colours were venerated by all—Hindus, Muslims, Christians and Parsis. Further, the design was aesthetic and suited the genius, tradition and culture of India. Saiyid Mohammad Saadulla welcomed the inclusion of saffron in the flag and said it reminded the people that they must keep themselves on the "high plane of renunciation."

Frank Anthony, who served on the Flag Committee of the Constituent Assembly, said the flag did not contain any communal motives or significance. It was "a beautiful flag in its physical aspect and also in its motives." The best way to shame those who attribute other motives to the colours of our national flag is to cite the opinions of these learned individuals who designed our flag almost seven decades ago.

It is sad to see people run down the national flag, which ought to be treated with the utmost reverence because it brings all Indians together and is therefore the most secular point of convergence. In a diverse nation such as India where every symbol, flag and book is seen as being denominational and divisive, two things that bring all citizens together is the national flag and the Constitution of India. Therefore, any attempt to denigrate the flag not only violates a specific law such as the Prevention of Insults to National Honour Act and the Flag Code but also strikes at the most sacred secular symbol of India.

Given this history of the flag and the deep connect the Congress party has with it, it was indeed shocking to see members of India's oldest party team up with the communists and a frustrated bunch of politically displaced academicians to mock at the idea of hoisting the tricolour in our university campuses. Is this really the party that fought for India's freedom?

The New Indian Express, 2 March, 2016

□

Nip Secession Demands in the Bud

After five decades, some reckless and irresponsible voices calling for secession are once again being heard in the South. While some southern political leaders have called for a separate 'Dravida Nadu' comprising all five southern states but within the Indian Union, some others have said that these five states must break away from the Indian Union because they are getting a raw deal from the North. The debate was initially triggered by Kamal Haasan, actor-turned-politician when he said that if all the southern states imbibed the "Dravidian identity", discrimination that they talk of would vanish and "our voices would become a loud chorus."

DMK working president M.K. Stalin joined the chorus and said he would welcome it if the Southern states were to come together and make a demand for a Dravida Nadu. Pawan Kalyan, a Telugu actor and leader of the Jana Sena Party, has also warned of a North-South divide. He is seen endorsing the idea of a 'United States of Southern India' in the hope of getting a better deal from New Delhi.

However, M. Muralimohan, another Telugu actor-turned -MP of the Telugu Desam Party has taken this debate to an unacceptable level by talking of secession. He said the South felt discriminated and that if this continued, the five southern states would declare themselves as a "separate country".

The reason for the discontent appears to be the approach of the 15th Finance Commission to the devolution of funds to states. The southern states certainly have a right to demand fair distribution of funds from the central pool of national resources. While these issues need to be discussed and debated, they cannot become the reason for the break-up of India. These demands for a separate identity for the South are indeed surprising, because one believed that the nation had taken giant strides towards integration over the last 70 years and effectively smothered voices that preached disintegration. After Independence, the first time the nation heard the demand for secession at a formal gathering was during the maiden speech of C.N. Annadurai in the Rajya Sabha on 1 May, 1962 when Jawaharlal Nehru was the prime minister.

The DMK leader took the first opportunity that came his way to talk about the most controversial demand of his party — secession of Tamil Nadu (then called Madras). Much to the shock of many members, Annadurai said, "Let us have a re-thinking. We have a Constitution, of course ... but the time has come for a re-thinking, for a re-appraisal, for a re-valuation and for a re-interpretation of the word nation." And what is that re-appraisal?

Annadurai elaborated: "I claim to come from a country ... which I think, is of a different stock ... I belong to the Dravidian stock. I am proud to call myself a Dravidian ... Dravidians have got something distinct, something different, to offer to the nation at large. Therefore it is that we want self-determination." Further, he said if the South were to separate, it would not cause hardships because it was one geographical unit—the peninsula. Therefore, there would be no migration or refugee problem. He wanted India to become "a comity of nations instead of being a medley of disgruntled units here and there". Dravida Nadu, comprising the entire South would become "a small nation, compact, homogeneous and united".

Among those who took strong exception to Annadurai's observations was Atal Behari Vajpayee of the Bharatiya Jana Sangh. Speaking in the Rajya Sabha a day after Annadurai's speech, he said the House had heard a "warning bell" the previous day—a demand was being made for the division of India once again an this would spell disaster. "The reason given for separating from India ... is that justice is not being done to Madras. We can go to any state, we will hear the same complaint." He said such complaints of discrimination could be heard even within states with one region complaining against another. "There can be some truth in these complaints, but these complaints cannot prompt us to challenge the existence of the nation ... and demand the balkanisation of India."

Vajpayee said, "I feel saddened that this voice is raised in the garb of self-determination. There is an attempt to give it an ideological stance and demand for separatism is placed at a higher pedestal and it was said that India is not a nation but a group of nations and the South can get separated from the North. I do not think any nation can negotiate with this kind of thinking. The Muslim League raised the issue of two nations and we fought against it. We never agreed to the theory of two nations". Vajpayee's views were backed by all sections of the House including many MPs from the South. A year later and following the Chinese aggression when national unity became the first priority, the DMK withdrew the demand for secession, became part of the mainstream political and electoral system and even came to power in 1967 in Madras State. With this, one presumed that the forces of integration had gained the upper hand.

About 56 years after this debate in the Rajya Sabha, we are once again hearing discordant voices and even talk of secession. It is thoughtless to even suggest this. The unity and integrity of India is non-negotiable. Three generations of Indians have toiled over the last seven decades to bind this nation together. No other society in the world is as diverse and democratic as ours and we cannot allow a few hot-headed delinquents to disrupt this glorious journey of unity in diversity. Every word of what Vajpayee said in 1962 in Parliament holds good even today. We must remind ourselves of his stirring call for unity and the current challenge to India's unity and integrity must be nipped in the bud.

The New Indian Express, 10 April, 2018

□

The Court and the Anthem

The recent order of the Supreme Court directing all cinema halls in the country to play the national anthem before the commencement of the show has triggered widespread debate among jurists and political commentators with several of them arguing th t the court has outreached itself and taken a position that is violative of the fundamental rights of citizens. Some of them even argue that it may be difficult to enforce the order.

The critics say that showing respect to the national anthem is one thing and insisting that it be played in every cinema hall in the country, is quite another. While there may be some merit in the argument that the court need not have gone so far as to direct that the national anthem be played before the show in every cinema hall, the court's order must be seen in the light of the intense political discourse in recent years over the claims of some sections of the citizenry that their religious beliefs prevent them from accepting India as their 'motherland" or from singing the national anthem. It is also significant because of its emphasis on the fundamental duties of citizens. The order, which has stirred a controversy, directed all cinema halls to display the national flag on the screen while playing the national anthem and said that all persons present in the hall are obliged to stand up and show respect to the national anthem.

This protocol, it said, had its roots in "national identity, national integrity and constitutional patriotism". The court said respect for the national anthem and the national flag reflects "love and respect for the motherland" and it instils a feeling of "patriotism and nationalism". Some observations made by the apex court in this order are quite distinct from an earlier judgement of the court on the issue of showing respect for the national anthem. In 1985, three children belonging to a sect called Jehovah's Witnesses were expelled from a school in Kerala for refusing to sing the national anthem. The students stood in respectful silence along with other children in the school assembly, but refused to sing the anthem because it was "against the tenets of their religious faith".

When their appeal to the High Court failed, they moved the Supreme Court. In this case—Bijoe Emmanuel & Ors vs State of Kerala & Ors—the court held that the expulsion order infringed the fundamental rights of the students under Art 19(1)(a) and 25(1), who, "because of their conscientiously held religious faith" do not join the singing of the national anthem. The action taken against them "is a violation of the fundamental right to freedom of conscience and freely to profess, practice and propagate religion". The court noted that the stand taken by Jehovah's Witnesses was not peculiar to India. In other nations, members of this sect refuse to vote or run for public office or serve in the armed forces. They refuse to salute the flag, stand up when the national anthem is played or recite the pledge of allegiance, because their religious beliefs forbid them to do so. The court said that the real test of a true democracy is the ability of even an insignificant minority to find its identity under the country's Constitution.

This has to be borne in mind in interpreting Art 25. It also touched on the fundamental duty to respect the national anthem and said proper respect is shown when a person stands up when the anthem is sung. "It will not be right to say that disrespect is shown by not joining in the singing". As regards the fundamental duties of citizens, the Bench that passed the recent order has made it clear it is the "sacred obligation" of every citizen to respect the national anthem and national flag. However, in the Emmanuel Case, the court said standing up when the anthem is sung is enough. "It will not be right to say that disrespect is shown by not joining in the singing".

Given the fact that India is not only the world's largest democracy, but also the world's most diverse nation, one thing will have to be borne in mind—that the only secular point of convergence for all citizens is the national flag, the national anthem and the country's Constitution. All other flags, anthems and books are exclusive to different groups and communities and have a tendency to promote divisiveness. Therefore, any individual or group which cites religion or any other reason to show disrespect or less respect to our national symbols, hits at the root of India's unity and integrity, and must therefore be firmly discouraged. If individual freedoms like freedom of expression and freedom to practice religion prevail over a citizen's duty to come to the common, secular meeting ground that our national symbols offer us, it would harm the integrative process in our diverse land. Further, some commentators would have us believe that the chapter on fundamental duties in our Constitution is unenforceable and therefore of little value.

Given India's diversity and the pressure that centrifugal forces are putting on ideas and institutions which bind us, this argument must be challenged. Several religious and social groups are subjecting our core constitutional values, which is the amalgam that binds us all, to such bombardment that national unity is under constant threat. In this scenario, this argument must the rejected. The apex court's reference to fundamental duties in its recent order must be welcomed because it raises the hope that the court could breathe life into this chapter. Fundamental duties enable aggregation of the citizenry towards common national goals and provide the glue to bind the most diverse nation in the world. May be, the time has come to re-visit the postulates in the Emmanuel Judgement.

The New Indian Express, 6 December, 2016

□

Chapter-8

THE DYNASTY

Bharat Ratna and the Congress First Family

While the announcement of the Bharat Ratna for Nanaji Deshmukh, Pranab Mukherjee and Bhupen Hazarika by the Narendra Modi government has been well received all over the country, there are some voices of dissent, especially within the Congress, with some accusing the Centre of promoting "loyalists". Nothing can be farther from the truth and, as the details that follow will reveal, it is best that Congress members are far more circumspect when the debate is about honouring India's real heroes.

Given Deshmukh's phenomenal contribution to the idea of rural self-reliance and the sacrifices he made to bring about agrarian reform, the real question is why he was not conferred the honour earlier. The same is true of Hazarika, who bridged the cultural gap between the Northeast and other states and made a huge contribution to national integration through his music and art. Former President and Congress veteran Pranab, the most qualified Congress leader for the office of PM, was edged out of the race by "accidental" PMs more than once due to the insecurities of a single political family. His judicious advice and non-partisan approach were invaluable at critical times for two PMs when he was President.

Now for some unpleasant home truths about the Bharat Ratna. As per the rules, the honour is conferred by the President on the recommendation of the PM. It was instituted in 1954. The very next year, PM Jawaharlal Nehru's government gave Nehru the Bharat Ratna in 1955. PM Indira Gandhi too gave herself the Bharat Ratna in 1971. Neither Nehru nor Indira considered Dr. B.R. Ambedkar, the architect of our Constitution, or Sardar Vallabhbhai Patel, the man who created an united India, worthy of the nation's highest honour. Rajiv Gandhi too was given the Bharat Ratna soon after his assassination.

Dr. Ambedkar was conferred the Bharat Ratna by the Janata Dal-led government of V P Singh, which was supported by the BJP. But why was he overlooked until then? Because, according to Dr Subramanian Swamy, "Till then no PM dared to overrule Nehru." Patel too was recognised by a non-Congress government in 1991. It was PM Chandra Shekhar who suggested the Sardar be given the Bharat Ratna posthumously and ex-President Venkataraman recalls in his memoirs that he "readily agreed to the proposal". Earlier that year, Chandra Shekhar had proposed that Bharat Ratna be conferred on former PM Morarji Desai. He was 96 when he received the honour.

The Modi government's decision to honour Hazarika with the Bharat Ratna reminds one of the Atal Bihari Vajpayee government's decision to honour Gopinath Bordoloi, a great patriot. Bordoloi worked closely with Patel to ensure Pakistan's claims to parts of Assam were scuttled and this key state in the Northeast remained united with India. But the Congress did not consider him worthy of the honour. He was conferred the award by the Vajpayee government in 1999.

Another great Gandhian and patriot—Jayaprakash Narayan—who led the movement for restoration of democracy in the 1970s after Indira imposed a dictatorship, was conferred the highest civilian honour by the Vajpayee government in 1999.

Although the Congress, under Mahatma Gandhi's leadership, was at the vanguard of the freedom movement, the party under the leadership of the Nehru-Gandhis became small-minded and spiteful. Between them, Nehru, Indira and Rajiv were in power for 38 years. In addition, Sonia Gandhi as Congress president was the de facto head of government while the 'Accidental Prime Minister' did the de jure functions for 10 years. The family also extracted its political pound of flesh when Narasimha Rao was PM.

However, even though many well-meaning citizens suggested that Vajpayee be conferred the Bharat Ratna, the Sonia-Manmohan combine dismissed the idea. Ultimately, Vajpayee was given the honour after the peoples' verdict of 2014 reduced the Congress to a rump in Parliament. On the other hand, the Modi government chose eminent Congress leaders of the past and present—Pandit Madan Mohan Malaviya and Pranab—for this honour.

While the Nehru-Gandhis conferred the honour on themselves, they never felt the need to honour some of the greatest Indians. India had to elect non-Congress governments to ensure that these leaders got their due.

It is also true that the Nehru-Gandhis never acknowledged the contribution of those belonging to political formations they disliked, although the Congress often harps on its commitment to diversity. Obviously, in the Congress lexicon diversity does not include political/ideological diversity. On the other hand, PM Modi and the BJP have displayed greater maturity and magnanimity.

Finally, the Congress has often been accused of using the award to promote its electoral prospects. A case in point is the conferment of the Bharat Ratna on former Tamil Nadu Chief Minister M.G. Ramachandran in 1988. Rajiv was desperate to win the support of MGR's party and garner votes in the elections the following year. B.G. Deshmukh, who was cabinet secretary at that time, recalls in his memoirs that "many in government as well as outside it viewed this as a political move by the Congress". Also, Deshmukh indicates that there was much opposition to awarding the Bharat Ratna posthumously as this would open the floodgates. But these arguments were overruled obviously due to political reasons. So, in regard to the Bharat Ratna, the best advice for Congress members would be: "Please keep your lips sealed!"

The New Indian Express, 29 January, 2019

□

Patel Deserves the Statue, and much more

The inauguration of Sardar Vallabhbhai Patel's statue—the Statue of Unity—in Gujarat on October 31 by the prime minister has raised the hackles of the whining, carping bunch of malcontents of the Nehruvian and Marxist mould who question the wisdom of erecting a statue—incidentally the tallest in the world—at a huge cost. But these complaints must be brushed aside because we owe our very existence as a nation to Sardar Patel. There are a lot more reasons as well—many of which were hidden by sarkari historians owing allegiance to a single political family. Here are some of them.

When the British left the country, they gave all the princely states three options—to declare their independence, accede to India or accede to Pakistan. To get such a motley group of over 550 maharajas and rajas—many of whom were on their own ego trips—to sign on the dotted line and become part of India was a Herculean task. However, Patel's steely determination, combined with his diplomacy and foresight, enabled him to get the princes to sign the Instrument of Accession.

The Nizam of Hyderabad and the Nawab of Junagadh had wanted to remain independent or to accede to Pakistan and a couple of maharajas in central India were keen to retain their independence. Patel put his foot down, sent in the armed forces when necessary and got these states integrated into India. "I do not want undigested lumps in India's belly", he is reported to have said in the context of Hyderabad becoming part of Pakistan.

The then PM Jawaharlal Nehru was not happy with the use of force, but the truth is that if 'Iron Man' Patel were not around at that time, no one would have been able to counter Nehru's pusillanimity and the map of India would have been in tatters on the very day of her Independence.

Is this not sufficient reason for building the Statue of Unity?

Apart from being tough as nails while dealing with issues relating to national unity, Patel had another extraordinary quality—his readiness to sacrifice for the larger cause. There is abundant evidence to show that he was the very epitome of selflessness, in contrast to the pettiness and selfishness of Nehru. On Gandhi's advice, Patel had to forego the opportunity to head the Congress on many occasions including 1929, 1936 and 1946 and make way for Nehru.

In 1946, it was clear that the person elected head of the Congress would be invited by the British to be the first prime minister of independent India. The party asked 15 Pradesh Congress Committees to propose names for the office; 12 of the 15 committees voted for Sardar Patel. The remaining three committees had no opinion. The story goes that Nehru went into a sulk and told Gandhi that he would not play second fiddle to anybody! Gandhi stepped in once again on behalf of Nehru and got Patel to withdraw from the contest.

Thus, although his party overwhelmingly wanted him to be the first PM after Independence, Patel sacrificed this for the sake of the party and national unity. Historians loyal to the Nehru-Gandhis have tried to hide these facts from the people all these years. So, for those who ask why spend so much on Patel's statue, the answer is: "Is this not sufficient reason to remember the Sardar in the most memorable way possible?"

As against Patel's large-heartedness, we now have evidence of how small-minded and spiteful Nehru was when dealing with Patel. When Patel died on 15 December 1950 in Mumbai, he directed officials from Delhi not to attend Patel's funeral in Mumbai. Even more shocking was the first order he issued after the Sardar's demise—that Patel's official car be returned to the foreign ministry forthwith. More was to follow. The best example of Nehru's small-mindedness relates to the Bharat Ratna. Nehru's government gave the Bharat Ratna to Nehru in 1955! Sardar Patel was conferred the Bharat Ratna by the Chandra Shekhar government in 1991.

Further, while the Nehru-Gandhis have helped themselves to much of Lutyens' geography, Nehru treated Patel's daughter Maniben in the most insensitive manner when she met him after Patel's death. In his memoirs, Verghese Kurien, the father of the milk revolution, tells us how shabbily Nehru treated her. After Patel died, Maniben picked up a book and a bag that belonged to him and went to meet Nehru. Patel had instructed her to hand them over to Nehru.

The bag contained Rs. 35 lakh that belonged to the Congress and the book was the party's book of accounts. Nehru took them and thanked her. "Maniben waited expectantly, hoping he would say something more, but he did not, so she got up and left." He did not even enquire as to how she was doing after the passing of Patel. Kurien found Nehru's behaviour "distressing".

Many years ago, this writer had put together a list of 450 government schemes, projects and institutions named after just three members of the Nehru-Gandhi family. This included a majority of social welfare schemes of the Union government, airports, national parks, educational and scientific institutions, and sports tournaments. Nothing was left out. Yet, all those party to this vulgar display of sycophancy are unhappy that the man who gave us the India we live in today is being honoured in a manner which is worthy of his stupendous effort.

Therefore, the time has come for India to make adequate reparation for the pettiness displayed by Nehru and his progeny towards Sardar Patel, the greatest son of India. The Statue of Unity is now a reality because of the Patel-like determination and commitment of PM Narendra Modi to give the Sardar his due. Modi must ignore these critics and take further initiatives like introducing the real Sardar to school children through history books. He must then begin the next big project to provide another extraordinary national hero—Subhas Chandra Bose—his rightful place. Bose too has been a victim of the chicanery of 'establishment historians'. The nation will always remember Modi for ensuring that India will eternally be grateful to its real heroes.

The New Indian Express, 6 November, 2018

□

The Forgotten Father-in-Law

When we look at the history of democratic institutions in the country, we come across several instances of MPs and MLAs in the Opposition who work hard to pin down the Government. But rarely do we find a ruling party MP firing all guns in his effort to expose a scam and to insist on transparency and accountability in the functioning of his Government. One such MP was Feroze Gandhi of the Congress, a crusader against corruption and India's first and undoubtedly the best investigative parliamentarian whose birth anniversary falls on September 12.

Feroze Gandhi must be remembered for many things—his participation in the freedom struggle which resulted in jail terms more than once; his painstaking research and commitment to probity in public life which cost Jawaharlal Nehru's Finance Minister TT Krishnamachari his job; the nationalisation of life insurance; and for bringing in a law to insulate the media from defamation and libel suits when they reported the proceedings of Parliament.

Incidentally, since the Congress never takes the name of such an impassioned campaigner against corruption, the younger generation may not know that he was Indira Gandhi's husband, Sonia Gandhi's father-in-law and Rahul Gandhi's grand father. Feroze Gandhi was inspired by Kamala Nehru to join the national movement for independence in the late 1920s. He was jailed on more than one occasion and even led an underground movement. He became a member of the Provisional Parliament in 1950 and was elected to the Lok Sabha in 1952 and in 1957.

Initially Feroze relished his role as a backbencher but became an instant hit with his maiden speech in the Lok Sabha in December 1955. Everyone was compelled to sit up and take notice when he spoke on the Insurance (Amendment) Bill. He held the House in thrall for close to two hours as he exposed the nefarious activities of private insurance firms and built an iron-clad case for the nationalisation of the life insurance business. He demanded strong measures to protect public funds that had been invested in these companies.

By the time he ended his speech, every member felt that private insurance companies were doomed. His arguments were so compelling that within two months the President promulgated an ordinance nationalising life insurance. Congratulating the Government, Feroze said: "To hold a horse you need a rein; to hold an elephant you need a chain." In the words of his biographer, Tarun Kumar Mukhopadhyay, Feroze's maiden speech sounded the death-knell for the private life insurance business. Following nationalisation, the Life Insurance Corporation (LIC) came into being. This was a signal achievement for an MP but more was to come when in the latter half of 1957, Feroze Gandhi received a tip-off about a scam in the Finance Ministry. He heard that LIC had suddenly bought shares of companies owned by HD Mundhra, an industrialist close to the Congress, at inflated prices. This prompted him to intervene during Question Hour and seek a special debate.

The Finance Minister's disingenuous response put Feroze on full alert and he sought a special debate on this issue. Initiating a discussion he said: "A mutiny in my mind has compelled me to raise this debate. When things of such magnitude, as I shall describe to you later, occur, silence becomes a crime."

To put it briefly, the story was that Mundhra, a businessman with a dubious record and who had funded the Congress' election campaign, ran into financial problems and wanted the Nehru Government to bail him out. He asked the Government to invest a crore of rupees in the shares of some of his companies. Although none of the Mundhra companies were doing well, the Government agreed to do this *via* the LIC.

However, while the negotiations were on, Mundhra bought

up shares of his own company in the Calcutta Stock Exchange and artificially jacked up the prices of his shares. Therefore, eventually, when the LIC went to the market, it bought them at prices much higher than what prevailed when Mundhra first approached the Government for help. This is what is called the LIC-Mundhra scandal.

Feroze Gandhi deployed his truly extraordinary investigative skills to track share prices of Mundhra companies over a fortnight to expose the Government. The then Finance Minister, Krishnamachari, tried to defend the deal by saying that LIC decided to enter the market to build up its portfolio and so, bought these shares. But Feroze Gandhi was not convinced. Why did you take a fancy only to Mundhra companies and why did you buy them at inflated prices? How can public money be squandered in this manner, he asked, pointing out that the prices of these shares slumped after LIC bought them.

The Government had no convincing answers. Anyway, to cut a long story short, Nehru was forced to institute a commission of inquiry which held Krishnamachari morally responsible for the questionable decision, leading to his resignation.

Feroze Gandhi had several more achievements in his parliamentary career, including the Bill he introduced to insulate the media from defamation suits when it covered Parliament. Journalists told him that while MPs had the privilege to speak freely in Parliament, reporting the proceedings faced defamation and libel suits. Given his deep and abiding commitment to democracy and Press freedom, he felt that the media should have no constraint while reporting Parliament and the people must get a faithful account of what transpires in legislative chambers.

Feroze Gandhi introduced the Parliamentary Proceedings (Protection of Publication) Bill to insulate the media. And in an extraordinary gesture, the Government adopted this Bill and saw it through in the two Houses. In each of these instances, Feroze Gandhi's meticulous collection of data and facts helped him to almost single handedly carry the debate on his shoulders until it reached its logical conclusion.

A variety of factors enabled Feroze Gandhi to effectively

pursue his goals as a representative of the people. The first was his crusading nature and his commitment to public welfare and democracy. Second, the diligence with which he gathered information to argue this case and the ease with which he connected with his sources deep within the Government. Lastly, his parliamentary prowess. That is why his fellow MPs and ministers in Jawaharlal Nehru's Government described him as "a dangerously well-informed man."

India needs to do a lot more to remember this MP-extraordinaire!

The Pioneer, 10 September, 2019

☐

The Man the Congress has Loved to Ignore, Forget

The Narendra Modi Government's decision to follow-up on the resolution passed by the Telangana State Assembly, that a fitting memorial should be erected for former Prime Minister, P.V. Narasimha Rao, will be widely welcomed by all those who believe that the nation must acknowledge the contribution of the real leaders and builders of modern India.

The contribution of Rao, the man who pulled India's economy out of the rut a quarter century ago, and laid the foundations for the country's spectacular economic growth, has never been acknowledged by previous Governments, including those headed by his own party, the Congress. Apart from being the chief architect of economic reforms, Rao's sagacious leadership in the 1991-96 phase also helped stamp out the secessionist forces in Punjab and save the country's unity and integrity.

Yet, despite those extraordinary achievements, the Congress, probably giving in to the insecurities of its own leaders, sought to effectively stamp out Rao from the national consciousness.

Rao came on the scene when all seemed lost and the nation was adrift on choppy seas. India's foreign exchange reserves had crashed to perilous levels and the nation was on the brink of default. It had dollars just enough to pay for petroleum imports for two weeks. The rate of inflation was 13 per cent, which soon climbed to 17 per cent. Industrial growth had come to a grinding halt and the Eighth Five-Year Plan had been abandoned. The economic crisis was so huge that Rao's predecessor had mortgaged gold to the Bank of England to raise a measly $200 million.

This was the time when doomsayers were having a field day because, apart from this gargantuan economic crisis, Rao had inherited the Punjab problem, where centrifugal forces were pulling the State away from India's orbit and there were innumerable other flashpoints, including the smouldering communal crisis and the post-Mandal casteist fires stoked by another predecessor, VP Singh. Rao was called upon to cope with all this, with his hands tied behind his back—he did not have the numbers in the Lok Sabha. The Congress had secured just 232 seats and was 41 short of a majority in the 1991 Lok Sabha poll.

Given this reality, only a cerebral and decisive Prime Minister could have ensured the country's political and geographic unity and economic recovery—both of which he achieved in a matter of five years. Rao picked up persons of calibre and gave them a free hand to craft policies that would result in a turnaround. He chose Manmohan Singh as his Finance Minister, shielded him from the fiercest political attacks in and out of Parliament, and asked him to re-work the economic policy. The two together opened up the economy to domestic and foreign investors and dumped Nehruvian socialist policies which had all but killed the entrepreneurial skills of Indians.

These policies, which were pursued with greater vengeance by Jawaharlal Nehru's daughter, Indira Gandhi, had reduced industrialists to a bunch of licence and permit grabbers who were called upon to master the art of bribing their way through the corridors of power. Such was the stranglehold of the state over the economy that the Government had a virtual monopoly in the manufacturing sector—from condoms to telephone instruments. Also, much of the services were in Government hands, be it telecommunications or airlines, thus pulling the economy down through their inefficiencies.

The Rao Government's first Budget of 1991 was a watershed as it began the process of dismantling the rusted Nehruvian framework, brick by brick. By the time his term ended, the grand revival of Indian business and industry had begun and hope was once again in the air. The long-term impact of his policies can be gauged from the fact that the country's foreign exchange reserves, which had dried up when he took charge, had climbed to $140 billion when he passed away in December 2004. A fortnight ago, it stood at a robust $345 billion.

Rao displayed similar grit in tackling the other big monster at India's door in the 1990s—secessionism in Punjab. The seeds of separatism were sown during Indira Gandhi's prime ministership and the plant flowered during Rajiv Gandhi's tenure. The State was virtually slipping away because the previous Governments had failed miserably to quell the forces that were out to wreck India's unity. Rao gave then Punjab Chief Minister Beant Singh and police chief KPS Gill a free hand to tackle the problem. This brought in dividends. But for Rao's shrewdness, Punjab could have become the first State to secede from India.

Following his demise, the media was full of reports of how the United Progressive Alliance Government headed by Manmohan Singh did not want Rao's last rites to be performed in Delhi. It was also widely reported that the Congress leadership prevented his body from being taken to the premises of the All India Congress Committee on Akbar Road. Rao was eventually cremated in Hyderabad.

The Narendra Modi Government has, therefore, its task cut out. Beginning with Rao, it must correct many of the injustices of the past, especially those pertaining to the marginalisation of some of the nation's real heroes and leaders, irrespective of which party they belonged to.

For starters, the Government must allocate land on Rajpath for both Netaji Subhas Chandra Bose and Sardar Vallabhbhai Patel. We have the Jawaharlal Nehru Bhavan, housing the Ministry of External Affairs on one side of Rajpath. On the other is the Indira Gandhi Centre for the Arts. A 100 metres away in this key area is the Rajiv Gandhi Bhavan. But what about Sardar Patel, the iron man, without whom we would never have had the India that he stitched together with grit, determination and extraordinary foresight? And what about Netaji Bose, the man who raised an army to oust the British and showed extraordinary courage and commitment to free India from foreign rule?

A grateful nation must at least now grant them their rightful place in the history books and on the nation's most prominent promenade. Anything short of such tributes will smack of ungratefulness. This is one of the many responsibilities that the Narendra Modi Government has to shoulder, but it is an important one because it will correct some of the injustices of the past and also rejuvenate our national consciousness.

The Pioneer, 12 May, 2015

□

The Congress Party and Hitler

Ever since Indira Gandhi assumed the role of a dictator during the Emergency and mutilated India's democratic Constitution to such an extent that it was beyond recognition, there was always a lurking suspicion that while members of the Congress Party paid lip service to democracy, they were actually inclined towards fascism. Thus, whenever the opportunity arose or when caught off guard, members of this party would bare their fangs and show their true colours.

The most shocking display of such fascination and respect for fascism by a very senior member of the Indira Gandhi Cabinet happened in the Lok Sabha on 24 March, 1982.

The House was debating the Demands for Grants of the Ministry of Home Affairs that day and the Home Minister, Giani Zail Singh was called by the Deputy Speaker, who was chairing the session, to respond to the issues raised by the members. A few minutes into his speech, Mr. Zail Singh decided to talk about things he and his party truly believed in. To the utter dismay of those in the opposition benches and the Press Gallery, Mr. Singh began singing praises of Adolf Hitler and Benito Mussolini. He praised their tenacity of purpose and the discipline they introduced in their countries. He described Hitler as a 'Mahaan Vyakthi' (a great man) and a 'Mahaan Deshbhakt' (a great patriot) and as the builder of modern Germany.

Since the minister was speaking late evening after the House had been through an arduous debate on the working of the Ministry of Home Affairs, many members were in a somnambulant mood and most MPs were anxiously looking at the clock and hoping that the minister's ritualistic reply would be over and done with, in a short while. Since a whip had been issued to ensure the presence of all their MPs, the Congress benches were full while the opposition benches were sparsely filled. None in the treasury or opposition benches expected any fireworks. After a hard day's work they just wanted the formality of the minister's speech and the vote on the Demands for Grants of that ministry to be gone through, so that they could head back to their official quarters in Lutyens' Delhi.

It other words, the passage of the Demands for Grants of various ministries was an annual parliamentary rite that had to be performed as ordained by the rule book and the sooner it was over, the better.

But, they were all pulled out of their stupor when Chandrajit Yadav, a socialist and member of one of the breakaway factions of the Janata Party drew the attention of the Deputy Speaker, Mr. Lakshmanan to Mr. Zail Singh's remarks and asked him to stop the minister in his tracks. Some members of the Congress too woke up to the situation and demanded that the minister's remarks praising Hitler should be expunged. Until Mr. Yadav blew the whistle, the Deputy Speaker too was oblivious to the "perceptive" observations of the Home Minister. He immediately realized that if the remarks remained on the records of the House, it would do permanent damage to the image of the Congress Party. Although the observations of the Home Minister were not defamatory (they were just laudatory of Hitler) or against any rule of the House, Mr. Lakshmanan took a snap decision to expunge the remarks. Several members of the opposition protested against the Deputy Speaker's decision but the latter refused to yield to their entities. Within minutes of the expunction decision, the Deputy Speaker sent the Press Officer of the Lok Sabha to the Press Gallery to inform media persons of the expunction and to warm them not to publish a word of what the minister had said about Hitler.

I was the parliamentary correspondent of the Indian Express and was reporting the proceedings of the Lok Sabha that day. The Press Officer conveyed the Deputy Speaker's directions generally to all those present in the Press Gallery and then walked up to me and said "Mr. Indian Express, I hope you have heard the Deputy Speaker's order!" I said, "Of course, I have heard it!"

Ironically, Mr. Zail Singh made this laudatory references to Hitler while trying to counter the allegation of an opposition MP, Mr. Niren Ghosh of the Communist Party of India (Marxist) that the country was heading towards total dictatorship and asked the Congress Party if it wished to follow in the footsteps of Hitler. Mr. Zail Singh refuted the charge and said "we are not moving to dictatorship and the government had no intention to introduce a presidential form of government. He claimed that the Congress Party had never discussed changing the Constitution and that Indira Gandhi was "the most democratic" leader. This was indeed a false claim given the dictatorship imposed by Indira Gandhi between 1975-77 after imposing the Emergency and the shocking constitutional amendments which she introduced at that time, which had robbed the democratic Constitution of its very soul.

However, although he did the mandatory lip service to democracy, he could not hold back his true feelings towards Adolf Hitler and spoke freely about how he admired the Fuehrer.

After the rumpus in the House, the much-chastened minister abandoned his enchantment with Hitler and resumed his speech on the work of the Ministry of Home Affairs. I returned to my office, called the Editor, Mr. Nihal Singh and told him of what had transpired in the Lok Sabha that evening. I told him that although the Deputy Speaker had expunged the remarks, it was incumbent on us, in public interest, to report what had happened and face the consequences. I told him that my report of the proceedings could result in cancellation of my Lok Sabha pass, but more importantly, it could attract Breach of Privilege notices against the Editor, Publisher and Correspondent. Mr. Singh heard me and without the slightest hesitation said 'Go ahead'.

I put out the story that Home Minister Zail Singh had praised Hitler during his speech in the Lok Sabha and that the Deputy Speaker, bowing to pressure from the Congress benches had expunged the remarks. It was carried prominently in many editions of the Indian Express the next morning on the front page. The headline in the Delhi Edition said: Zail Singh Praises Hitler, Everything Expunged.

I woke up to many congratulatory messages from many colleagues within the organisation who were aware of the drama the previous evening, but I had become persona non grata for correspondents of other newspapers who covered the Lok Sabha, for having violated the Deputy Speaker's directions and thereby putting them in a situation whereby they had to explain to their editors as to why they had not reported the incident. As a result, I got a cold reception when I took my seat in the Press Gallery the next morning. Some correspondents seated nearby warned me that several Congress MPs had given Breach of Privilege notices against the newspaper and that my goose was cooked!

As soon as Question Hour ended, there was much tension in the House as many MPs drew the attention of the Speaker, Mr. Balram Jakhar to their Breach of Privilege notices against the Indian Express, while leading members of the opposition questioned the Deputy Speaker's decision to expunge Mr. Zail Singh's remarks when they did not violate any parliamentary rule. Some opposition MPs even accused the Home Minister of having violated the oath he had taken under the Constitution.

Mr. Madhu Dandavate pointed out that under Article-99 of the Constitution of India, every member of the House, including the Home Minister, had taken a oath of allegiance to the Constitution of India, which believes in the democratic system. Therefore, when Mr. Zail Singh "says anything counter to the spirit of the Constitution, by praising or saying something which is commendatory to Hitler's fascist system, it runs counter to the spirit of the (Indian) Constitution".

He also took exception to the expunction of the Home Minister's remarks the previous evening and said under the rules of the House, any words which are defamatory, unparliamentary and indecent can be expunged by the presiding officer. The Speaker's powers in this regard are not unlimited. They are governed by the rules.

As the verbal clash between the ruling party and the opposition intensified, the Speaker informed the House that the Home Minister would make a statement. The Law Minister, Mr. Shiv Shanker, who was seated next to Mr. Zail Singh pulled out a note from his file and gave it to the latter to read. Far from challenging the Indian Express for reporting his remarks, the Home Minister tendered an abject apology for praising Hitler the previous day. He said he regretted his remarks about Hitler and was withdrawing those remarks. He said: "Sir, I seek to clarify about what happened yesterday during the course of my reply to the debate on the Demands for Grants of Home Ministry. My extempore observation about Hitler then was only provoked by the heat and the impulse of the debate." He then went on to assert that his party had always fought against fascism, imperialism, racialism etc. and said 'the remarks and observations made by me were unintentional........and off the cuff and did not mean to convey my real feelings, thoughts and sentiments. I regret for all that transpired and withdraw my expressions about Hitler. This is to explain myself and set the record straight."

The opposition benches responded with loud protests and the Speaker sought to pacify them by saying that the Home Minister was withdrawing his remarks. "He has expressed regret as well as withdrawal," the Speaker said. This led to a fresh bout of exchanges between him and prominent MPs in the opposition benches. Mr. Atal Behari Vajpayee, the leader of the Bharatiya Janata Party (BJP) cryptically asked the Speaker: "Expunge Kardiya Tho, Withdraw Kaise Kar Sakthe Ho (If the remarks have been expunged, how can he withdraw them now?). He further told the Speaker "This is not the way to run the House. Whatever has been expunged, you bring it back to the proceedings."

Mr. Madhu Dandavate, Mr. Harikesh Bahadur and several others in the opposition benches protested against the expunction order of the Deputy Speaker and demanded that the Speaker rescind that order and restore the Home Minister's remarks on Hitler in the House's proceedings. Mr. Harikesh Bahadur vociferously told the Speaker "What has been expunged cannot be withdrawn.....when it is not on record, what is he withdrawing." He said the Deputy Speaker cannot exercise his powers arbitrarily.

The Minister's statement led to a fresh uproar in the House. Mr. Atal Behari Vajpayee of the Bharatiya Janata Party and Mr. Madhu Dandavate of the Janata Party told the Speaker that they were unable to understand as to what the apology was all about, since his remarks the previous evening had been expunged. They demanded that the expunged portions be restored, so that the apology would make sense. Mr. Vajpayee said this was not the first time the Deputy Speaker had erred. "Only recently, he had expunged his own remarks".

Thereafter, the Speaker announced that he had received many breach of privilege notices against the Indian Express. He read out a brief order citing rules of the House which prohibit publication of expunged remarks and said the media should always be conscious of it and adhere to it. He chided the Indian Express for having violated the orders of the Deputy Speaker. However, he said, in view of the statement (apology) made by the Home Minister, he was dismissing all the notices given by the members against the newspaper!

Thus ended a rather tense hour for me in the Lok Sabha Press Gallery, but I was happy that I had managed to put the Home Minister's real feelings towards Hitler in the public domain. The next day, newspapers across the country reported all that had transpired on March 25 including the Home Minister's apology and alluded to the minister's remarks on Hitler the previous day.

Neither Indira Gandhi nor anyone else took umbrage at the Home Minister's fascination for Hitler and Mussolini. Instead, just two months after this incident, Indira Gandhi chose Zail Singh as the candidate for the office of President of India. When his candidature was announced, Mr. Singh declared his unswerving loyalty to Indira Gandhi and said he was willing to sweep the floor, if she ordered him to. Mr. Singh won the election effortlessly and took oath as the President of India on 25 July, 1982.

Excerpts from A. Surya Prakash, Fascist Tendencies in the Congress Party, Prabhat Prakashan, New Delhi, 2018

□

The Congress and the Hijackers

On 20 December, 1978, Bhola Pandey of Azamgarh and his friend Devendar Pandey of Ballia hijacked Indian Airlines flight IC 410 from Lucknow to Delhi soon after it took off from Lucknow. There were 132 passengers on board. The hijackers, who appeared to be armed, made several demands and forced the aircraft to land at Varanasi. They said they were members of the Youth Congress. They wanted Indira Gandhi to be released from jail; all criminal cases against her and Sanjay Gandhi to be withdrawn; and the Janata Party Government at the Centre to tender its resignation. They demanded that the authorities should convey their regards to Sanjay Gandhi and summon the Chief Minister of the state for talks. The Chief Minister of Uttar Pradesh, the Inspector General of Police and the Chief Secretary took a special flight to Varanasi and arrived at that airport soon after 1 a.m. the following morning, to negotiate the release of the passengers. The hijackers also demanded that arrangements be made for them to address a press conference at the airport lounge and that the Prime Minister and All India Radio should be informed of the hijacking.

Following protracted negotiations with the Chief Minister and senior state officials, the two hijackers released the passengers and surrendered.

Both the hijackers have been rewarded repeatedly by the Congress Party with party tickets to contest Uttar Pradesh Assembly and Lok Sabha elections.

When the Lok Sabha met on December 21, the hijack was on top of every one's mind. Several members sought an immediate discussion. Prime Minister Morarji Desai told the Speaker he had no objection to a debate "because it is the most serious thing that has happened". Mr. K.P. Unnikrishnan said the hijacking incident was indicative of a far deeper malaise that was creeping into the political firmament, namely "the climate of violence that is being deliberately created... ." It was then agreed that the House would have a full-fledged discussion after the minister in-charge made a statement on the hijacking of the aircraft and its aftermath.

The Minister of Tourism and Civil Aviation Mr. Purushottam Kaushik explained the sequence of events beginning with the hijack of the aircraft soon after it took off from Lucknow the previous day. That week was marked by large-scale violence in many states triggered by members of the Congress Party in protest against the arrest of Ms. Indira Gandhi in a breach of privilege case and her disqualification from Parliament on December 19. She was sentenced to imprisonment till the propagation of the House and also expelled from the Lok Sabha. The Pandeys hijacked the plane on December 20 to protest against Parliament's decision to punish Ms. Gandhi. On December 21, Congress mobs went to the extent of hurling bombs into the Calcutta residence of Mr. Samar Guha, the Chairman of the Committee of Privileges of the Lok Sabha, which had indicted Ms. Gandhi. Congress goons also went on the rampage in Bangalore and Hyderabad and targeted public property. Several persons were killed in these incidents. These violent incidents became the subject matter of an intense debate on 23 December, 1978 in the Lok Sabha.

Mr. Kaushik told the House that the flight IC 410 took off from Lucknow at 17.45 hrs on December 20. Five minutes later, the flight control centre got a message that some passengers were trying to force their entry into the cockpit. At 18.18 hrs Lucknow reported that the flight was being hijacked to Patna. Subsequently, Varanasi reported that the flight was landing at that airport and not at Patna. The flight landed at Varanasi at 19.01 hrs. The local police cordoned off the aircraft and the services of a psychiatrist were requisitioned from the defence authorities. There were 132 passengers on board. Soon after the hijacking was reported, the Central Anti-Hijacking Committee assembled in the control room in Delhi to issue necessary directions on how the hijackers should be dealt with.

While all this was on, one passenger–Mr. Modi–managed to escape from the aircraft with the help of an air hostess and told those in the Varanasi Airport Control Tower that two persons–one wearing a white pyjama and kurta and another wearing a white dhoti and kurta –had boarded the aircraft and they carried printed pamphlets in Hindi and English containing demands for release of the "national leader" and seeking wide publicity for their actions. The hijackers identified themselves as Bhola Nath Pandey of Azamgarh and Davender Pandey of Ballia and said they were from the Youth Congress. They wanted the Chief Minister of Uttar Pradesh to reach the Varanasi Airport; arrangements must be made for them (the hijackers) to hold a press conference in the airport lounge; and All India Radio must be informed of the hijacking. The Air Traffic Control at Varanasi kept up the conversation with the hijackers via the pilot, Captain Batliwala. Since the hijackers demanded the presence of the Chief Minister of Uttar Pradesh, the chief minister left Lucknow by a state aircraft for Varanasi around midnight and landed in Varanasi at 1.02 hrs. He was accompanied by the Chief Secretary, the Inspector-General of Police and a relative of one of the hijackers. The hijackers declined the request of the authorities to allow women and children to de-board or to allow serving of food and tea to the passengers. The hijackers, in turn, wanted the chief minister to enter the aircraft alone, which was not accepted. Finally, arrangements were made for them to talk to the chief minister. They demanded that Indira Gandhi should be released forthwith and all criminal cases against her must be withdrawn; the Janata Party government must tender its resignation; and lastly, that the aircraft should proceed back to Lucknow and they must be allowed to meet the press. The chief minister agreed to take them to Lucknow in the state aircraft if all the passengers were released. The hijackers initially rejected the chief minister's offer and demanded that the aircraft be refueled. The Central Committee told the negotiators in Varanasi not to refuel the aircraft and to continue negotiations.

Some time later, the hijackers released some passengers and demanded that the U.P. state aircraft be brought alongside the

Indian Airlines plane. Evenmtually, they released all passengers, surrendered their "weapons" and boarded the state aircraft. The hijackers landed at Lucknow at 8.03 hrs on December 21. On their arrival at Lucknow, the two hijackers were hoping for a big media event but just two reporters and three cameramen turned up to hear their story and they "looked disappointed at the poor press response." The police then took them into custody.

The House took up a full-fledged discussion on the hijacking and the climate of violence in various parts of the country, on December 23.

Initiating the discussion, K.P. Unnikrishnan said the hijacking was a political act by persons associated with the Congress(I) party (as the Congress led by Indira Gandhi was called at that time) and not an isolated act committed by some mindless young men. He said he condemned the conduct of these hijackers and told MPs belong to the Congress (I) also to condemn it "because we have to protect certain democratic norms, certain values and way of life, which is at stake today". He said these two hijackers were closely working with a confidant of Indira Gandhi to oust former H.N. Bahuguna, former Chief Minister of Uttar Pradesh and were also active in a shramdhan camp in Amethi. He said there was a clear pattern of political conduct in what the hijackers had done and the violence that had erupted all over the country was "basically taking the shape of a movement against legitimate function of parliament"(punishing a person for breach of privilege). The moment a decision is taken in a parliamentary democracy...... there are certain parameters of dissent and you cannot cross them, if you want parliamentary democracy to survive." He said the hijackers passed through security without being checked;

MPs belonging to other political parties condemned the hijacking and said that such trends smacked of fascist tendencies, which the Congress Party had in any case displayed in abundant measure during the dreaded Emergency imposed by Indira Gandhi for 21 months from June, 1975. Mr. Kanwarlal Gupta wondered whether in view of the hijacking and violence triggered by the Congress Party, democracy would survive in the country. "It is a question of democracy versus fascism, democracy versus dictatorship" he said.

However, leading lights of the Congress Party including Mr. R. Venkataraman, who later became President of India and Mr. Vasant Sathe, sought to rationalize the conduct of their party members and even tried to dismiss the hijacking incident as nothing more than a joke.

Leaders of this party went to extraordinary lengths to defend Bhola Pandey and Davender Pandey during this debate, which was revealing in terms of the respect that the Congress Party had for Parliament and its committees. It showed that despite the humiliating defeat of the party in the March, 1977 Lok Sabha election, when it was punished for imposing a dictatorship on India, the Congress (I) Party had learnt no lessons. The debate once again exposed the Congress mindset, its fascist inclinations and revealed a lot about the party's respect for the rule of law.

Among those who stood up to defend the violence unleashed by the party was Congress veteran R. Venkataraman, who went so far as to talk about the right of every citizen to express dissent. He said there was a sharp opinion in the country that the punishment meted out to Indira Gandhi was harsh and disproportionate and this had caused resentment in the country and "this resentment has given expression to itself in various ways."

"It is a lesson we have learnt from Gandhiji.....when in South Africa, he protested against discriminatory laws and courted imprisonment.....When Gandhiji broke the salt laws in the country for the purpose of agitating the peoples's right to freedom, he exercised the right to dissent. Therefore, the people of the country feel that a certain punishment is out of proportion or is unwarranted (expulsion of Indira Gandhi from the Lok Sabha and her arrest) and they have a right to dissent and to take recourse to such things as to bring forth their point of view....."

After this near shameful justification of country-wide violence, including the hijacking, Mr. Venkataraman claimed that the Congress Working Committee had passed a resolution condemning violence. However, "if in spite of it (the resolution), certain people take to certain measures, it is not because of the bidding, it is in spite of it." Therefore, he claimed, the party was not to blame. He then went on to claim that "there are always recalcitrant and intransigent elements in every party. There are always extreme elements in every party and extreme elements cannot be shown or brought up as an argument for condemning the party as a whole."

This argument later sounded hollow because the Congress Party went on to reward "the recalcitrant and intransigent and extreme elements"—the hijackers-with party tickets to contest not just the state assembly election in Uttar Pradesh but the Lok Sabha polls four times in a row! It shows that those who hijacked the aircraft in 1978 are deeply loved and respected by the Nehru-Gandhis and the Congress Party.

Finally, Mr. Venkataraman dismissed the hijacking as nothing more than a joke. He said when they first heard the news about the hijacking, there was great deal of anger in the country. "But, ultimately, when it turned out to be nothing more than a toy pistol and a cricket ball, Sir, it has become the joke of the year." On hearing this, the Speaker said "fortunately you were not in the plane".

Mr. Vasant Sathe, another senior parliamentarian in the Congress ranks, said at the outset that he was not justifying the conduct of the Pandeys but said he did not know how to describe the incident. Was it hijacking, skyjacking or sky joking?

According to him, it was "a prank by misguided young men" because they had deployed on a cricket ball and a toy pistol. Mr. Janardhana Poojary blamed the ruling Janata Party government for the violence that culminated in the hijacking. He said there was an overwhelming sentiment across the country in favour of Indira Gandhi and people were willing to sacrifice their lives and their property for her sake.

Lok Sabha records show that Mr. K.P. Unnikrishnan informed the House of the political connections and antecedents of the two Pandeys. He said they were closely connected with a confidant of Indira Gandhi and were 'very active' in the campaign to oust Mr. Bahuguna from the chief ministership of Uttar Pradesh.

Mr. Yadvendra Dutt spoke of how members of the Congress Party were saying that "if Indiraji goes to jail, rivers of blood will flow". The Congress had just a single point programme "release the queen bee or the honey bees will die. Is this not sycophancy of the highest order?".

Mr. Dutt compared the Congress Hooligans to the jackbooted

storm-troopers who marched on the streets of Munich and Hamburg during Hitler's reign to create the impression that democracy was useless. "That is exactly what they want to show……. that Mrs.Gandhi (is) above law and ……..above everything." He said Indian Airlines flights must have armed guards and hijackers must be shot dead.

Dr. Saradish Roy said when the House was to take up discussion on the report of the Privileges Committee regarding the breach of privilege committed by Indira Gandhi, the Congress Party made it known that if she was punished by the Lok Sabha, "the roads will be flooded with blood." He accused Ms. Gandhi of trying to reverse a decision of parliament through street action. He said she rigged the elections in West Bengal in 1972 and ran the state through a brutal "a semi-fascist regime." "All those who opposed her……were assassinated."

Mr. Saugata Roy said Mr. Dharam Bir Sinha, a former MP was on the hijacked plane. He told him that the hijackers were dressed in khadi kurta and pyjama. They came out of the cockpit and addressed the passengers and told them why they were hijacking the plane. They said they wanted to focus the attention of the world to Ms. Gandhi arrest. "There may not have been specific instructions; but these young men had a specific purpose in mind - to demand the release of Mrs. Gandhi." He said he heard from Varanasi that groups of Congress Party supporters went to the Varanasi airport that day and raised slogans like "Pandeyji ki ja."

Mr. P.G. Mavalankar, a member of the Committee of Privileges which found Indira Gandhi guilty of breach of privilege of the House, said "there was ample proof of her guilt". He did some plain speaking and said he was shocked to hear of the bomb attack on the house of Mr. Samar Guha, Chairman, Committee of Privileges. He said the House must stand as one and condemn this incident and build up public opinion against such behaviour. He said neither Mr. Guha nor other members of the Committee of Privileges would be intimidated by such conduct. He said such protests were highly objectionable "as they lead to disruption, dislocation and sabotage and we cannot tolerate it." He said some public decency and standards of morality had to be maintained in politics. Mr. Mavalankar was also amused at Mr. Venkataraman talking of the right of dissent in a democracy after Indira Gandhi had crushed dissent during the Emergency and jailed MPs who spoke against her in Parliament.

Prime Minister Morarji Desai lambasted Mr. Venkataraman and other Congress MPs who were trying to down play the hijacking. He said it was fortunate that the incident did not end in a disaster. "If the pilots had lost their nerve, anything could have happened." This was the gravity of the hijacking. He said he was pained to hear Mr. Venkataraman's comment that the incident was a joke. "How was it a joke? Such a thing can never be defended, whether it was a toy pistol or whether a ball was presented as a bomb. How was it possible for the pilot to know that it was a toy pistol? They could not take a risk. If anything had happened, I do not know how many lives would have been lost." He also referred to the large scale violence unleashed by the Congress Party in the country including the bomb attack on the house of the Chairman of the Committee of Privileges of the Lok Sabha; the violence in Karnataka and the attack on the house of another MP, Mr. Shejwalkar in Gwalior the previous night; and attempts to burn the office of the Janata Party in Delhi.

He said the hijacking was not just the work of two irresponsible boys. "There are bound to be people behind it because I know messages which have been sent by them." The Prime Minister was hinting at the involvement of other people, possibly higher up in the party's hierarchy.

The Congress hatched a plot to split the Janata Party in Parliament in 1979 and succeeded in doing so by weening away Chaudhary Charan Singh and his followers. The Congress Party tempted him with prime ministership if he broke away with his MPs. It offered him support to form the government. These moves led to the fall of the Morarji Desai Government. Mr. Charan Singh was sworn in as prime minister by the President, but he never faced Parliament as Prime Minister because the Congress Party withdrew support before the next session and thus forced elections. Meanwhile, the Charan Singh Government, under pressure from the Congress Party, initiated the process to withdraw the case against the hijackers.

The case against the two Pandeys was dropped. Thereafter,

the Congress Party honoured both of them by giving them tickets in the 1980 Uttar Pradesh Assembly election. They were elected to the assembly. Davendra Nath Pandey too has held key posts in the Uttar Pradesh Congress Committee apart from successfully contesting elections to the state assembly. Since then Bhola Pandey has been a favourite of the Nehru-Gandhis and given tickets to contest Lok Sabha elections in 1999, 2004 and 2009. On all these occasions, he has been unsuccessful. Further, Bhola Pandey has had his brush with the law on several occasions since the hijacking. For example, he was arrested and remanded to judicial custody by a local court in Ballia in March, 2009 following a non-bailable warrant in an extortion case dating back to 1982. Though remanded to judicial custody, the magistrate permitted him to file his nomination papers for the Lok Sabha election.

However, his clout with the Nehru-Gandhis is such that he was once again given the ticket for the Salempur Lok Sabha seat in 2014! Who knows? Given their persistence, the Nehru-Gandhis may well succeed in their efforts to bring the man who hijacked a plane in 1978 into their ranks in Parliament!

Excerpts from A. Surya Prakash, Fascist Tendencies in the Congress Party, Prabhat Prakashan, New Delhi, 2018

□

The Italian Connection

There is much talk of how Rajiv Gandhi as Prime Minister took his Italian relatives on a holiday to Lakshadweep and compromised national security by misusing the aircraft carrier INS Viraat and other Navy assets and also had naval officers in attendance to cater to the needs of the holiday-makers.

But there is an even greater scandal concerning the wholly illegal involvement of his Italian brother-in-law in the so-called training of the Special Protection Group (SPG) that managed the proximate security of the Prime Minister—a matter which would have certainly compromised the protocols of the special force and exposed it to foreign agencies.

Former Cabinet Secretary BG Deshmukh narrated the story of how the SPG became vulnerable to unknown and unauthorised foreigners in his autobiography, A Cabinet Secretary Looks Back. He said that as Cabinet Secretary, the special force was under his charge and one day in October 1986, he was told by an officer of this force posted in the Prime Minister's residence that a few of them were going to Italy for "special training." He immediately checked with Rajiv Gandhi and the latter said this was being arranged by the "Prime Minister's House." Deshmukh was not at all happy with this arrangement because the special force was a force that protected the Prime Minister of India, not Rajiv Gandhi, the individual. Therefore, he said the expenses must be borne by the Government. He also told Rajiv Gandhi that the Intelligence Bureau could handle it but later suggested that the Research and Analysis Wing (RAW) be entrusted with the job and the payments be made from the secret funds.

Rajiv Gandhi asked him to speak to Capt Satish Sharma, his close friend. Sharma told Deshmukh that Joshi, Director, RAW, should speak to a certain Italian (whom he named) "and settle the details." When Deshmukh asked Sharma who this Italian was, the latter "had a hearty laugh" and said Joshi would know. "Joshi ...said, it might have escaped my memory that this person was Rajiv Gandhi's brother-in-law." Later, Deshmukh said, Joshi came back to him after a week and said when RAW's Geneva office asked the Italian to pick up the amount in US dollars, the Italian said Joshi should himself "make arrangements to bring the amount in Italian currency and deliver it in Italy."

Deshmukh recounted what happened next: "Joshi was not at all happy with this as it would entail carrying about a quarter of a million dollars in Italian currency in a big suitcase, which was sure to invite trouble." The Cabinet Secretary told Rajiv Gandhi that the arrangement was not acceptable, "specially because the amount was so large. He (Rajiv Gandhi) flushed and told me to forget the whole affair." Later, Deshmukh learnt that officers did not go to Italy but an Italian expert came to India—"of course, he became rather unpopular with the SPG for he would throw his weight around." Deshmukh also realised that thereafter instructions had gone out to keep him out of the loop on all such "sensitive (read family) matters!"

In other words, Prime Minister Rajiv Gandhi wanted RAW to pay a quarter of a million dollars to his brother-in-law in Italian currency supposedly to train the SPG. And what were the qualifications of this brother-in-law with regard to proximate security of a Prime Minister? No one had a clue!

Deshmukh concluded his narration of this shocking incident by saying that "in the Mughal-darbar-like functioning of the Gandhis, he had committed the cardinal sin of checking with the king himself, the message he conveyed to me through his aides."

Deshmukh is a credible and reliable witness to the Rajiv Gandhi era in national politics. He belonged to the Maharashtra cadre of the IAS. He was called by Prime Minister Rajiv Gandhi to Delhi in 1986 and appointed Cabinet Secretary. A year later, the Prime Minister was coping with the Bofors scandal. In 1989, he was appointed Principal Secretary to the Prime Minister. Therefore, when the Bofors kickbacks allegation became public in April 1987, he was in the thick of it, participating in key meetings and advising Rajiv Gandhi on the way forward when the Opposition mounted an attack on the Prime Minister and accused him of taking bribes for the Swedish company.

The senior civil servant said he became aware of the fact that the Prime Minister's House had access to funds from abroad when the question of hiring Rajiv Gandhi's Italian relative to "train" the SPG came up. There were two sources for these funds—money stashed away by the family in foreign banks consequent to garnering commissions on foreign deals and the other being the secret funds of the Government of India. The secret funds are deployed for such purposes because they are not subject to inquisitive probes by the Comptroller and Auditor-General of India.

Hailing as he did from Maharashtra, Deshmukh was aware of how the Congress collected funds in the state. In the initial years of her prime ministership, Indira Gandhi depended heavily on Maharashtrian leaders like Rajni Patil and Vasantrao Naik. Later, when she gained complete control of the party and the Government, she decided that it was far better to collect funds for the party by "claiming cuts from foreign deals."

Consequently, trusted officers were posted in key Ministries like defence production. Also, Deshmukh said the practice of taking kickbacks earned India notoriety in foreign countries. So much so that when India decided to buy submarines from West Germany, the German Defence Ministry told the supplier the amount of commission that it would have to pay. The general talk in international circles was that in Latin American and African countries, the commission was above 10 per cent. India was placed in the five to 10 per cent bracket.

So, the scandal about commission payments by Bofors was no surprise. Deshmukh said that although he did not believe Rajiv Gandhi took the money, he said there was strong circumstantial evidence that he (Rajiv Gandhi) knew the names of the recipients but was reluctant to expose them. One could only surmise that the beneficiaries could be the Congress "or a close relative or friend of the Prime Minister's family", Deshmukh concluded. Indeed, he says a lot here without taking names. It appears, the dramatis personae of L'Affaire SPG were once again the same! For the sake of our Prime Minister's security, all this needs to be probed.

The Pioneer, 21 May, 2019

□

National Herald Case and its Grave Implications

The drama that was played out outside the premises of the Patiala Courts in New Delhi last week may send a political message to the supporters of the Congress party that it is fighting fit, but the issues raised by Dr Subramanian Swamy have grave implications for our democratic well-being and the working of political parties. Dr. Swamy's case relates to the assets of Associated Journals Ltd (AJL), the company that published National Herald. It got prime government land at concessional rates on Bahadur Shah Zafar Marg in New Delhi. This was given to it specifically for the purpose of publishing a newspaper. It also acquired properties in prime locations in other cities to build its offices. AJL published National Herald and several other publications but it closed the printing and publication of these newspapers in the year 2008.

But by then, the total assets of AJL stood at over `2,000 crore. However, this company owed a debt of `90 crore to the Congress party, as a result of interest-free loans given by the party to AJL from time to time. The party, subsequently assigned the huge debt to a Section 25 (of Companies Act) company called Young Indian (YI). This it did on receipt of a paltry sum of `50 lakh. Further, and here comes the twist, Congress president Sonia Gandhi and her son Rahul Gandhi each own 38 per cent of the shares of Young Indian (total 76 per cent between them).

Flowing from these facts, some questions arise: Why did AJL, which had assets totaling over `2000 crore, not dispose of some assets and wipe out the liability of `90 crore? Further, why did the Congress party, which had loaned out `90 crore to AJL assign the debt to the company called Young Indian in return for just `50 lakh?; Why did the Congress party advance money to a public limited company and indulge in the above mentioned commercial transactions? Is it a fact that at the end of this rigmarole, a company, Young Indian, in which Sonia Gandhi and Rahul Gandhi have 76 per cent control, has come to acquire real estate assets worth thousands of crores, including assets in prime locations in Delhi, Lucknow, Bhopal, Mumbai, Patna, Panchkula and other places?

But, these transactions have many disturbing implications. The Memorandum of Association of AJL barred the company from entering into any transaction which is not for furthering its objective of publishing newspapers; the land for National Herald House was given by the government at concessional rates, specifically for publishing a newspaper. However, National Herald House is now owned by Young Indian, which has decided not to publish the newspaper and has instead, rented it out to multi-national companies. All this happened during the Manmohan Singh regime. Following Dr Swamy's petition, the Metropolitan Magistrate said it appeared that Young Indian had been created "as a sham or a cloak to convert public money to personal use" and therefore, there was sufficient ground for proceeding against them. Accordingly, the accused persons were summoned by this court.

However, Ms Gandhi and others approached the Delhi High Court against the order of the Magistrate. But the High Court dismissed the petitions. Its observations are worthy of notice: It said "probity of a legendary national political party is under scanner in these petitions. This case is one of its own kind." Ab initio, the top lawyers of the Congress party tried to ward off trouble by raising the issue of locus standi.

They said Dr Swamy had no locus standi as he was not an aggrieved party. He had not been cheated or deprived of his rights as a shareholder of AJL. Justice Sunil Gaur of the High Court brushed aside these objections and said the question of locus standi "pales into insignificance" because of the Supreme Court's observation that freedom of a private citizen to proceed against the corrupt cannot be restricted.

The court held that "it will not be fair to say that a private citizen is free to proceed against corrupt public servants but not against a political party, when it is accused of serious offences of cheating, misappropriation etc. such as in this case where the office-bearers of a political party having criminal overtones are under scrutiny." The judge made a series of significant observations, which are worthy of reproduction, in view of the gravity of the charges levelled by Dr. Swamy against Sonia Gandhi, Rahul Gandhi and others and also because of the implications that his case has for our democracy. The court significantly observed that the allegations against the office-bearers of the party were that they siphoned off funds of the party "in a clandestine manner." The impropriety of extending interest-free loans to a public limited company by the Congress party in a democratic set up, particularly when the source of the Congress party's fund is largely from donations given by public, was the issue at hand and so, any citizen, could legitimately question the siphoning off funds by the political party.

The court further said: "What crops up in the mind of a prudent person is as to where was the need for extending interest-free loans to a public limited company engaged in a commercial venture of publishing newspapers. Also, writing off such a huge debt "can legitimately attract allegations of cheating, fraud etc." The court noted that the assigning of the loan to Young Indian "is certainly questionable and justifiably attracts the allegations of cheating, misappropriation, criminal breach of trust etc."

Further, why were genuine shareholders marginalised in the extraordinary general meeting of AJL, which was attended by just seven shareholders? Also, when lakhs of citizens give donations, is it not criminal misappropriation of Congress party's funds?

As regards the grave questions raised by the judges, Sonia Gandhi, Rahul Gandhi and other accused need to answer each of these allegations to the satisfaction of the court. They cannot be brushed aside by political drama and television camera-oriented street atmospherics. Dr. Swamy's accusations raise the larger question of where and how political parties should be allowed to spend their money.

Can they enter into business activities or enable companies owned by their office-bearers to acquire properties or businesses? In recent years, the national political parties have been receiving donations running into a few thousands of crores. Can they start commercial activity, loan out monies to corporate entities, buy and sell corporate assets etc.? What will happen to our democratic process if tax-free funds held by political parties enter the balance sheets of companies or even the stock market?

The New Indian Express, 24 December, 2015

□

The History of Modern Indian Corruption

The Court of Appeals in Milan has sent two senior officials of Finmeccanica, the Italian aerospace company, to jail for false accounting and corruption in the Rs. 3,600-crore Agusta Westland helicopter deal. It now transpires that the company had set apart 30 million Euros towards bribes to Indians to win this contract.

Corruption in defence deals is nothing new in India, but the AgustaWestland bribery case stands out for a very special reason, namely, that bribe-givers have been packed off to jail by an Italian court even as Indian investigators are groping in the dark as they search for the bribe-takers. This has happened in the past too.

But, while we are seized of the case at hand, we need to look at the larger issue, namely, the modern Indian history of corruption, and get to the genesis of bribes and commissions. There are many prominent witnesses to this history of corruption, who provide us valuable evidence of how and where it all began. These witnesses include, former President R. Venkataraman, former Cabinet Secretary B.G. Deshmukh, former CBI Director Mr. A.P. Mukherjee, former Ambassador and a member of the Nehru family Mr BK Nehru and Mr. JRD Tata. The most important witness to this history is Mr. R. Venkataraman. In his autobiography, My Presidential Years, he provides us a nugget of information that holds the clue to corruption and bribery in big international deals. He refers to a conversation he had with JRD Tata, when the latter called on him at Rashtrapati Bhavan.

Commenting on Prime Minister Rajiv Gandhi's statement on Bofors, Mr. Tata told the President "it would be difficult" for the Congress Party to deny the receipt of commission, because, since 1980, industrialists were not approached for political contributions. Consequently, the general feeling among industrialists was that the party was financed by commission on deals. Although Mr Venkataraman held key portfolios, including Defence, in the Indira Cabinet, he does not challenge or repudiate the comments of Mr. Tata. He just slips it in and allows his readers to digest the information! The testimony of Mr. B.G. Deshmukh, who was Cabinet Secretary from 1986 to 1989, is even more damning. In his autobiography titled, A Cabinet Secretary Looks Back, Mr. Deshmukh deals with the Bofors scandal involving corruption in the purchase of field guns from this Swedish company in 1986 and links it to Indira Gandhi's policy of not collecting party funds within the country, preferring instead to take cuts on global deals.

According to him, the genesis of the Bofors affair lay "in the practice initiated by Indira Gandhi for collecting funds for the Congress Party." According to him, collection of party funds was more transparent in Jawaharlal Nehru's time. In his view, at the beginning of her tenure as PM, Indira Gandhi realised that she needed funds to fight elections "to establish herself as the undisputed leader of the Congress Party." Once she established herself, Deshmukh says, Indira Gandhi "decided that a far better way to collect funds for the party was through claiming cuts from foreign deals." This system, according to him, "earned notoriety" in foreign countries. "In the HDW Submarine case, I was told the West German defence ministry had intimated to the defence supplier the amount of corruption that would be required to be paid in selling defence equipment. Commission on such deals was 10 per cent or more in Latin America and Africa, whereas India was placed in the 5-10 per cent bracket," he says.

Mr. Deshmukh's reference to HDW is significant because like Bofors, this deal too became controversial following a telex message which indicated HDW would have to give a commission of seven per cent in order to clinch the contract. In his autobiography, B.K. Nehru too refers to collection of party funds by the Congress and quotes Rajiv Gandhi as having told him that in the 1980s, "crores and unaccounted crores" had been collected for party purposes.

Much of this gets further corroboration in former CBI Director Mr. A.P. Mukherjee's book, Unknown facets of Rajiv Gandhi, Jyoti Basu and Indrajit Gupta. He says Rajiv Gandhi told him at the height of the Bofors controversy in 1989 that a big all-India party needed "substantial amounts of money. When he discussed it with colleagues, they said commissions to middlemen should be banned but commissions to be given as a matter of routine practice by the suppliers of major defence materials could be pooled under the care of some non-government entity which could be utilised solely for the purpose of meeting the inescapable expenses of the party." Mr. Mukherjee says Rajiv told him that he endorsed this idea.

Later, after the fall of the Rajiv government, the VP Singh Government secured the help of the Swiss and British governments and got evidence of the Bofors' payments trail. One trail established that Bofors had remitted US $ 7.3 million to the Swiss Bank account of Maria and Ottavio Quattrocchi, close friends of Sonia and Rajiv. So, there is sufficient evidence to establish that commissions on international deals have been 'de rigueur' since the 1980s.

There are some who, for domestic political reasons, despise everything that is Italian. That would not be the right approach. The recent Agusta Westland judgement shows we have much to learn from Italy. We must hope that the investigators will follow the leads and complete the process initiated by the court in Milan. On reading the judgement, one thing is for sure, if the investigators track down the final beneficiary, the Italians will not mind it!

The New Indian Express, 10 May, 2016

□

Bofors Ghost Still Haunts the Dynasty

A confidential assessment made by the West-European Division of the Central Investigation Agency (CIA) of the US in the late 1980s had said that although there was sufficient and clinching evidence of bribery and commissions in the Bofors Scandal, the Swedish government called off the investigation in order to protect the image of the then Prime Minister Rajiv Gandhi.

According to Manu Pubby of the Economic Times who got to see recently declassified CIA records, the documents said that "Stockholm wanted to save (Rajiv) Gandhi the troubles caused (to) him by the Swedish leak" and ward off a possible bribery indictment. Therefore, in order to achieve this, the two governments worked out a scheme to keep details of the payments secret.

The documents said that "almost certainly" payments were made by Sweden to win the India deal. It said the Swedish National Audit Bureau had concluded that as much as USD $ 40 million had been paid in commissions to middlemen.

However, in order to save Rajiv Gandhi, the Swedish government terminated its probe two years after the scandal broke out. The CIA documents only corroborate the fact that Bofors paid commissions and bribes to win the India deal.

The Bofors story dates back to the early 1980s when the process of procuring field guns for the Army began. Although Sofma of France was ahead in evaluations, Bofors clinched the deal in the final stages. Investigations by the Central Bureau of Investigation

(CBI) in Sweden and Switzerland, following brilliant international investigation by Geneva-based journalist Chitra Subramaniam, clearly established that Bofors had paid commissions. The CBI procured bank documents that established Ottavio Quattrocchi as one of the beneficiaries.

These investigations by media persons and the CBI provided damning evidence that took the allegation of commissions and bribes right up to the doorsteps of the Nehru-Gandhis. For example, the investigators found that Bofors entered into a contract with a company called AE Services in the latter part of 1985 and offered this company three per cent commission, if the Indian contract was concluded before 31 March, 1986. In other words, it was a time-bound deal.

AE Services had to deliver the contract within that deadline and strangely, the Rajiv Gandhi government signed the contract with Bofors on 24 March, 1986—just one week before the expiry of this deadline! Two months later, India paid 20 per cent of the contract sum to Bofors, and Bofors, as per its contract with AE Services, promptly transferred 3 per cent of this amount—$7.383 million to the bank account of this company in Nordfinanz Bank, Zurich. The CBI found that AE Services, in turn, transferred this money to the bank account of a company called Colbar Investments. And who owned Colbar Investments? Maria and Ottavio Quattrocchi, the dear friends of Sonia and Rajiv Gandhi!

The Delhi Bench of the Income Tax Appellate Tribunal which also probed payment of commissions also fully corroborated the money trail.

The bribery scandal broke out in April 1987, when the Swedish Radio declared that it had evidence of Bofors having paid bribes to people in India to clinch the deal. As Rajiv Gandhi's image plummeted and he struggled to keep afloat in the swirl of scandal, another strange development took place. An AE Services official wrote to Bofors and said it did not want any more commission on the India deal!

The question on every Indian's lips since 1987 is: How did Quattrocchi, an Italian, manage to swing the Bofors deal, before the expiry of the deadline set by the company? Who helped him achieve this rather extraordinary feat?

Why did Bofors pay this Italian a commission when we purchased guns for our Army? And finally, why did Quattrocchi forego subsequent payments that were "legitimately" due to him, after the scandal broke?

As everyone is aware, the Opposition went after Rajiv Gandhi, saying he had taken bribes in a defence deal and this led to the defeat of the Congress in the 1989 election. So many individuals involved in this scandal are no more. Rajiv Gandhi; Ottavio Quattrocchi; Martin Ardbo, who was President of Bofors when the deal was signed and whose diary entries provided vital clues to the Swedish police; the former Defence Secretary S.K. Bhatnagar; and Win Chadha, the company's agent in India.

With the passing of each of these individuals, there would be speculation that the saga of Bofors would now end. But no such thing has happened. No financial or bribery scandal will fade out of public memory until there are adequate reparations for the losses suffered by the exchequer. Unless this happens, a scandal is deathless. It will linger in the public mind and will be passed on, possibly with some embellishments from one generation to another. While this is generally the case, it is more so in cases concerning national security.

The taking of bribes or commissions when India bought guns for her soldiers is deemed an act of treachery (Desha Droha) and is never forgiven. Despite this clinching evidence of the money trail, Maria Quattrocchi claimed after her husband's death in 2013 that her husband was "hounded" for over 20 years.

The ghost of Bofors will continue to haunt the Nehru-Gandhis until they own up that bribes and commissions were paid to their near and dear ones by the Swedish arms manufacturer. The only Prayaschittha is honest admission by the family. Until then, as the latest evidence from the CIA files shows us, the ghost of Bofors will continue to haunt them and extract its price in political terms for the decisions made in 1986.

The New Indian Express, 14 February, 2017

□

Why is Congress hiding its MoU with China's Communists?

While the Congress is facing yet another challenge from within with long-time party loyalists doubtful about its future, the news about the Memorandum of Understanding (MoU) entered into by the party with the Communist Party of China (CCP) in 2008 has now become a matter of concern because of two pertinent reasons. Firstly, the Congress is just not willing to disclose the contents of this MoU with the CCP, which not only controls the Chinese government but runs that country in every sense of the word. Secondly, there is the news about donations received by the Rajiv Gandhi Foundation (RGF) from the Chinese Government.

The MoU was signed on behalf of the party by Rahul Gandhi, its general secretary at that time, and by an official of the CCP in the presence of his mother and party president, Sonia Gandhi and the then Chinese Vice-President Xi Jinping. Despite mounting public demand, the Nehru-Gandhis are chary of releasing this MoU. What are they afraid of? To begin with, the Congress must explain why the RGF, which, like the party, is a closely held enterprise of the Nehru-Gandhi family, took a donation from China—a nation that has spurned India's hand of friendship and repeatedly challenged India's territorial integrity for over seven decades.

Posting a picture of the MoU-signing ceremony, the noted lawyer Mahesh Jethmalani tweeted and said it was imperative for the party to disclose the details. More ominously (for the Congress), the lawyer noted that "China was and is in Indian law, an enemy country. The CCP is an enemy association. The CCP supports the occupation of Indian territory and lays claim to other territory. Any agreement/MoU with the CCP validates the CCP's stand and is an unlawful activity punishable under the UAPA (Unlawful Activities Prevention Act)," says Jethmalani. He has also suggested a CBI probe into possible offences under the Prevention of Corruption Act and the Foreign Contribution Regulation Acts of 1976 and 2010.

This question becomes all the more relevant at a time when Indian soldiers laid down their lives while countering yet another attempted incursion by the Chinese in the Galwan Valley in Ladakh and the continued aggressive posture of the Chinese army along the Line of Actual Control (LAC). There is also a domestic angle to the scandal involving funds flowing into this family's trust, which is even more appalling. This relates to the diversion of funds from the Prime Minister's National Relief Fund (PMNRF), which is primarily meant to lend succour to people in times of natural calamities, etc., to the RGF when the party headed the coalition that ran the Union government from 2004 to 2014.

Apart from the Nehru-Gandhis, Manmohan Singh, who was the prime minister at that time, must explain how he allowed such gross misuse of a public fund directly under his charge. The news about the donation from the government of China to the Congress has stirred a hornet's nest as it has raised questions about the sanctity of the transaction and its possible impact on India's sovereignty, unity and integrity. The Congress, which was at the vanguard of the freedom movement, has for long enjoyed the trust and love of the people for the enormous sacrifices made by its leaders to secure the country's freedom.

However, this reverence began to fade away when, after the advent of Indira Gandhi, the party became a clone of a private limited company that was tightly held by the Nehru-Gandhi family and which allowed the family's insecurities and pettiness to permeate its activities. Consequently, they made India a de facto monarchy and with the help of courtiers in academia and the media, worked overtime to obliterate the contribution of great leaders outside this family. This reached such vulgar proportions that every major government scheme, public building, national institutions, universities, scholarships and sports events were named after members of this family. So, the question now is whether senior leaders of the Congress, who want it to put its house in order, see the impact of all this on the overall image of the party and demand answers from the family.

The sense of entitlement of the family is such that Sonia Gandhi and not Prime Minister Manmohan Singh attended the Beijing Olympics. The Chinese played host to her, her son Rahul Gandhi, her daughter Priyanka Gandhi Vadra and son-in-law Robert Vadra. Tweeting about this, Shobha Karandlaje, BJP MP, has said, "This wasn't just a mockery of the office of the Prime Minister, but a subversion of India's democratic system & ethos". There is seething anger in the country regarding the hegemonistic attitude of China and its perfidy after signing agreements vis-a-vis patrolling and other arrangements along the LAC for maintenance of peace. Why is this party at odds with this national sentiment? Will the current churning in the party lead to a change of heart? Also, will the current crop of dissidents, who want the party to put its house in order, see the impact of all this on the overall image of the Congress and demand answers?

The New Indian Express, 27 August, 2020

□

Home Rule not Rome Rule, Mr. President

The American Constitution stipulates that only natural born citizens and those who have been resident in America for 14 years prior to his or her nomination are eligible to the office of President. The Singapore Constitution says that "a person who is not a citizen of Singapore born in Malaya shall not be elected President," and the law in Finland is that the President of the Republic must be "from among the natural born citizens of Finland." These are just three of the innumerable examples available the world over to show how constitutions bar naturalised citizens from high public offices. India's Constitution has no such exclusion clause possibly because the founding fathers, who had waged a relentless struggle against European colonialists, never thought that there would come a day when a foreigner acquiring Indian Citizenship would offer himself or herself as a candidate for the Presidency or Prime Ministership. For the very Saline reason, parliamentarians Saw no need Lo place such restrictions on naturalised citizens in the electoral laws they made in the early 1950s. As a result, foreigners who acquire Indian citizenship can legitimately aspire for high constitutional offices in India.

It is this glaring lacuna in the country's laws that has emboldened Congressmen to give Ms Sonia Gandhi a carte blanche and encourage her to make a bid for prime ministership.

Though on the face of it there is no constitutional impediment, there are a few sensitive is sues which President KR Narayanan will have to take into account before inviting her to form the next Government. The first of these is her vulnerability under the Citizenship Act and the fact that since she is not an Indian citizen by birth, her citizenship is conditional. The second is the issue of legitimacy, not in Narrow legal terms but in tie larger sense. The third is sue is that Indians know very little about her.

Though this writer had occasion to examine this issue in detail on an earlier occasion, Ms Gandhi's strenuous efforts to lead the next Government warrants a reiteration of the restrictions that India's citizenship law imposes on her. As in all other countries, there is a hierarchy of citizens in India. Under The Citizenship Act, 1955, all those born in India are classified as "Citizens by Birth". Foreigners who marry Indian Citizens and live here are classified as "Citizens by Registration". Ms Sonia Gandhi falls in this category. The Act also recognises two other categories of citizens—"Citizens by Naturalisation" and "Commonwealth Citizens". Foreigners and citizens of Commonwealth countries who live in India for long years and apply for citizenship come in these two categories respectively.

Those born in India acquire Indian citizen ship at birth and carry it to their graves. They do not have to apply for it and their citizenship is unconditional. Further, there is no law or authority which can deprive them or their citizenship. But that is not the case with citizens like Ms Sonia Gandhi. Foreigners like her have to apply for citizenship and fulfill certain conditions in order to secure it. Secondly, their citizenship is subject to certain conditions.

Ms. Sonia Gandhi married Rajiv Gandhi in 1968. Under the Citizenship Act she was entitled to apply for Indian Citizenship after five years. She, however, retained her Italian Citizenship for about 15 years after marriage. When she eventually put in her application and it was granted, she become a "Citizen by Registration." And as per the law, this is given subject to certain "conditions and restrictions."

The Act says that those who acquire citizenship through false representations can be punished with imprisonment up to six months.

In other words, while natural-born Indians CAT never be deprived of their citizenship, citizens like Ms. Gandhi always face the danger of their citizenship being questioned or challenged under any of the four grounds mentioned in Section 10. Therefore, oven though there is no constitutional bar on her becoming the Prime Minister, Ms Gandhi bas to live with the vulnerability that comes with her category of citizenship. President KR Narayanan must consider whether India should have a Prime Minister whose citizenship is conditional and challengeable at any point of time.

The second problem is that under this law, the Government has the right to proscribe additional conditionalities on her, depending up on how Italy, the country of her birth, treats Indians who become spouses of Italian citizens. Section 5 of the Act says: "Provided that in prescribing the conditions and restrictions subject to which persons of any such country may be registered as Citizens of India under this clause, the Central Government shall have due regard to the conditions subject to which citizens of India may, by law or practice of that country, become citizens of that country by registration."

This means that it is incumbent on the Government to examine the conditions and restrictions imposed by the Government of Italy on Indian spouses of Italian citizens while granting them citizenship and ensure purity. If Indians who secure Italian citizenship are restricted in any manner from holding elective posts or entering public office, the same will have to apply to Ms Gandhi. Should the fate of the Prime Minister of India be dependent upon the vagaries of Italian naturalisation laws?

President Narayanan will therefore lure to consider whether he should have a Prime Minister whose citizenship is subject to so many "ifs" and "buts".

The second issue is one of legitimacy. They office of the Prime Minister is such that the incumbent is often required to remind the people of their patriotic duties and recall the phenomenal sacrifices made by preceding generations to drive out the British French, Dutch and Portuguese colonialists. Can a European born Prime Minister carry conviction?

Finally unlike home-grown leaders like Messrs PV Narasimha Rao, HD Deve Gowda, IK Gujral and Atal Bihari Vajpayee, about whom so much is known. Sonin Gandhi has remained an enigma throughout her 31 year stay in India. Even though many Indian leaders would hope that much of what they do remains a secret, there are really no secrets in India's social and political milieu. Even a short notice, it is possible to line up at least a few of Mr. Rao's school males or to get a complete lowdown on another leader's soul mates. In Ms Gandhi's case, her life has remained a closed book. This would be perfectly in order for one leading a private life, but it can hardly fit into the demands of a vibrant democratic environment in the world's largest democracy, Indians know very little about her, so little that they do not have the faintest idea of even something as innocuous as her educational attainments. Nor are Indians acquainted with her natal family. Little is known about her parents and siblings, about their occupations or political persuasions.

These are glaring shortcomings for someone who aspires to be the Prime Minister of India Should the President invite her to form the Government, all this is certain to cramp her style and reduce her manoeuvrability, despite all the affection that Congressmen may shower on her Further, nothing can be more in congruous than an Italian-born Prime Minister for a resurgent India, which, after 200 years of colonial rule and 50 years of post Independence dithering is all set to take on the Western world in a host of areas that range from commerce and strategic affairs to computer technology and English literatures such is the magic in the Indian label these days that any Indian with a technical skill is a much sought after person the world over. This new found self-confidence has, for the first time after Independence, given respectability to the label which says "Made in India".

A Prime Minister who is "Made in India" would be in harmony

with India's rhythm. Anything else could mean dissonance and even cause untold damage to the national psyche. What Indian reeds today is Home Rule, not Rome Rule. President Narayanan therefore has the historic and enviable task of ensuring that his decision is in consonance with the current explosion indigenous pride.

The Pioneer, 23 April, 1999

□

"The Stuff" Sonia Gandhi is Made of

Sonia Gandhi was probably attending middle school in Orbassano when Atal Bihari Vajpayee first made his parliamentary debut in India in 1957. Today, he is not only the senior-most parliamentarian and a gifted speaker but also a man of immense experience. More importantly, he has the image of a benign mass leader with a human touch and with the capacity to rise above ideology and politics in times of stress and conflict. In short, he is India's tallest political leader and statesman at this point of time. And what does Ms Sonia Gandhi—the Indian come lately-have to say about him? According to her, Mr. Vajpayee is a "liar", a man prone to *Gaddari* (treacherous acts) and one who is leading India down the road to destruction.

One wonders whether there is another naturalised citizen in any society around the world who would make such remarks about a man held in reverence by millions of people. Also, is there another society outside India that would tolerate such impertinence from a reluctant citizen?

In fact. Ms Gandhi's disrespect for prime ministers and protocol is nothing new. Unlike natural-born Indians who go to the Prime Minister's Residence should the latter express a desire to meet them, Ms Gandhi has made prime ministers like PV Narasimha Rao and HD Deve Gowda wait at her doorstep. Television cameras also showed her look the other way when Mr. Vajpayee greeted her after he took oath of office in March, 1998.

Alongside this tirade against the prime minister during

the current campaign, Ms. Gandhi has also been emboldened to train her guns at natural-born Indians who question her right to become India's Prime Minister. Some weeks ago, she told Star TV in an interview that those who rake up the foreigner issue do not know "the stuff I am made of." Apart from the implied threat, there is a factual inaccuracy in her statement. Many natural-born Indians are aware of "the stuff" she is made of and are therefore on nigh alert vis-a-vis her vaulting political ambitions.

Sonia Gandhi is the daughter of Stetano Maino, a building contractor who lived in Orbassano near Turin in Northern Italy. The Mainos are an orthodox Catholic family. Mr. Maino was an ardent admirer of the Italian Fascist Dictator Benito Mussolini. He fought alongside the Nazis on the Russian front in World War II. In 1977, when Javed Laiq, an Indian journalist visited him at his home, Mr. Maino had bound volumes of Mussolini's teachings in his drawing room and he reminisced about the good old days. He told Laiq that except the neo-fascists, he had no respect for the other political parties in democratic Italy. All these parties he said were "traitors". This is the political environment in which Sonia Gandhi grew up. It is therefore amusing to hear her talk of the fascist Forces in India.

Sonia married Rajiv Gandhi in 1968 and was elgible for citizenship in February, 1973. But she did not apply for Indian citizenship until 7 April, 1983. Obviously, she was never comfortable with the thought of becoming an Indian. Yet, because of her political ambitions, she kept her 15 year reluctance a closely guarded secret and hoped that no one would ever rake up this issue. It was left to *The Pioneer* to make these ates public and to put an end to the pre ailing confusion over this issue. Now that is public knowledge that she preferred to retain her Italian Citizenship even though she as the daughter-in-law of India's Prime Minister and even lived in the Prime Minister's House, she is now indulging in a t of obfuscation.

She claimed in a TV interview the other day that she accepted Indian citizenship the day she became India Gandhi's *bahu* and that plying for citizenship was a mere "technicality". All Italy-bound Indians must test theory of citizenship at the touchstone an Immigration! It is difficult to find er naturalised citizen who indulges in such brazen dishonesty but then this is the stuff she is made of.

Ms Gandhi clung to her Italian citizenship for fifteen years after marriage but strangely was anxious to gain voting rights in India. Though only Indian citizens can be voters, she smuggled herself into the voters' list in New Delhi in January, 1980. Luckily, some one detected the fraud and complained to the Chief Electoral Officer. Following the complaint her name was deleted from the voters list in 1982. However, Ms. Gandhi returned to the voters' list prepared in 1983 with 1 January, 1983 as the qualifying date, again without being a citizen of India on that day.

But this desire to eat the cake and have it too is apparent in her conduct in other matters as well. She held shares in two Indian companies and was also appointed Managing Director of these firms in gross violation of the Foreign Exchange Regulation Act in 1974.

Ms Gandhi, therefore, has shown little respect for Indian laws during her stay in India as a foreign national and this gives us some idea or "the stuff" that she is made of. If a foreign national is allowed to violate our laws with such impunity, with what moral authority can the government enforce the law in respect of natural-born Indians? How was Sonia Gandhi given Indian citizenship in the first place when this was her conduct as a foreign national? If the government attaches any importance to the rule of law and to national security, there is need for a thorough probe into these matters followed by corrective action.

However, it must be clarified that throwing challenges is not a newly acquired trait. In 1987, Sonia accompanied Prime Minister Rajiv Gandhi, on an official visit to Hyderabad. There were many VIPs standing in a line to welcome him at the airport. Among them was P. Upendra, a prominent leader of the Telugu Desam. Soon after Rajiv shook hands with Upendra, Sonia stepped back and to the utter shock of the Telugu Desam MP, administered a severe warning to him. According to a report in Newstime dated 23 December, 1987, she turned to Upendra and said: "I will see your end if I am alive for what you said about me in Parliament."

Upendra had not made any re marks against her. She mistook him for some one else but the fact remains that she threatened an MP for what she thought he had said in parliament. If anyone else had done this, the Privileges Committees of Parliament would have thrown him in jail, but that is be sides the point. The point to note is that there was sufficient evidence even 12 years ago of "the stuff" that she is made of.

Indians are an accommodating and generous people but it is foolish to constantly test the tolerance levels of the natural-born in any society. Under the citizenship law. Ms. Gandhi, after all, is a citizen of the second class. Unlike natural-born Indians who acquire their citizenship at birth and retain it unconditionally until death, Ms. Gandhi's citizenship is conditional. If ever she is found violating any of the conditions stipulated in this law, her citizenship is liable to be can celled. She must also remember that the Indian tax-payer shells out over Rs. 4 crores a year to provide her a home and security. It is therefore an irony that instead of being grateful, the SPG cocoon in which she lives emboldens her to hold out threats to natural-born Indians.

Generally speaking, naturalised citizens should never forget their *aukat*. More so, if they live on the munificence of a country's taxpayers. But, as we now know this is not "the stuff" she is made of.

The Pioneer, 10 February, 1998

□

A Thorn in our Flesh, a Gift from Nehru

The recent remarks of the IAF chief, Air Chief Marshal Arup Raha, that Pakistan-occupied Kashmir (POK) would have been with India if the country had opted for a military solution to settle the Kashmir issue, rather than taking the moral high ground and rushing to the United Nations for a settlement are indeed significant.

In unusually candid remarks on the conflict in Kashmir in 1947, when Pakistan sent in hordes of raiders into the state the IAF Chief said that India did not follow a pragmatic approach to secure its interests. As a result, PoK has now be come a "thorn in our flesh". According to the Air Chief, our foreign policy was enshrined in the charter of the UN, charter of the Non-Alignment Movement as well as the Panchsheel doctrine. In his view, "we have been governed by high ideals and we really did not follow a very pragmatic approach...to security needs". As a result, we had ignored the role of military power in maintaining a conducive environment.

Recalling how the IAF was pressed into service at a critical moment in October, 1947 to rush troops and equipment to the Kashmir Valley, he said the problem still persists because when a military solution was in sight, the country went to the UN for a peaceful solution, which never came about.

The IAF Chief's remarks revive the debate on some controversial decisions taken by the country's political leadership at that time, which has burdened the nation with a festering problem for 70 years.

The problem began soon after independence. Following partition, all Indian states were given the option to accede to either India or Pakistan. Maharaja Hari Singh of the state of Jammu and Kashmir was considering the idea of an independent state but was unable to make up his mind. While he kept dilly-dallying on the issue, he was confronted with the Pakistani invasion of his state. Pakistan pushed thousands of heavily armed tribesmen in October, 1947 across the border in a bid to capture the state by force. These tribesmen led by Pakistani Army regulars attacked Muzaffarabad and soon captured large parts of the state.

The Jammu and Kashmir state army, which comprised of Muslims and Dogras, was called upon to defend the state's borders, but was crippled by desertions by the Muslims, who joined the invaders and even provided them logistic and other support. Despite the desertions, the state army led by Brigadier Rajinder Singh offered valiant resistance at Uri for two days. But once this resistance collapsed, the intruders captured Baramulla and were soon on the outskirts of Srinagar. They also cut off power supply to Srinagar

Thus, within days, Maharaja Hari Singh realised that his indecisiveness was costing him the state. He then pressed the panic button and made a desperate appeal for Indian forces to help repel the invaders. Despite the grave implications that these developments had for India's strategic interests, the Jawaharlal Nehru Government took the view that it had no locus standi to go to the rescue of this state, unless the state acceded to India. The Maharaja finally signed the Instrument of Accession on October 26 and New Delhi launched a massive airlift of troops to Srinagar from the early hours of October 27. Home Minister Sardar Patel's assertiveness ensured that the Indian Army arrived in Srinagar just in the nick of time. Within a fortnight. Baramulla and the heights of Uri were re-taken. Air Chief Marshal Raha's comments relate to these events.

However, while the army was on the job, Prime Minister Nehru took the fateful decision on 1 January, 1948—much against the advice of Sardar Patel—to complain to the UN Security Council.

Before he approached the Nehru went to Lahore on 8 December, 1947, to plead with counterpart, Liaqat Ali Khan to initiate steps to de-escalate tensions by issuing an appeal to the Pakistani intruders in Kashmir to withdraw. According to Mr. V.P. Menon, Secretary in the Ministry of States at the time, Khan pleaded helplessness on the grounds that he ran a moderate government that was already under attack by the media for its failure to fully back the Azad Kashmir movement. Instead, he wanted India to appoint an impartial administration in the state. Nehru returned empty-handed from Lahore and thereafter decided to go to the UN.

This hurt India's interests on two counts: one, it internationalised the Kashmir dispute; and two, it stopped the Indian Army from finishing the job of throwing out the intruders. In fact, it is said that the ceasefire was ordered at a time when the army needed just a few more days to complete its task. Further, the decision to beseech the UN showed India up as a weak state that needed third party intervention to throw out an aggressor.

Most Indians who are acquainted with the events that unfolded in Kashmir in the last quarter of 1947 are aware of how Kashmir got divided and how PoK became a thorn in India's flesh. Air Chief Marshal Raha has only re-kindled those unpleasant memories of the pusillanimity of the Indian State from the very day of our independence and how this has been the unfortunate template for dealing with issues concerning India's strategic interests.

Also, despite our democratic experience over 70 years, the Nehruvian establishment's tradition of burying the truth is still so entrenched in the national capital that eyebrows are raised even when a serving Chief of our armed forces speaks of what went wrong 70 years ago. But we must thank Air Chief Marshal Raha for his candidness, because in security and military-related matters, only unvarnished truth will serve the national interest!

The New Indian Express, 13 September, 2016

□

Chapter-9

THE EMERGENCY

1975: A Haunting Tyranny

At the stroke of midnight on June 25, 1975, the idea of India was dealt a lethal blow when a presidential proclamation, at the behest of then Prime Minister Indira Gandhi, declared a state of internal Emergency and India lost its freedom to authoritarianism. A Surya Prakash's book, in his own words, provides readers some case studies from independent India's darkest political era which illustrate the terrible woes that befall a nation when democracy is snuffed out.

Every year, 25 June marks the anniversary of the dreaded Emergency that was imposed by Indira Gandhi to snuff out democracy and to gain absolute power after she was found guilty of corrupt electoral practice. She got a pliant President (Fakhruddin Ali Ahmed) to issue a proclamation under Article 352 of the Constitution to impose an 'Internal Emergency' and thus turned a vibrant democracy into a dictatorship. The Emergency, which lasted 21 months, constituted the darkest hour of India's democracy.

During the Emergency the Constitution was mutilated, Parliament was reduced to a rubber stamp and the media was gagged. Even the judiciary failed to stand up to the tyrannical regime. As a result, the people of India lost their basic freedoms and came face-to-face with fascism.

India's tallest leaders were arrested soon after the President signed the proclamation. Those arrested included Jayaprakash Narayan, Atal Bihari Vajpayee, Chandra Shekhar, Charan Singh, lK Advani, Madhu Dandavate, Ramakrishna Hegde, Morarji Desai,

Biju Patnaik, Nanaji Deshmukh and Sikander Bakht. Balasaheb Deoras, the Sarsanghchalak of the Rashtriya Swayamsevak Sangh (RSS) and a large number of leaders of the RSS and the Bharatiya Jana Sangh (later the Bharatiya Janata Party) were jailed during the Emergency. As on 12 February, 1977, the Government said that of the 6,330 persons belonging to banned organisations and political parties who were detained under MISA, 4,026 were from the RSS (3,254) and the Jana Sangh (772). Many of those who hold prominent positions in the RSS, the Union Government and the BJP today suffered jail terms during the Emergency.

Author's Experience of Emergency

My memories of the Emergency go back to that eerie feeling on the morning of 26 June, when V.N. Subba Rao, my Chief Reporter in The Indian Express, Bangalore, called to say that an Emergency had been imposed and many national leaders had been arrested. He summoned me to the office to chase these stories. Soon thereafter, we heard that censorship had been imposed and that all our copies had to be sent to the chief censor. Out to humiliate the media, the Government appointed KCK Raja, Inspector General of Police (IGP), Karnataka, as the chief censor in the State. Raja had a battery of police inspectors and sub-inspectors and information department officials working as 'chhota censors'. The 'censors' would cut out anything that looked like criticism of Indira Gandhi or which showed the Government in poor light, and return them to the newspaper. The senior editorial staff had to ensure that the censors' instructions were carried out. Thus, the Inspector General of Police became my editor throughout the Emergency!.........

My other recollection of the Emergency was my meeting with Lawrence Fernandes, brother of George Fernandes, after he was released by the Corps of Detectives, Karnataka, in March 1977. This happened after the announcement of a parliamentary election and lifting of censorship. He had been brutally tortured in police custody and broke down several times during a late-night interview at his Richmond Town home. When the interview was published, the people were shocked and the Union Government was furious. It directed the editor to carry the Government's version on front page the next day. The Indira Gandhi Government was confident of returning to power in the election due in March 1977 and the State's Home Secretary echoed this sentiment when he called to say that the Government would "deal" with this issue, after the election results came in. Such was the climate of fear during the Emergency that my mother and sister thought that the police had arrived to pick me up! Those were indeed harrowing times for my mother, Parvatamma and father AN Anantaramaiah, who were deeply worried about the safety of their journalist son and constantly feared a midnight knock!.....

Lest we Forget

Recounting the horrors of the Emergency and how the midnight arrests on 25 June 1975 changed the political landscape, Bharatiya Janata Party (then Bharatiya Jana Sangh) leader LK Advani said that night he received an urgent message which said Jayaprakash Narayan had been arrested, as also Morarji Desai and Raj Narain. "The arrests are continuing ... I ... hastened to Atalji's room to convey the news to him ... we conferred briefly and decided that neither of us should evade arrest ... Atalji and I prepared a joint statement condemning the arrest of J.P. and other leaders, denouncing the Emergency and affirming that June 26, 1975 would have the same historic significance in the annals of independent India as 9 August, 1942 had in the pre-Independence days when the Quit India movement was launched to force the British to leave the country." Advani is right. If we are to protect ourselves from such tyranny hereafter, we need to remember the story of the Emergency. It must be told and retold so that the idea of democracy gets replenished, generation after generation....

Justice J.C. Shah, who headed the commission of inquiry which investigated the excesses during the Emergency ... did a commendable job in probing the tyranny unleashed by Indira Gandhi at that time, beginning with the dubious and wholly unconstitutional conduct of President Fakhruddin Ali Ahmed in signing the proclamation, even though the advice had not come from the Union cabinet, and following the various atrocities that occurred in the name of family planning, city beautification, etc. He also probed the conduct of many politicians and bureaucrats who became part of an extra-constitutional coterie that was headed by Indira Gandhi's son, Sanjay Gandhi, and operated out of the Prime Minister's residence....

Paying an eloquent tribute to Justice Shah, Era Sezhiyan, one of India's leading parliamentarians, said it (the Shah Commission Report) would read like an investigative report. "It is a magnificent historical document to serve as a warning for those coming to power in the future not to disturb the basic structure of a functioning democracy". It was also a hopeful guide for those suppressed under a despotic rule, to redeem their freedom by a spirited struggle.

India's founding fathers had warned citizens of such exigencies like the Emergency if they were not alert. Dr. Sarvepalli Radhakrishnan, a member of the Constituent Assembly, said "Our opportunities are great but let me warn you that when power outstrips ability, we will fall on evil days ... a free India will be judged by the way in which it will serve the interests of the common man ... unless we destroy corruption in high places, root out every trace of nepotism, love of power ... we will not be able to raise the standards of efficiency in administration."

This warning holds good for all time. Fortunately, the people used the first opportunity that came their way in 1977 to restore democracy. The threat from dynasticism, nepotism and corruption to India's much-cherished democracy is not over yet. We need to be ever on our guard. The purpose of this book is to keep the flame of eternal vigil alive.

Constitution Mutilated

In 1976, when India was groaning under the impact of Indira Gandhi's dictatorship, the Congress appointed a Committee headed by Swaran Singh to review the Constitution. The Committee worked at great speed, consulted party MPs, party chief ministers and Pradesh Congress chiefs and came up with a horrendous list of amendments to cripple the judiciary, destroy the federal character of the Constitution and to give Parliament untrammelled power to alter this document.

The Swaran Singh report set the tone for the infamous 42nd Amendment that destroyed the very soul of the Constitution. While all this was on, citizens were barred from holding meetings to discuss the proposed amendments and the media was prohibited from criticising the proposals....

A major recommendation of the Swaran Singh Committee was that "the constituent power of Parliament to amend the Constitution as provided in Article 368 should not be open to question or challenge". In order to achieve this, the Committee said Article 368 should be amended to categorically prohibit judicial review. Further, the high courts should be barred from entertaining writ petitions challenging the constitutional validity of a Central law "and any rule, regulation and byelaw made thereunder."....

In short, the Swaran Singh Committee was hitting at the very foundations of the Constitution by suggesting measures to weaken the judiciary and to alter the federal features in the Constitution. Armed with such dangerous recommendations from a party Committee that was deliberating the issue when Indira Gandhi's dictatorship was at its worst, the Congress Government led by her pushed through the Constitution (Forty-second Amendment) Act that virtually sanctified authoritarian rule and knocked the bottom out of India's democratic Constitution....

The first thing Indira Gandhi did after imposing the Emergency was to push through the 39th Amendment to bar courts, with retrospective effect, from entertaining election petitions against the Prime Minister. This was to overcome the verdict of the Allahabad High Court, which had found her guilty of corrupt electoral practice.

The extraordinary aspect of this episode was the speed with which this deed was accomplished. The Bill was introduced in the lok Sabha on 7 August, 1975 and, much against rules, debated and passed the same day.

It was passed by the Rajya Sabha on 8 August and, hold your breath, ratified by the legislative assemblies of 17 states the very next day, a Saturday. Then an obliging President gave his assent on 10 August and an even more obliging bureaucracy notified it that very day—a Sunday....

Taken together, these amendments robbed the Constitution of its soul and turned India into a dictatorship. This Amendment knocked out the principle of equality before law enshrined in Article 14.... The basic features of the Constitution were subjected to much greater bombardment in the 42nd Amendment that was passed by Parliament in November 1976, after the lok Sabha had extended its life. This Amendment, which mutilated the Constitution, was done after the Swaran Singh Committee conducted a spurious constitutional review. It introduced a new article to deal with "anti-national activity" (a euphemism for political opponents), put constitutional amendments beyond judicial review, stripped the high courts of their powers and bolstered the emergency powers of the executive. But the most obnoxious clause was the one which empowered the President to amend the Constitution when necessary.

Here is a glimpse of what Congress MPs said in Parliament in 1976 on some constitutional matters:

Indira Gandhi: Shri Gokhale and others quoted Jawaharlal Nehru's admonition to the Constituent Assembly not to tie down future generations. So, revision and adjustment in changing conditions are part and parcel of our Constitution. Those who want to fix it in a rigid and unalterable frame do not know the spirit of our Constitution and are entirely out of tune with the spirit of new India.

Vasant Sathe: We are sovereign. We have the constituent power ... and we do not want anybody to tell us this or that.

A.R. Antulay: The Constitution has to be changed at every interval of time. Nobody can say that this is the finality. A Constitution which is static is a constitution which ultimately becomes a big hurdle in the path of progress of the nation.

NKP Salve: The means of amendment of the Constitution are the very means of conservation and preservation of the Constitution. The sovereign legal rights of Parliament are unhampered or unimpeded by any doctrine of eternal immutability of the basic structure.

Swaran Singh: We cannot shirk that responsibility. We should not at all be apologetic about changing the Constitution.

CM Stephen: Now the power of this Parliament (through the 42nd Amendment) is declared to be out of bounds for any court. It is left to the courts whether they should defy it. I do not know whether they will have the temerity to do that but if they do ... that will be a bad day for the judiciary. The committee of the House is sitting with regard to the enquiry into the conduct of judges and all that. We have got our methods, our machinery.

D.B. Chandre Gowda: The framers of the Constitution ... rightly thought that the future generation would not accept the Constitution as accepted by them on 26 November, 1949.

Priyaranjan Das Munshi: The Government has shown the courage and wisdom to bring in such a bold measure and those who brought this measure should be considered as the greatest patriots of the country for all time to come.

Singer Kishore Kumar Targetted

In January 1976, the Ministry of Information and Broadcasting decided to rope in celebrities from the film industry to do films for television eulogising the Emergency and Indira Gandhi's Twenty-Point Programme. It also wanted playback singers to sing jingles in praise of the Government and its schemes.....(It was learnt that) Kishore Kumar was not prepared to be associated with this initiative in any manner....

CB Jain, joint secretary in the Ministry, spoke to Kishore Kumar and told him of what the Government had in mind.... Kishore Kumar refused to meet the Ministry's officials....Jain told the Shah Commission that Kishore Kumar was "curt and blunt" and his refusal to meet him (Jain) and other officers was "a grossly discourteous behaviour". On returning to Delhi, Jain met SMH Burney, Secretary, MIB, and told him that not only was Kishore Kumar not cooperating with the Ministry, but his behaviour with the Ministry officials was also "grossly discourteous and uncalled for"....

The Secretary, MIB, decided to punish the man who was the most versatile and entertaining playback singer and who was adored by India. Burney ordered that all songs of Kishore Kumar "should be banned from AIR (All India Radio) and Doordarshan" and all films in which Kishore Kumar had acted were to be "listed out for further action".

Even more extraordinary was this bureaucrat's order that "the sales of gramophone records of Shri Kishore Kumar's songs were to be frozen". The purpose of this action against Kishore Kumar was twofold. One, to teach him a lesson; and two, more importantly, to ensure that this action against Kumar had the necessary impact on the entire film industry, meaning that everyone better get the message and fall in line. Burney gloated in his note that these measures "had tangible effect on film producers". Following Burney's diktat, All India Radio banned Kishore Kumar on 4 May and Doordarshan on 5 May. MIB officials also contacted Polydor and HMV record companies "to discuss ways and means to freeze the sale of Shri Kishore Kumar's records". While Polydor remained noncommittal, HMV, the renowned gramophone record company agreed "to stop getting Kishore Kumar to record any individual recording or solo items on HMV's own initiative".....

Drama in PM House

Siddhartha Shankar Ray later told the Shah Commission that the Prime Minister had told him on two or three occasions prior to this meeting that "India required a shock treatment" and something had to be done. Some sort of emergency power or drastic power was necessary. One such occasion when she mentioned the need for "shock treatment" was prior to 12 June, 1975—the day Justice Sinha of the Allahabad High Court had delivered his judgement. Ray told her that they could manage the situation with the existing laws....

Indira Gandhi's oft-repeated claim that the law and order situation in the country had deteriorated and that this warranted the imposition of Emergency remained unsubstantiated by facts. Actually, it turned out to be a blatant lie. The Shah Commission exposed her falsehood fully. It found that official records were telling a different story. It examined the fortnightly reports sent by the Governors in the States to the President and by the chief secretaries of States to the Union Home Secretary. These reports indicated that the law and order situation was "under complete control" all over the country.

In the weeks and months preceding the Emergency, the Home Ministry had not received any reports which said that the situation had deteriorated. The claim that things had deteriorated on the economic front were also without basis. There was nothing alarming on the economic front. The Shah Commission found that the Wholesale Price Index (WPI) had declined by 7.4 per cent between 3 December, 1974 and the last week of March 1975 as per the Economic Survey for the fiscal year 1975-76 which was prepared by the very same Government....

"Eventually, they completed the task of writing Mrs Gandhi's speech and Ray stepped out of the room. At that point he heard from Om Mehta, the Minister of State for Home Affairs, that orders had been issued to lockup the high courts the next day and to cut off electricity connections to all newspapers."....

The Prime Minister wanted the President to sign the proclamation. She told the President that she was not consulting the Cabinet "due to shortage of time", and that therefore, she was permitting a departure from the Transaction of Business Rules in exercise of her powers under Rule 12 thereof...

"Om Mehta confirmed that it was happening and went on to say that 'tomorrow all the high courts will be closed, the doors locked.' Siddhartha Shankar Ray was horrified and asked to see Indira again. Her aides informed him that she had gone to her room and could not be disturbed. Ray insisted. As they waited for Indira, Sanjay came out and spoke to Siddhartha. "You people do not know how to run the country". Before his mother arrived, he left.

Agitatedly, Ray told Indira of Om Mehta's information. She was taken aback, asked Ray to wait till she found out what was happening. She was away for about 20 minutes; when she returned Siddhartha noticed that her eyes were red and that she had been weeping. "Something very hard has happened. She told him, 'Siddhartha, the electricity to the newspapers will not be cut and the high courts will remain open'."

The Rajan Case

There were hundreds of cases of police torture during the Emergency, but there were some cases that shocked the conscience of the nation. Among them were the cases of P. Rajan in Kerala and lawrence Fernandes in Karnataka. The barbarity displayed by the police in both cases, and in particular in the Rajan case, has few parallels...

The case of torture and murder of P. Rajan, a student of the Regional Engineering College, Calicut, was probably the most brutal and heart-wrenching. The picture of a retired teacher—Rajan's father TV Eachara Warrier—trudging from office to office with his son's photograph and pleading for help from the Kerala Home Minister to the inspector of police to trace his son, who was seen being dragged into a police jeep, came to symbolise the horrific consequences of dictatorship. When democracy metamorphoses into despotism, the law enforcers become the most prominent law breakers....

It is said that the police in Kerala were on the lookout for students with ultra-left leanings because of some attacks on rural police stations. They had heard that there was a student by the name Rajan among the radicals and that a person going by that name was a student at the Regional Engineering College. Armed with this information, a police party swooped down on the college hostel in the early hours of 1 March, 1976 and picked up Rajan and another student....

A couple of MPs raised the issue of the disappearance of Rajan in Parliament as well, but no individual or institution was willing to order a probe or make any tangible effort to find the young man...

But, what did they do to Rajan's body. Mathrubhoomi, a popular newspaper in Kerala reported the chilling confession of the contract driver who drove Rajan's body to some place 38 years ago. The driver said Rajan's tortured and mutilated body "was first dumped in an ice chamber and later ground and fed to pigs in a Government factory, 'Meat Products of India', Koothattukulam."

Sterilise or be Damned

One of the worst features of the Emergency was the forcible sterilisation of the population. Sanjay Gandhi was convinced that unbridled population growth was pulling India down. Whatever was being done on the development front would be neutralised by the untrammelled growth of population. He felt that unless drastic measures were taken to contain the population, India would have no future. Therefore, since he was the de facto head of the Congress party, he directed all chief ministers and party leaders to work out a strategy for mass sterilisation of both men and women. The chief ministers evolved a simple strategy. They fixed quotas for all and sundry, including government servants, policemen, teachers and municipal employees. Everyone had to fulfil his or her quota—meaning, they had to induce men and women to go to family planning camps and have themselves sterilised. Everyone was barking orders to everyone else down the administrative chain. The message that went round was that all those who failed to meet their quotas would be punished. They could lose their jobs or get demoted or face some other penalty. The same was true for members of the public. Anyone resisting the call to 'The Camp' would be marked and 'taken care of' in some way or the other....

The leaders in States such as Haryana, Delhi and Uttar Pradesh, were desperate to earn brownie points for ruthless implementation of the young leader's idea. Such was the level of sycophancy that chief ministers of these States doubled or even trebled the sterilisation quotas fixed for their States by the Centre. For example, the Union Government fixed a quote of 0.4 million sterilisations for Uttar Pradesh for 1976-77. The State proudly announced that it had revised its quota to 1.5 million! No wonder then that some of the most frightening stories of forced sterilisations came from these States....

The Ministry of Coercion

There was (yet another) Nazi-style operation undertaken by the Information and Broadcasting Ministry...This extraordinarily hush-hush operation was undertaken on 7 February 1977 and the 22 translators (whose services were utilised to translate the Congress party's election manifesto for the 1977 Lok Sabha elections) belonged to the Directorate of Advertising and Visual Publicity and All India Radio. They were summoned from their offices to a central point, told that they were chosen for an "important assignment", bundled into cars and taken to Vishwa Yuvak Kendra in New Delhi's Chanakyapuri area....

The translators realised that they had been roped in to translate the Congress party's election manifesto only when they got the cyclostyled sheets in hand. They were also immediately supplied stationery and seated at desks....For a few moments there was stunned silence in the room but that was the only permissible reaction in those authoritarian days. No one protested. There was not even a murmur. Quickly, everyone got down to the task at hand. The man who was assigned the task of coordinating this operation was Narendra Sethi, Director, DAVP.

Witn sses who appeared before the Shah Commission narrated their tales of woe. KS Srinivasan, senior copywriter, DAVP, said he was summoned on 7 February 1977 by Sethi and told that all his officers should be in readiness to undertake an urgent assignment. "Neither the duration and nature of the job nor the destination where they were to be taken was disclosed to them". However, Sethi reminded them that they were 'Government servants' and that therefore, they were "'under an oath of secrecy" and that they should not tell anyone that they had been taken out of their offices 'for a special job'. He took Ms Mukherjee, Dr J Mangamma and DN Swadia, assistant editors in DAVP, in his staff car to a building near Teen Murti, New Delhi.

Ms Mukherjee told the Commission that since she had abruptly left the office on an assignment that could take a lot of time, she had to inform her family, lest they get anxious about her not returning home from work at the usual time. So, she sought the permission of (two) strangers to call home...she was not to disclose where she was or the nature of the task given to her. Swadia too had a similar problem.... When he made the call, he was "flanked by two unknown persons".

Justice Khanna's Heroic Role

I would be doing grave injustice to the history of the Emergency, if I did not acknowledge the immense contribution of Justice HR Khanna, one of the great heroes of the second freedom struggle... This judge not only made an immense sacrifice to preserve core constitutional values and to uphold the democratic rights of citizens, but also fought a lone battle to defend the citizen's right to life and personal liberty even as his brother judges bartered away this right in that forgettable majority-decision of the Supreme Court...

The Supreme Court was called upon to determine whether citizens could move courts to safeguard their right under Article 21 of the Constitution, when the Emergency was in force. While four of his colleagues on the bench said 'No', Justice Khanna dissented and said "... the Constitution and the laws of India do not permit life and liberty to be at the mercy of the absolute power of the Executive".

While all the articles in Part III of the Constitution dealing with Fundamental Rights are important, Article 21 is rather special. It says: "No person shall be deprived of his life and personal liberty except according to procedure established by law." This is a constitutional provision that highlights the distinction between democracy and dictatorship, between rule of law and the law of the jungle. Such is the importance of this fundamental right that no nation that does not have such a provision in its Constitution can ever claim to be a democracy. Yet, the first thing that Indira Gandhi did after she imposed the Emergency was to get the President to rubber-stamp an order suspending all fundamental rights including the right to life and personal liberty.

Once this order was passed, thousands of political workers, journalists and social activists who were jailed by the Government moved the high courts challenging this order and claiming that Article 21 cannot be suspended. Many political leaders such as L.K. Advani and Madhu Dandvate were among the petitioners. The Supreme Court directed the transfer of these cases to itself. A five-judge bench comprising the Chief Justice A.N. Ray and Justices H.R. Khanna, M.H. Beg, Y.V. Chandrachud and P.N. Bhagwati heard these petitions. During the hearing, Niren De, the Attorney General, contended that so long as the Emergency was in force, no citizen could knock on the doors of a court to seek enforcement of the right to life and personal liberty.

Any democrat would have been aghast to hear such an argument. But most of the judges heard the Attorney General in silence. Justice Khanna notes in his autobiography Neither Roses Nor Thorns that he found some of his colleagues, who used to be very vocal about human rights and civil liberties, "were sitting tongue tied" and "their silence seemed rather ominous". Justice Khanna therefore decided to confront the Attorney General. He asked him whether, in view of his submissions, there would be any remedy "if a police officer, because of personal enmity, killed another manIJ" Justice Khanna says the Attorney General's answer was unequivocal. Consistent with his argument, he said, "There would be no judicial remedy in such a case so long as the Emergency lasts". De further said, "It may shock your conscience, it shocks mine, but consistent with my submissions, no proceedings can be taken in a court of law on that score."

Although it 'shocked' the conscience of the Attorney General, it did not stir the conscience of the majority on the bench.... Justice Khanna dissented. Justice Khanna's sacrifice for the sake of democracy and constitutional principles is best exemplified by the fact that after Justice Beg, the other two judges who concurred with the Government in this case—Justices Chandrachud and Bhagwati—also went on to become chief justices of the Supreme Court. Justice Khanna's sacrifice will never be in vain if we disseminate the story of his judgeship to every new generation because his heroic virtues are certain to inspire many citizens in different walks of life to stand up and be counted when there is a threat to democracy and the rule of law.

The Pioneer, 25 June, 2017

□

Playing with Constitution and Prospering too

June 25 marks yet another anniversary of the Internal Emergency imposed by Indira Gandhi in 1975, which turned the world's largest democracy into a dictatorship. During those 21 months, Indira Gandhi jailed her political opponents and journalists, imposed censorship on the Press, ensured that the fundamental rights guaranteed by the Constitution stood suspended, and turned India into a police state. Once citizens lost the right to seek relief in courts, politicians, bureaucrats and police officers took law into their hands and indulged in various atrocities. As mass sterilisation of the population was ordered and homes of the poor were demolished to 'clean up' cities and to promote Sanjay Gandhi's ideas, India came face to face with an autocratic regime.

In the absence of democratic vents, many indulged in gross misuse of authority. The Shah Commission of Inquiry, which probed the atrocities after the end of the Emergency, identified many villains. Among politicians, it identified Bansi Lal, Defence Minister in the Indira Gandhi Government, and V.C. Shukla, who was the Minister for Information and Broadcasting. And among officials and police officers, R.K. Dhawan, Additional Private Secretary to Indira Gandhi; Delhi's Lt Governor Krishan Chand; his Secretary, Navin Chawla; P.S. Bhinder, DIG of police; and K.S. Bajwa, Superintendent of Police, CID, Delhi Police, came in for severe indictment at the hands of the Shah Commission.

It said for purely personal reasons, Bansi Lal "grossly

misused his position as Chief Minister and abused his authority". He had descended to "a petty, vindictive level to satisfy a personal grudge". He was such a terror that his successor, B.D. Gupta told the commission that he stood "in constant fear of being detained under Misa (Maintenance of Internal security Act) by Bansi Lal".

The commission found Shukla guilty of gross misuse of power for his vindictive action against journalists and independent newspapers; playback singer Kishore Kumar; and for forcing Government employees to work for the Congress.

About Bhinder, it said his conduct was "a serious blot on the fair name of any administration". In regard to police firing at Turkman Gate, Delhi, Bhinder pressured the magistrates to sign and pre-date the firing order. When he sensed some reluctance, Sanjay Gandhi stepped into the picture and forced them to sign the papers.

R.K. Dhawan wanted magistrates to sign Misa arrest warrants without looking into the ground of arrest. A District Magistrate said he got the impression that any delay or resistance on his part was "fraught with danger for me personally". The panel said unscrupulous operators were short-circuiting the chain of command.

Because of his proximity to Sanjay Gandhi, Navin Chawla, Secretary to the Lt Governor, had become an extra-constitutional authority. He threatened to jail IAS officers who did not toe the line. Such was his clout that the Lt Governor confessed before the commission that he took 'instructions' from his Secretary! Though Chawla had no position in the jail hierarchy, he was exercising extra-statutory control in jail matters. The Tihar Jail Superintendent told the commission that Chawla had suggested the construction of some cells with asbestos roofs to 'bake' certain persons. Further, Chawla had on one occasion suggested that certain troublesome detenus "should be kept with the lunatics".

Wrapping up its inquiry into the conduct of Bhinder, Bajwa and Chawla, the Shah Commission said their conduct was "authoritarian and callous". It said they grossly misused their position and abused their powers in cynical disregard of the welfare of citizens and in the process "rendered themselves unfit to hold any public office" which demands an attitude of fair play and consideration for others. "Effective dissent was smothered, followed by a general erosion of democratic values. High-handed and arbitrary actions were carried out with impunity... Tyrants sprouted at all levels overnight—tyrants whose claim to authority was largely based on their proximity to power..."

This severe indictment notwithstanding, the careers of all these villains blossomed after Indira Gandhi's return to power in 1980, except that of Krishan Chand. Though he did any number of unconscionable acts during his tenure as Lt Governor, his conscience pricked him after the Shah Commission severely indicted him. On the night of July 9, 1978, he walked out of his South Delhi residence, jumped into an abandoned well and committed suicide. Here is a low down on what happened to the other key members of that notorious gang:

Bansi Lal: He bounced back after the Emergency, became the Minister for Railways in the Rajiv Gandhi Government and had two stints as Chief Minister of Haryana in the 1980s and 1990s. He even has a canal named after him. He died in March 2006.

VC Shukla: His high-handedness during the Emergency had no adverse effect on his career. He once again became a Minister in the Rajiv Gandhi Government and thereafter was a member of the VP Singh and the Narasimha Rao Cabinets. He died in May 2013.

RK Dhawan: He joined Indira Gandhi once again on her return to power in 1980. Later, he became a member of the Rajya Sabha and a Minister in the PV Narasimha Rao Government.

Navin Chawla: Although he was completely devoid of democratic credentials, the Manmohan Singh-Sonia Gandhi combine appointed him as an Election Commissioner in 2005. Chawla later went on to become the Chief Election Commissioner despite a formal objection by his predecessor, who severely doubted his neutrality.

PS Bhinder: The Shah Commission's indictment appears to have done wonders for this police officer. On Indira Gandhi's return to power, he became Delhi's Commissioner of Police and retired as Director General of Police.

Jayaram Padikkal: The DIG (Crime Branch), Kerala Police, was the prime accused in the case of torture and murder of P. Rajan, a student, in police custody. He went on to become the Director General of Police. He died in 1997.

What an irony that the heroes of the Emergency, such as Justice HR Khanna, who stood up for an individual's right to life and liberty in the Habeas Corpus Case during the Emergency, had to pay the price, but the villains prospered. Indira Gandhi superseded him for the office of Chief Justice of the Supreme Court.

Also, as stated earlier, Bansi Lal, VC Shukla, RK Dhawan, Navin Chawla, PS Bhinder and KS Bajwa climbed the political and administrative ladder without letup or hindrance post-1980, and all of them wore their misdeeds during the Emergency as a badge of honour. If this is our response to such a horrendous assault on our Constitution and democratic way of life, is our democracy safe? One wonders whether there is any parallel to this in any other country.

The Pioneer, 20 June, 2017

□

Emergency must be Taught in Schools

Union Minister of State for Parliamentary Affairs Mr Mukhtar Abbas Naqvi's suggestion that a chapter on the Emergency must be introduced in school textbooks should certainly be welcomed by all those who cherish our Constitution and our democratic way of life.

Speaking on the sidelines of an event held in Lucknow to mark the 41st anniversary of the imposition of the dreaded Emergency, where many "Loktantra Senanis" (those who fought against the Emergency) were felicitated, Mr. Naqvi said that successive generations must be told about the atrocities that were committed during those terrible 19 months when democracy stood eclipsed in India.

He said 75 per cent of the country's population was unaware of why and how emergency was imposed and what happened while it lasted. Schoolchildren should know the truth about this dark phase in India's post-independence history, just as they learn about the freedom movement and about those who fought for India's independence.

India came under a dictatorial regime after the Allahabad High Court unseated Prime Minister Indira Gandhi in June, 1975 for indulging in corrupt electoral practices in her Lok Sabha constituency, Rae Bareli in the 1971 election. Mrs. Gandhi however decided to defy the Constitution and democratic norms and remain in power, whatever the means. She fell back on a never-used provision in the Constitution, and imposed an

"Internal Emergency", which enabled her to introduce draconian laws, imprison all her political opponents and critics and unleash a reign of terror across the country. Gandhi's Emergency regime crushed all the major institutions including the Parliament, the judiciary, the Executive and the media. Today's generation needs to be told how the Constitution was mutilated and how every institution buckled under pressure. This will also educate young Indians on what actual "intolerance" is all about and also about the vulnerability of those who man these institutions to threats and inducements.

During this ugly period in the nation's history, Parliament became a rubber stamp, and passed some of the most atrocious constitutional amendments. It began with the 38th Amendment that prohibited a judicial review of the emergency proclamation. The 39th Amendment barred the Supreme Court from hearing any petition against the election of the Prime Minister. The 41st Amendment went even further. It said no civil or criminal proceedings could be instituted against the Prime Minister for anything done by her before or after she entered office. In other words, the Prime Minister became a super citizen, who would be above the law.

Today's high school children need to know that India once had a Prime Minister who put herself above everyone else. Then came the 42nd Amendment, many provisions of which would only bring utter shame to those who voted for it. As everyone is aware, Mrs Gandhi had a rubber stamp President called Fakruddin Ali Ahmed, who signed on the dotted line when she sent him the notification for imposition of the Emergency.

He did not even ask her how she could come to him with such a major proposal without getting the same cleared by her Cabinet. Assured of such a compliant President, Mrs Gandhi got Parliament to pass a provision which enabled the President to amend the Constitution through an execute order. Hitler and Mussolini got their Parliaments to empower them in this manner.

Those in school today must know Parliament and the President were made rubber stamps and how the judiciary and the media were stifled. Today's generation must also know how, while on the one hand, Mrs Gandhi strangled the judiciary through these constitutional amendments, the judiciary, at very critical moments, let down the Constitution, the people and democracy itself.

Many judges buckled under pressure at that time and Shiv Kant Shukla v ADM (Additional District Magistrate), Jabalpur, also known as the Habeas Corpus Case, offers the best example. In this case, a five-judge bench of the Supreme Court upheld the Indira Gandhi government's contention that during the Emergency, no citizen had the right to challenge his or her detention or to move a writ of habeas corpus.

This, after the Attorney General told the court that so long as the Emergency was on, no citizen could seek relief in a court of law, not even when a policeman shoots a citizen dead in the police station. Only one of the five judges—Justice HR Khanna—dissented. Justice Khanna, who was in line to become the Chief Justice of India, was superseded by Mrs Gandhi.

All the other four judges, who wrote a judgement that snuffed out a fundamental right given to citizens by the Constitution, became chief justices of the Supreme Court. The younger generation must be told that despite the terror that prevailed then, we had an extraordinary judge like Justice Khanna, who stood by the citizens' fundamental right, unmindful of its implications for his career. "Mrs Gandhi's dictatorship, both in its personalised and institutionalised forms is now complete", Jayaprakash Narayan declared woefully, when he heard the Supreme Court verdict in this case.

Similarly, the younger generation must be told of the journalists, writers, artists etc who stood up to the brutal regime, went to jail and faced many travails, so that democracy may return. As many as 1,11,000 persons were detained under MISA and the Defence of India Rule, the dreaded laws which were used to intimidate citizens. That is why the fight against Indira Gandhi's Emergency is called the Second Freedom Struggle. Children who learn of the heroic deeds of many of those who fought against Indira Gandhi's dictatorship, will be inspired to stand up for their freedoms.

The New Indian Express, 5 July, 2016

□

Lessons from the Row over Indu Sarkar

The current campaign by the Congress against Madhur Bhandarkar's film Indu Sarkar and the initial cuts suggested by the Central Board of Film Certification (popularly called the Censor Board) are indeed most unfortunate. Bhandarkar's film is a human drama in the backdrop of the Emergency. It is not a film on the Emergency. Therefore the protests being engineered against the release of the film and the needless intervention by the Censor Board are indicative of how fragile the constitutional right to freedom of expression is in our country.

Indira Gandhi turned a vibrant democracy into a dictatorship between 1975-77, jailed all her political opponents and perpetrated some of the worst acts of tyranny that India has seen after independence.

Forty years have gone by since we regained our freedom and our Constitution, yet, not a single movie has been produced on the darkest days that our democracy witnessed during the Emergency. Finally, when a popular and talented director like Madhur Bhandarkar decides to do a movie on a story which has the Emergency as the backdrop, all kinds of objections are being raised. The Congress does not want freedom of expression to extend to the dissemination of truth about the most dreadful phase in India's democratic life, when a fascist regime ruled the country.

One can well understand the discomfort of a political party, but how can the Censor Board have a problem with this? Some of the objections raised initially by the Censor Board are indeed absurd. The Censor Board objected to the following words and expressions: Bharat ki ek beti ne desh ko bandhi banaya hua hai (a daughter of Bharat has chained the country); Aur tum log zindagi bhar maa-bete ki gulaami karte rahoge (And all of you will be slaves of the mother and son all your life). Fortunately, these cuts were restored after review.

The Emergency has been extensively written about. There are many books and thousands of newspaper columns describing the atrocities committed on the people at that time. Why cannot a film director have the same freedom of expression as a newspaper columnist or an author? Further, we are told that the Censor Board initially had asked for deletion of this dialogue: Main toh 70 saal ka bhooda hoon, meri nasbandi kyun kawra rahe ho? (I am 70 years old, why are you sterilising me?) This dialogue too eventually escaped the Censor Board's scissors, but why was the board objecting to this in the first place? Forcible sterilisation was one of the worst crimes perpetrated during the Emergency. During the Emergency, lakhs of people in the country, including government servants and teachers, were compulsorily sterilised.

People with two or more children were forcibly dragged to sterilisation camps. Secondly, in order to speed up the programme, targets were fixed for every state. The Shah Commission, which investigated many of the Emergency crimes, reported that school teachers who refused to undergo vasectomy operations were jailed under the MISA (Maintenance of Internal Security Act) law. They were released after they showed doctor's certificates that they had been sterilised!

Where do we go from here? We must ask the government to implement the recommendations of the committee headed by Shyam Benegal in regard to film censorship. This committee has made it clear that the role of the Central Board is only that of a film certification board. It is not a censor board.

It should not suggest cuts, but only limit itself to film certification. It can reject certification if a film violates Section 5B (1) of the Cinematograph Act.

The Censor Board's diktats with regard to a documentary on Amartya Sen are equally absurd. Suman Ghosh, the documentary maker has told the media that the Censor Board wanted words and expressions like "Gujarat", "Cow" and "Hindutva view of India" beeped out! We are all aware of the raging debate in the country of cow vigilantes and the acts of lawlessness perpetrated by hooligans in the name of the cow in recent months. Prime Minister Narendra Modi has himself come out strongly against such hooliganism and asked state governments to firmly deal with those who indulge in such violence. Why is the Censor Board then behaving in this holier than thou fashion?

Therefore, the sooner the Benegal Report is adopted, the better it will be for the film industry. The Congress' serial protests against Madhur Bhandarkar in Pune, Nagpur etc only suggest that the party has not undergone much change since the days of the Emergency. During the Emergency, the party banned Kishore Kumar from All India Radio and Doordarshan and even asked gramophone companies not to market Kishore Kumar's records.

The Indira Gandhi government also banned films like Kissa Kursi Ka and Aandhi. Now, the Congress wants Bhandarkar's film banned. As regards Indu Sarkar, the movie has opened in theatres across the country, but the Congress Party's protests continue, despite an apex court order clearing the film. However, more than the Congress' cacophony, it is the deafening silence of the flag-bearers of freedom of expression (of course of recent origin) and of the Lutyens' citizenry that is baffling.

Most of them have gone into the woodwork. Shall we take their silence as acquiescence vis-a-vis the demand for ban on the film? Over the last four decades, they had ensured that the horrifying details of the Emergency were kept away from the Indian public. Why do they want the story of India's tryst with fascism to remain buried forever? Whatever their intentions, it is best to tell them the truth—something akin to a statutory

Chapter-10

GOVERNANCE

Tune in to Mann Ki Baat

An answer to people who think notes ban was done hastily and the push for e-payments came only after the move.

Ever since Prime Minister Narendra Modi announced his government's decision to demonetise high denomination notes, his political opponents have been accusing him of acting recklessly and taking a momentous decision without adequate thought or preparation, thereby disrupting the lives of millions of Indians, ruining small businesses and causing long-term harm to the Indian economy.

This criticism may not hold if one re-visits his public utterances before November 8 and also examines the growth of black money and wealth between 2004-2014 and the consequences of continued Manmohan Singh style pussy-footing for the nation's economy.

So first, the question as to whether Modi had foolishly rushed in where angels fear to tread or whether demonetisation was part of a well-thought out strategy. There were several occasions when Modi touched upon the issue of ewallets or electronic banking prior to November 8, but there was one occasion during which he made his intentions absolutely clear. That was on May 22 during his show on All India Radio—Mann Ki Baat.

For those who listened to him that day, November 8 would have held no surprises. Obviously, Modi was mulling this option quite some time ago, because even as early as May—a full five months prior to demonetisation—he had urged people in his radio programme to move from cash to a less-cash economy when he said: "We will have to change our old habits... the world is moving towards a cashless society... through electronic technology... there is no question of our wallets getting stolen.

The 'Pradhan Mantri Jan Dhan Yojana' has ensured that almost every family came into the banking system and got a Ru- Pay Card, which is useful both as a debit and credit card; also, with the very small instrument called Point of Sale machines now in vogue, one can make payments.

Then there is the Bank on Mobile—the Universal Payment Interface banking; and finally, there is the Aadhar card and the fact that practically everyone in the country has a mobile phone. There is no need to carry around any cash. Therefore, by synchronising Jan Dhan, Aadhar and the mobile (J.A.M), we can move ahead towards a cashless society" He virtually prepared the minds of his listeners that day to what was coming when he said, "If we learn and adapt urselves to use these services, then we will not require currency... businesses will function automatically... underhand dealings will stop, the influence of black money will be reduced.

So I appeal to my countrymen, that we should at least make a beginning. Once we start, we will move ahead with great ease." He also called upon people to overcome the fear of the unknown. He said 20 years ago who would have thought that so many people would have mobile phones. "Yet, we caught on to it and now we cannot do without cell phones. Maybe this cashless society assumes a similar form. But the sooner this happens, the better it will be," he said. Could any prime minister have been more explicit than this about his intention to launch a major assault on black money, demonetise currency and nudge the society towards a less-cash economy?

The second line of attack on Modi is demonetisation is wholly unnecessary and that he had needlessly put the nation's economy in peril. This was best answered by S. Gurumurthy, a well-known writer and commentator on economic and political issues. According to him, Modi was compelled to administer a dose of "bitter tea" because of the pathetic economic management by his predecessor, Dr. Manmohan Singh. If Modi had not taken the tough decision, it would have been disastrous for India's economy. In his lecture at the Vivekananda International Centre in Delhi last week,

Gurumurthy presented data to show how Dr. Singh had failed. Here are some of his main arguments:

Though GDP grew at an envious rate during 2004- 2010, it never created new jobs because much of the alleged growth was brought about by asset inflation. Real estate and gold prices sky-rocketed and created a false notion of growth. As a result, while the GDP grew by 8.4 per cent per annum, the number of jobs it created was a meagre 2.7 million. Further, the amount of black money in the economy ballooned and generated black wealth.

There was a huge unrecorded economy which demonetisation is putting an end to. The clue to huge asset inflation lay in the rising unmonitored High Denomination Notes (HDN) cash stock with the public. Explaining why demonetisation was inevitable, he said HDNs with the public more than doubled from 34 per cent in 2004 to 79 per cent in 2010. On November 8 it was 87 per cent. The average annual rise in HDNs was between 51-63 per cent from 2004-2013.

Also, even more worrisome was the Reserve Bank's opinion that two-thirds of the `1,000 notes and one-third of the `500 notes—that is over `6 lakh crore—never returned to banks after they were issued. The unmonitored HDNs roaming outside banks—black cash —drove up gold and land prices.

The curse—asset inflation inspired jobless growth—seemed irreversible until a method was found to catch the unmonitored high denomination currency that was fuelling this false sense of growth. Even a week after this lecture, which was widely reported, there has been no credible response to the question—why did HDN shoot up between 2004-2014? But now we know why hoarders of black money, including political parties, were taken unawares by the November 8 announcement. They never listened to Narendra Modi's Mann ki Baat!

The New Indian Express, 20 December, 2016

□

Don't Forget the Prophet of Boom

Friends and admirers from across the country paid rich tributes to former PM P.V. Narasimha Rao on his 97th birth anniversary last week and recalled his sagacity and statesmanship in pulling India out of the economic crisis of 1991 and for stamping out terrorism and secessionism in Punjab. PM Narendra Modi was the first off the mark with a glowing tribute to his predecessor on Twitter. Modi said, "Remembering our former PM Shri P.V. Narasimha Rao on his birth anniversary. Shri Rao is widely respected as a statesman who provided valuable leadership during a critical period of India's history. Blessed with immense wisdom, he made a mark as a distinguished scholar as well."

The TRS government in Telangana observed the day by holding events to remind the people about Rao's judicious and philosophical leadership at a critical moment in India's history and took immense pride in the fact that Rao was not just a Telugu bidda, but also a Telangana bidda. Its Chief Minister K. Chandrasekhar Rao said that "the people will remember forever and ever" the great services rendered by Rao. The chief minister has earlier urged the Centre to confer the Bharat Ratna on Rao.

On the other hand, the Congress, the party to which Rao owed allegiance all through his life, was not so enthused. It seemed to be dragging its feet when it put out a tweet hours later remembering Rao for pushing through legislative measures in Parliament although he headed a minority government. The party underplayed the fact that he had courageously opened up the economy, retrieved Punjab from the clutches of hardcore terrorists and laid the foundation for a new India. This is in line with its policy of underplaying the contributions of party leaders not belonging to the Nehru-Gandhi family.

Rao became prime minister at a very critical time. When he took oath as PM, the country's foreign exchange reserves were perilously low—`2,100 crore—just enough to pay bills for a fortnight. The previous government headed by Chandra Shekhar had mortgaged gold to raise foreign exchange of US $200 million. Rao realised that India's economy would go into a spiral if he continued with the moth-eaten socialism of the Jawaharlal Nehru and Indira Gandhi variety.

The country could emerge out of its economic crisis only if he dismantled the licence-permit raj and encouraged foreign direct investment. He chose Manmohan Singh as his finance minister and backed him to the hilt, shielding him from critics within the Congress and the communists who saw him as an American lackey. The Rao-Singh combine systematically opened up the economy and things started looking up. Indians began to feel that they could compete with the rest of the world. In short, Rao enabled Indians to transit from hopelessness to hope.

However, the Congress has always been reluctant to give him his due. This is generally in line with the attitude of the party to outstanding national leaders who did not belong to the Nehru-Gandhi family. Starting from the days of Nehru, the party has systematically tried to wipe out Sardar Vallabhbhai Patel, Subhas Chandra Bose, B R Ambedkar, Syama Prasad Mookerjee and a host of other leaders from the national psyche.

Over the years, every party statement and document has eulogised Nehru, Indira and Rajiv Gandhi and generally ignored the work of others, including that of Rao, who was one of India's best prime ministers. This is most unfortunate because the contribution of each of these leaders is phenomenal. The political map of India would not be what it is but for Sardar Patel, and Dr. Ambedkar's contribution to the drafting of the Constitution is too well known. The new India that we see today would never have been possible if Rao did not have the gumption to discard the policies of the Nehru-Gandhis and to put the country on a new growth trajectory. The country's foreign exchange reserves stood at nearly US $140 billion when he died in 2004.

The BJP has cashed in on the reluctance of the Congress to acknowledge the immense contribution of its own leaders and has almost effortlessly appropriated them. The first was Sardar Patel. This process began sometime ago, when Atal Bihari Vajpayee and L.K. Advani were at the helm of the party. Modi stepped up the efforts to accord due recognition to Sardar Patel by launching a major project in Gujarat to remember the Sardar which includes erection of the tallest statue in the world. It is now too late for the Congress to retrieve one of its most valuable treasures. Slowly but surely, the party has allowed one of its icons to slip out of its hands.

Dr. Ambedkar is the icon of the BSP and he also finds pride of place in the BJP's scheme of things. Both these leaders have virtually been snatched away from the Congress pantheon and India's oldest party is finding it difficult to shake off the image of belonging to just one parivar—the Nehru-Gandhi family. Rao is yet another icon which the family-centric Congress has virtually discarded. Never one to miss out on an opportunity, the BJP, in recent years, has made it a point to remind the nation of the stellar contribution of Rao.

The Modi government has already decided to act on the Telangana Assembly resolution to build a fitting memorial for Rao. Going by the alacrity of PM Modi on Rao's recent birth anniversary and the warmth and respect that he has displayed for his predecessor, it is only a matter of time before the BJP wrests this Congress icon as well. In any case, India should not forget this Prophet of Boom!

The New Indian Express, 3 July, 2018

□

Time to Revamp Rusty Bureaucracy

More than hoarders of black money, the Prime Minister, Narendra Modi's announcement on November 8 to demonetise high value currency to strike at the root of illicit wealth appears to have stunned his political opponents. Coming within weeks of the surgical strike against Pakistan, through which he signalled his ability to take decisive action, the blow that he struck against hoarders of black money a fortnight ago has put him way ahead of the competition. It is true that the roll out of the scheme has been rather clumsy and different organs of the government are struggling to cope with the challenges posed by demonetisation, resulting in long queues outside banks and hardship for people wanting to exchange old currency for new.

Yet, the large mass of people all over the country have given the idea a big thumbs up, because barring a few diehard critics of Modi, nobody is doubting his intentions. This is indeed extraordinary, because it is difficult to recall the last time an Indian prime minister commanded the trust of the people across the length and breadth of India and that too when people from every strata of society have been hit by the sudden absence of liquidity in the system. Meanwhile, the Opposition has begun to whip up tensions over the non-availability of new currency leading to long queues outside banks. So far, the people have refused to fall for the bait, but the government machinery needs to do much more if it is to prevent trouble on the streets.

However, going by how the demonetisation plan has worked out in the first two weeks, one thing is obvious: The country now has a prime minister who thinks out-of-the-box and who is determined to end the status quo mentality of the Nehruvian establishment that he has inherited. But, he does not have the kind of machinery which he needs to carry out his policies. Although he has given the bureaucracy many a pep talk, it is mired in the inertia and the sluggishness of the past seventy years and is finding it difficult to cope with him. The massive problems encountered in the roll-out of the demonetisation scheme is a pointer to the fact that the prime minister and the administrative machinery through which he operates are not running at the same pace.

Modi has publicly declared his intention to take several more tough measures to achieve the goal of cleaning the body politic, which means we must be ready for many more big ticket programmes. But, does the prime minister have the administrative apparatus to carry out his plans? Going by the experience of the past fortnight, it seems some innovative strategies will be necessary to upgrade the management skills of the government. One way of dealing with this is to ensure lateral entry of management experts, who are currently outside the government system.

Given India's complexities and the pace at which Modi wants to bring about change, a good mix of the best minds in government and the private sector may be necessary to manage specific schemes. In order to do this, the prime minister will have to break the shackles of tradition and entice the best minds within and outside the government to come in and help him achieve his goals. Within the government, he could look at officials in the various services with strong technology and management backgrounds and get them to work alongside those who come in from outside the system. From the private sector, Modi could look at individuals who have specialised in the rural market or those who have found innovative ways to capture the market at the bottom of the pyramid. In this, the prime minister can look at the way the US president picks his team.

Many of those who get the top jobs in the administration come from the private sector, fit into the system, and get on to doing something else after their tenures in government are over. Rather than seeing the chosen one as an intruder or an outsider, the American bureaucracy welcomes the new entrant and goes about its business in the most normal way. Since Modi is given to questioning the efficacy of existing practices, he could look at the possibility of opening the doors of government to management specialists hired specifically to manage national programmes. This can happen if he can end the stuffiness of the Indian bureaucracy, which has the reputation of resisting "outsiders" and killing their creativity.

In India, the bureaucracy resists the idea of lateral entry into the bureaucracy. Political bosses are okay in the sense that they are a necessary evil, but the entry of "foreign bodies" into the administrative set-up must be resisted and challenged. Those who do not have a 'batch", a "service" and a "year" to refer to, have no business being in government! This will have to change. The new India that Modi wishes to build will need a new administrative machinery.

Given the Indian reality, the new structure will have to be a proper blend of bureaucrats who have grappled with problems at the grass roots and management specialists from outside government, who are not weighed down by bureaucratic baggage. In other words, it will have to be a combination of the old and the new, the traditional and the radical. In order to achieve this, the prime minister will have to shake up the system and trigger a paradigm change in the way government works. This will be the next big surgical strike that he will have to undertake, in order to have the machinery that can execute his plans. Let us keep our fingers crossed!

The New Indian Express, 22 November, 2016

□

Don't Test our Patience

Addressing the historic 75th session of the United Nations General Assembly (UNGA) recently, Prime Minister Narendra Modi yet again made a forceful plea for reforming this international body and making the UN Security Council (UNSC) more representative and balanced. Modi had flagged this issue six years ago when he addressed the UNGA for the first time as India's Prime Minister in September 2014. On that occasion, he told the member countries that no one country or group of countries can determine the course of the world. There has to be a genuine international partnership. This is not just a moral position but a practical reality and these efforts should begin with the UN. "We must reform the United Nations, including the Security Council, and make it more democratic and participative", or else it could "face the risk of irrelevance" if it remained resistant to change. The Prime Minister was obviously emphasising India's right to be a permanent member of the UNSC, a status enjoyed by the P-5—US, UK, France, Russia and China—who are also armed with extraordinary veto powers.

He returned to this theme once again when he addressed the UNGA last month. Referring to the circumstances prevailing in 1945 when the UN came into being, he told his audience that members were now in a completely different era—the 21st century. Therefore, the international community must ask itself whether the character of the institution, constituted in 1945, was relevant even today? He spoke of the regard that the people of India have for the UN and said they wonder whether the reform process will ever reach its logical conclusion. "For how long will

India be kept out of the decision-making structures of the United Nations?...When we were strong, we did not trouble the world; when we were weak, we did not become a burden on the world. How long will such a country have to wait?"

The Prime Minister was echoing the sentiments of 1.35 billion citizens of the country when he hinted that India's patience was running thin. Indians find it difficult to fathom why their country is kept out, especially when it has such strong credentials. It is the world's largest and most vibrant democracy with 911 million electors, of whom over 600 million exercised their franchise in 2019. It is also the most diverse nation in the world with unparalleled ethnic, cultural and linguistic diversity and home to all the major religions in the world. Indians speak 121 languages and 270 dialects. Further, India accounts for 18 per cent of the global population and will overtake China and become the most populous nation by 2027. Add to this its economic and military strength—it is the fifth-largest economy and one of the top five military powers in the world. Finally, it is a founding member of the UN, one of the 26 signatories at the first conference in 1942 and has made a phenomenal contribution to the organisation's peace-keeping efforts across the world. Are these not enough reasons for India to be a permanent member of the UNSC?

As proud citizens of the world's largest and most vibrant democracy, Indians also have the right to demand that the UN remain faithful to its own fundamental postulates. Is it not strange that the Preamble to the Charter of the United Nations reaffirms faith "in the equal rights of men and women and of nations large and small..." and yet, actively promotes a hierarchy of nations and consequently, of human beings? How can India, which has equality as a fundamental precept in its Constitution, accept this form of graded membership?

Further, Article 2 of the Charter says the UN is based on the sovereign equality of all members. How is this achieved when a nation with almost one-fifth of the global population is not a permanent member of the UNSC whereas two European nations—UK (67 million) and France (65 million), each with a population equivalent to just one of India's 28 states (Karnataka)—are permanent members of the UNSC?

Articles 108 and 109 of the UN Charter are also wholly undemocratic because even if two-thirds of the members of the UN agree to amend the Charter, any of the five permanent members of the UNSC can use its veto power to block the amendment. This is absolutely undemocratic and unworthy of being part of any civilised institution in the democratic world. Why should the world's largest democracy put up with this?

These articles enable members of the P-5 to play politics and stonewall reform. That is why the efforts of the G-4 (India, Brazil, Japan and Germany) to support each other's bid for a permanent seat in the UNSC have not thus far fructified.

The international community must understand that India's patience, despite all its philosophical underpinnings, is not inexhaustible and that there is a new India emerging—optimistic, self-confident and self-reliant (atmanirbhar). It is true that seven decades ago, given India's economic plight after centuries of colonisation, it lacked the gumption to stand up and demand its rightful place. But that is not the India of today. This is not a tame India. This is a bold India. A billion-plus citizens of this nation are no longer willing to accept these inequities as part of their karma and reconcile themselves to the second-class status thrust on them 75 years ago.

India is shaking off the delusions of the past. It has shed its innocence and gullibility that was in full display during the "Hindi-Chini Bhai Bhai" days and has realised that it must become strong and resilient to promote peace in its neighbourhood and the world. The Chinese are getting a taste of this, and as the momentum picks up, other nations too will begin to sense it. This is irreversible. Having nudged his countrymen towards this new thinking, Modi is sensing the change. That is why he made a specific reference to the aspirations of the people vis-à-vis UN reform.

India will celebrate the 75th anniversary of its independence in 2022. The UN must use the occasion to redeem itself, acknowledge that democracy is the most civilised political system ever devised by man and invite India to the high table.

The Pioneer, 6 October, 2020

□□□